Contents

 KU-538-905

Part 2: General Skills

COUNSELLING AND COMMUNICATION SKILLS FOR MEDICAL AND HEALTH PRACTITIONERS

Edited by

Rowan Bayne, University of East London
Paula Nicolson, University of Sheffield
Ian Horton, University of East London

BPS BOOKS — THE BRITISH PSYCHOLOGICAL SOCIETY

First published in 1998 by BPS Books (The British Psychological Society), St Andrews House, 48 Princess Road East, Leicester LE1 7DR, UK.

Copyright © The British Psychological Society

All rights reserved. No part of this publication may be reproduced or transmitted, in any form, or by any means, without permission.

This book is sold subject to the condition that it shall not, by way of trade or otherwise, be lent, resold, hired out, or otherwise circulated without the publisher's prior consent in any form of binding, cover or electronic form, other than that in which it is published and without a similar condition including this condition imposed on the subsequent purchaser.

ISBN 1 85433 256 2

Whilst every effort has been made to ensure the accuracy of the contents of this publication, the publisher and authors expressly disclaim responsibility in law for negligence or any other cause of action whatsoever.

Typeset by Words & Graphics Limited

Printed in Great Britain by Arrowhead Books Limited

List of figures

List of tables

The Contributors

Rowan Bayne	Senior Lecturer in Counselling and Psychology, Psychology Department, University of East London.
Jenny Bimrose	Head of the Centre for Training in Careers Guidance, Psychology Department, University of East London.
Christa Drennan	Counsellor in independent practice.
Pamela Griffiths	Senior Lecturer in Rehabilitation Counselling, Brunel University.
Ian Horton	Principal Lecturer in Counselling and Psychotherapy, Psychology Department, University of East London.
David Hogan	Consultant psychologist in private practice.
Richard Kwiatkowski	Senior Lecturer in Occupational Psychology, University of East London.
John McLeod	Professor of Counselling, Keele University.
Jim Monach	Lecturer in Mental Health Studies, University of Sheffield.
Rowena Murray	Senior Lecturer, Centre for Academic Practice, University of Strathclyde, Glasgow.
Paula Nicolson	Senior Lecturer in Medical Psychology, University of Sheffield.
Harvey Ratner	Co-director of the Brief Therapy Practice, London.
Sallie Rumbold	Nurse/Co-ordinator, Fertility Unit, Homerton Hospital London.
Verena Tschudin	Senior Lecturer, Department of Health Sciences, University of East London.

Acknowledgement

A warm thank you to Susy Ajith who became Thara's mother as this book took shape. Susy again helped in two ways: she word-processed skilfully and she treated us calmly and positively.

Introduction

This book reviews in a practical way some key aspects of counselling and communication for medical and health practitioners. We asked the authors of each chapter to bear in mind, when considering ideas and research findings relating to their subject, the question, 'In what way might it be useful for a health professional to know this?', and to emphasise practical applications in the form of frameworks and guidelines. A new curriculum for trainee doctors in the United States (Marcus, 1997) defines nine areas of medical competency. Six of these are themes in this book:

- effective communication
- self-awareness, self-care and personal growth
- problem-solving
- social and community contexts of medical care
- moral reasoning and ethical judgment
- life-long learning

We see these areas of medical competency as centrally relevant to all health professionals, especially as roles and settings are changing with, for example, nurse-practitioners playing a larger role, and health centres bringing together a wider range of health professionals. The areas also recognize, as we do, that medicine – like counselling and communication – is still at least as much art as science, let alone a straight-forward technology. Medical techniques and treatments work best when allied with psychological care (Parry, 1996). Both elements are vital: the technical aspects of illness and treatment for the parts of the body that have gone wrong, on the one hand, and the person who is ill and their social context, on the other.

The book is organized in three sections: background, general skills, and specialized skills and settings. The first chapter is background in the sense of summarizing several fairly standard aspects of counselling and communication in medical and health care settings. The other chapter in this section, on health professionals looking after themselves, is background in a different sense; it is part of the context in which other skills and expert knowledge can flourish or be impeded. Its position early in the book has a symbolic value: we hope medical and health practitioners will regard looking after themselves as a priority and a professional responsibility.

The second section contains discussions of skills that most health professionals can use routinely. We have included both fresh approaches to familiar topics (listening, mental illness, multiculturalism and groups) and new directions (stories, psychological type).

Section three is about relatively specialized skills and settings. Again, there is a mix of the familiar and the probably new. Four of the chapters represent, respectively, approaches to communicating with a particular age group (children and adolescents), about a sensitive topic (sexuality), about a problem with some unusual features (infertility), and the current trend towards brief counselling (solution-focused brief therapy). The fifth chapter in this section argues for and presents a more open approach to ethical issues and decision-making, echoing the book's earlier themes of appropriate openness and greater acceptance of difference. The final chapter reviews rehabilitation counselling, again echoing earlier themes – in this case, of models of coping with loss and an integrative approach to counselling.

References

Marcus, J. (1997) Doctors take a lesson in caring. *Times Higher Education Supplement* March 14, p9.

Parry, G. (1996) *The Review of Strategic Policy on NHS Psychotherapy (and Counselling) Services in England*. Wetherby, UK: Department of Health.

PART I

BACKGROUND

Chapter 1

Counselling and communication in health care

Ian Horton and Rowan Bayne

In this introductory chapter, we summarize several aspects of counselling and communication that are not the main focus of other chapters. These are:

1. what counselling is; counselling in health care settings; an integrative model of counselling that we use in training and practice; counselling versus counselling skills; role conflict; referral; supervision and counsellor training.
2. three basic sets of communication skills: gathering information, 'informational care' and 'emotional care' (the last two terms are from Nichols, 1993); and ideas and skills for responding to people who are: angry, violent or potentially violent; suffering a loss; too withdrawn; too talkative; or making a complaint.

Knowledge of the technical and medical aspects of particular disorders, treatment options for them and their side-effects, and of the wide range of patients' fears and worries are deliberately omitted. They are covered well by Davis and Fallowfield (1991) and Broome and Llewellyn (1995), and in a recent series of books on particular illnesses, for example Shillitoe (1994) on counselling people with diabetes.

Counselling

What is counselling?

Counselling is a way of helping people with psychological problems. It is a particular way of relating and responding to people who are temporarily in the role of client. Through talking, clients are helped to explore their problems, develop a clearer understanding of them and then to use their strengths and resources to resolve or cope more effectively with them. Counselling can enable people to make choices or changes in how they think, feel or behave, or it can help to reduce confusion and enable people to live more fulfilling lives.

Counselling practice is highly diverse. It can be delivered to individuals, couples, families and groups, usually in face-to-face contact but also over the telephone and even through books and self-help manuals (McLeod, 1993). There are many disparate views on what is meant by counselling and how, and indeed if, it is different from psychotherapy. Traditionally, counsellors were seen, at least by some, as working with people who were less severely ill, people with situational or life adjustment problems rather than mental illness *per se* (NHS, 1996). However Patterson (1986: xiv) concluded:

> ... there are no essential differences between counselling and psychotherapy in the nature of the relationship, in the process, in the methods or techniques, in the goals or broadly conceived outcomes, or even in the types of clients involved.

Similarly, Inniss and Bell (1996) conclude that the differences *within* psychotherapy are at least as great as, if not more complex and intense than, any possible differences *between* counselling and psychotherapy. It seems clear that what Thorne (1992: 244) described as 'the apparent hopelessness of the quest for differences' is more about professional status, prestige, privilege and money than it is to do with scientific theory and technical practice. Counselling and psychotherapy are both psychological and therapeutic in nature and are recognized as forms of psychological intervention or treatment. However, some perceived differences exist in particular settings. For example, in primary care within the NHS the term 'counsellor' is often used in preference to 'psychotherapist', as it is perceived as less stigmatizing and off-putting to general practice patients (NHS, 1996).

Counselling in health care

One of the primary locations for counselling (and psychotherapy) is both within and alongside medicine. McLeod (1993) points out that even when counsellors work independently of medical organizations, they frequently establish some form of link with medical and psychiatric services for advice and consultancy and to facilitate client referrals when necessary. Within the NHS there is a growing demand for psychological therapies, which are seen as complementing physical treatments. Langlands (1996: 3) suggests that the demand for counselling and psychotherapy is rising in both primary and second-ary care as a consequence of the high level of distress caused by mental illness and of increasing public expectations. In the 1990s formal counselling (or psychotherapy) has been offered increasingly in primary health care settings, with many more GPs considering the psychological therapeutic dimension of their work with patients and acknowledging the importance of counselling and communication skills (Curtis Jenkins and Einzig, 1996).

Within the NHS three approaches to the provision of counselling and psychotherapy interventions have been identified (NHS, 1996: 2.5.2). The first is provided as an integral component of wider health care plans. These plans may involve such people as psychiatrists, specially trained mental health nurses, occupational therapists, clinical psychologists, doctors and nurses. For example, a health care plan may include some form of counselling or therapeutic intervention while the patient is still in hospital receiving medical and nursing care; another example might be a programme of cognitive-behavioural counselling for anxiety, which is complemented by pharmacological management. The second approach is eclectic psychological counsel-ling, which is different from the first approach in that it is not part of a wider health care plan. The second approach usually follows an assessment of patient/client needs that informs a therapeutic plan that may incorporate a range of different psychological strategies and techniques. The third approach is also a separate and complete treatment intervention, but is based on a particular school of counsel-ling or psychotherapy with a well-developed body of theory and related practice. This type of approach is usually undertaken by a specialist practitioner trained in the particular approach.

Diversity of theoretical models

All forms of counselling or psychotherapy are based on a particular theoretical model or models. Counselling strategies and interventions are not employed in a vacuum but need to be underpinned by some theoretical rationale that defines the purpose and intended effect on the client. A comprehensive model or theory of counselling has four elements (Neimeyer, 1993):

1. Basic assumptions : about human development and counselling.
2. Formal theory: that accounts for functional and dysfunctional human development and takes a position on the aetiology of psychological problems and how they are maintained.
3. Clinical theory: that explains the principles and mechanisms of psychological change, including the function of the therapeutic relationship.

4. Skills and strategies: that are used to facilitate the change
   process.

Counselling practice is not only diverse in how and where it is provided, but also in terms of the theoretical orientations on which it is based. Norcross and Grencavage (1990) reviewed various surveys which revealed that between 1959 and 1986 the number of different theoretical models of counselling rose from 36 to over 400. Since that time the number has steadily increased, with many new approaches being introduced largely through a process of 'creative synthesis' or integration of concepts and methods drawn from existing approaches. However, it is possible to organize the theoretical models into various broad traditions that have a common core of basic assumptions and formal theory. For example, a fourfold categorization of approaches is psychodynamic, cognitive-behavioural, existential-humanistic and multi-cultural (Ivey, Ivey and Simek-Morgan, 1997). Their view is that 'each theory has some value for most clients', a view central to a fifth group of approaches: integrative-eclectic.

While counselling is generally effective (Lambert and Bergin, 1994; Mellor-Clark and Barkham, 1996), it has not been possible to demonstrate the superiority of one approach over any other (except for a few specific presenting problems). What seems likely is that the diverse models of counselling share common ingredients that contribute to successful therapeutic outcomes. For example, the strength and quality of the relationship between counsellor and client has been shown to be consistently associated with positive outcomes (Bergin and Garfield, 1994). There is therefore a strong trend for practitioners trained in a particular model to integrate ideas and strategies from one or more of the other models.

An integrative process model of counselling

An integrative process model is outlined here. It provides a way of thinking about the counselling process. It is essentially a map of clinical practice, indicating what the counsellor needs to be doing at each stage of the process. See Figures 1.1 and 1.2 for basic and elaborated versions of the model. The model provides an organizing framework for integrating explanatory concepts about the origin and maintenance of psychological problems with strategies and techniques from other approaches. As an atheoretical model of process it does not undermine the integrity of different theoretical approaches (Horton, 1996). As an integrative process model, it is particularly useful for health care professionals who see counselling as a function of a wider professional role. A version of a similar model developed by Egan (e.g. 1975) is used as a framework in Chapters 11 and 14.

Stage One: Explore

The counsellor accepts and empathises with the client and is genuine*. The client explores her or his emotions, thoughts, behaviour and experiences related to a problem.

Stage Two (if necessary): Understand

The counsellor suggests, or helps the client to suggest, themes and patterns or other ways of looking at the problem**, and decide what, if anything the client wants to do about it.

Stage Three (if necessary): Act

The counsellor helps the client to decide exactly what to do***, taking costs and benefits for self and others into account, and to evaluate the results.

---

*   See Chapters 3 and 5 for discussion of these core qualities of the counsellor.
** These skills are called Challenging skills in Chapter 3.
*** Action skills in Chapter 3.

Figure 1.1: An integrative model of counselling (basic version).

The elaborated model is conceptualized as a matrix of developmental stages and themes that have been shown to be associated with positive outcomes. The beginning, middle and end stages of counselling are characterized by stage-related process goals or tasks that need to be achieved at each stage and for each of the three themes: therapeutic relationship, content of client presenting-problems, and therapeutic planning and reflection. In the first stage the counsellor needs to work towards establishing an effective working relationship with the client, assess client needs, and together with the client define the problem in a way that is amenable to the development of a therapeutic plan. In

Theme	Stage 1 tasks	Stage 2 tasks	Stage 3 tasks
1. Relationship	Establish	Maintain and use	End
2. Content	Assess problem and client resources	Facilitate learning and change	Consolidate and apply learning
3. Therapeutic planning and reflection	Develop therapeutic plan; negotiate client goals	Monitor and revise plans; reflect on process	Evaluate process and outcomes

Figure 1.2: An integrative model of the counselling process (elaborated version).

the second stage the relationship is maintained and, if appropriate, used as a window on the client's presenting problems. The counsellor seeks to facilitate learning and change, reflects on the efficacy of the process, monitors and if necessary revises the therapeutic plan. In the final stage the counsellor and client will need to address issues about ending, discuss ways of consolidating or applying learning and change, and evaluate the process and outcomes.

The model is a conceptual map and is not intended to prescribe a rigid structure. It does not reflect the experience or reality of the actual counselling process, which tends to be fluid. Movement through the overlapping stages is seldom linear or necessarily sequential. Counsellors need first to learn what strategies are necessary to achieve the particular process goals or tasks and then develop the personal qualities and skills necessary for implementing them. Active listening skills and relationship-oriented strategies provide a solid foundation for counselling.

Counselling and counselling skills

Many health care professionals use counselling skills in the context of a relationship that is focused primarily on other, non-counselling concerns (McLeod, 1993). For example, a district nurse may visit a patient's home to give medical care, but find him or herself listening to family problems and giving emotional support. Nursing consists of a multiplicity of functions and roles that require the ability to relate to and co-operate with others (Nurse, 1980). The concept of 'interpersonal relationships', and communication as a set of therapeutic skills, are now part of nursing terminology (Quinn, 1985). Physiotherapists and other health care professionals can also make effective use of counselling and communication skills and sometimes work with patients in a counselling mode over a fairly lengthy period, yet it remains part of a wider (medical) treatment plan.

The essential difference between counselling and using counselling skills is that counselling needs to be explicit, that is, both the person in the role of counsellor and the person in the role of client know that what they are doing is counselling and that they are working together within contracted or agreed boundaries of time, privacy and confidentiality. Counselling does not involve advice, or information-giving (as a primary aim) or practical help. The focus is on the client's psychological problems.

Role conflict

Doctors, nurses, physiotherapists, occupational therapists and other medical and health practitioners may be effective counsellors with their patients, but it is important to recognize that there are inherent risks. It can be very difficult for the health professional in the role of expert, with in-depth knowledge of a particular mode of treatment, efficient and skilled in performing tasks for others, and responsible for the treatment, then to switch roles, and provide a counselling relationship in which the responsibility is on the *patient* to work through and come to terms with painful and emotional aspects of her or his life and for which the health practitioner, in the role of counsellor, cannot provide any solutions or practical help.

But it is not easy for the patient either. Patients have expectations that the health care practitioner will know what to do to make things better. In a sense, patients have to switch roles and expectations too. As counselling clients rather than medical patients they can no longer expect things to be made to happen for them in the same way. They may become confused, angry or disappointed with the health care practitioner, who may feel inadequate in the role of counsellor.

Health practitioners as counsellors put themselves in a potentially powerful position over the person who temporarily accepts their help. This can feel rewarding but it is also seductive. The critical aspect of this issue is that basic human needs, such as feeling respected, wanted and loved, are met adequately in the counsellors' own personal lives, otherwise there is a real danger that they will try to satisfy these needs through their work with clients. Counsellors need to recognize this danger so that they can control it. If they remain unaware of their underlying motivations, they and their clients can become psychologically dependent. Clearly it is quite right and proper for counsellors to gain a sense of satisfaction from the work they do, but they also need to be alert to their own 'process' i.e. their motives, reactions, etc. and the ways in which they might misuse the relationship with their clients to satisfy their own needs as human beings. This is one of the reasons for regular clinical supervision (see later in this chapter).

Another role conflict is about pressure of work. Medical and health practitioners tend to be very busy. In the late 1990s, within the ethos of quality control and accountability, there is great pressure to get things done as quickly and efficiently as possible so that more can be done for more people. Employers and managers expect results. It is often tempting, and it feels easier, to do something for others or tell them what to do rather than to help them do it for themselves. A difficulty is that sometimes it takes weeks to establish an effective psychological relationship with clients and allow them time to explore and work through their problems at their own pace and to find what is for them the best way to cope more effectively. It can be hard for busy health care practitioners to put aside work pressures and justify to themselves and their managers that counselling is the most appropriate option. Many will not have time to offer counselling. Their skill is in recognizing when counselling would be appropriate and in making the necessary referral.

Referral

Counsellors themselves need to be able to recognize the limits of their ability. No one is the best person available for every client or every type of problem. It is essential to be able to identify those situations and circumstances in which it is ethically responsible and appropriate to refer a client to someone else (see Bayne *et al.* 1994: 127–129 for guidelines on referral). However, practitioners may have mixed feelings about referral. They may feel inadequate or ambivalent, experiencing a sense of both failure and relief about referring a client. Clients, too, may experience a whole range of emotions about being referred. While it can bring a sense of hope and relief, referral can also be disruptive and disappointing. Clients can feel hurt, rejected and reluctant to start again with someone else they do not know or trust.

Referrals for psychological help need to be made as soon as possible. Whenever the possibility of referral arises, it is always appropriate to discuss it with the client (Bayne *et al.*, 1994). Referral can be seen as a process in which the health care practitioner may be able to provide a 'bridge' of short-term supportive counselling in which clients are helped to resolve any emotional blocks about being referred and, if necessary, helped to make their own approach or application to the agency or other counsellor. Obviously, the health care practitioner needs to develop personal contacts and an adequate referral resources file.

Supervision

Regular supervision or consultative support is an integral part of professional and ethical practice throughout the working life of a counsellor, and irrespective of the counsellor's level of experience or qualifications. In the UK it is a breach of ethics to practise as a counsellor without supervision (BAC, 1996 a).

Helping people to cope with psychological problems makes considerable emotional demands upon the person in the role of counsellor. Entering fully into a counselling relationship and listening to the often deep sadness and distress of others can in itself be distressing to the person listening; but it can also re-stimulate problems and issues in the counsellor's own life. There may be some part of a counsellor's experience and feelings that remains hidden below the surface or is on the edge of awareness. These 'unconscious experiences' influence behaviour and may be independent of conscious awareness (Greenberg and Safran, 1987: 47). One purpose of supervision is to help counselling practitioners become aware of these feelings and the way in which they may affect their counselling. A second purpose is to enable counsellors to monitor and evaluate the strategies and techniques they use with clients and to generate options and possibly more effective ways of responding to their clients' needs.

Supervision needs to be a formal contractual arrangement with someone who is appropriately experienced in counselling and supervision. The formality is important. Casual conversations with a colleague or friend to let off steam about a 'difficult client' is professionally inappropriate and a breach of confidentiality (BAC, 1996a) as well as being much less likely to be effective. In addition, the supervisory relationship should be separate from other work or social roles or relationships. Counsellors should not receive supervision from their line managers – at least not from their line managers alone. This is still a problem in the health service. Line managers can provide general management supervision, but ideally counsellors should receive additional clinical supervision and psychological support from someone with whom they have no other relationship. Supervision can be provided in a one-to-one relationship or in a small group (BAC, 1996a). Qualified and experienced counsellors can work reciprocally in a peer group. Supervision normally takes place once a month.

Initial attitudes towards supervision can be ambivalent. Those being supervised are often pleased or even relieved to know that they will receive support and guidance on their work with clients. However, they may also feel apprehensive or threatened by what they see as exposing their professional competence to the scrutiny and possible criticism of others. The term 'supervision' is misleading. In common usage it implies subordination, control, direction and authority to inspect the work of others who are not competent to work on their own. In counselling, the term supervision has a different meaning. It refers to a consultative arrangement in which the counsellor is a participant not a recipient (Horton, 1993). Supervision is an opportunity and resource for the counsellor to monitor, develop and maintain the quality of her or his counselling practice and to achieve SUPER-vision rather than supervision (Houston, 1990: 1). Supervision is also an integral component of counsellor training.

Training

Counselling skills training is often a small component of the training for many medical and health practitioners, and some may wish to develop their work in this area. Many colleges, universities and private organizations offer short counselling skills and longer professional counsellor training courses. However, there is a bewildering number and variety of courses, and for anyone thinking about training as a counsellor it may be a useful first step to contact the British Association for Counselling for information about courses (see BAC in references for the address). BAC accredits courses and this not only provides some assurance of quality and standards, but it also means that the course satisfies the education and training requirements for individual counsellor accreditation and UK registration.

Professional counsellor training courses are usually of not less than two years part-time. They include in-depth training in one core theoretical model, skills training, professional studies, clinical practice with clients and related supervision, as well as self-development work, including personal counselling. Details of admission criteria, and the elements of training and assessment can be found in the BAC Booklet *Recognition of Counsellor Training Courses* (BAC, 1996b) and are discussed in Dryden, Horton and Mearns (1995).

Communication

Gathering information

Table 1.1 lists and briefly defines one way of formulating the relevant skills. It is probably fair to say that these skills are easier to acknowledge as ideas than they are to execute well, but also that most people can improve in their use of them, as well as in developing the related personal qualities or attitudes (eg. Connor, 1994; Maguire, 1981). These skills and qualities are used for building a relationship and either for gathering information (the emphasis in interviewing) or for helping someone explore and clarify (the emphasis in counselling).

Informational care

Nichols' review of the literature on psychological care in physical illness points to three conclusions (1993: 42–3):

- Recovery from illness can be hampered by psychological distress.
- Compliance with treatments and medical advice can be diminished by psychological distress.
- Expensive medical treatment is sometimes used when relatively cheap psychological care would have been more effective.

Informational care and emotional care are key elements of psychological care. Informational care involves putting effort and skill into keeping patients informed in a systematic, active and planned way

Table 1.1: Brief definitions of some of the skills of interviewing and counselling*

Preparation is considering such factors as the time available, aims, broad structure, mood (ideally, calm and alert) and place (ideally, private and pleasant).

Negotiating a contract is a concise statement about your aims and asking for your client's or patient's response, and then reaching a mutual understanding.

Attending is nonverbal: posture, eye-contact, etc.

Listening is paying full attention.

Observing is picking up non-verbal cues to attitudes, emotions, etc.

Reflecting is saying a word or phrase back to your client.

Paraphrasing is a rephrase of the meaning of what your client has said or clearly implied (verbally or non-verbally). Paraphrases can be of *content* (facts) or *emotions* (feelings) or both.

Being concrete is asking for detail or an example.

Silence is allowing time for reflection or just a natural pause.

Open questions invite longer statements, e.g. What happened next? What was that like? How did you . . . ?

A *summary* draws themes and points together and gives some 'shape'.

---

* There are no generally agreed terms in the counselling literature, For example, 'active listening' is used by some authors as we use 'paraphrasing' and as others use 'reflecting'.

---

about their illness and treatment, and routinely checking their knowledge and beliefs (Nichols, 1993). Powerful emotions are often involved – fear and grief especially – and they can have a 'crushing power' (Nichols, 1993: 17). However, keeping patients informed about procedures, side-effects, etc. is difficult. They may be anxious and prone to selective memory and wishful thinking. They may also be confused and disoriented by adjusting to a new way of life, especially in a hospital. Informational care therefore means a nurse assigned to particular patients and checking what each patient knows and wants to know, as well as providing carefully prepared leaflets.

Worry would not be banished, but the anxiety generated by *needless* uncertainty would go, and the experience of someone functioning in this way for our benefit would have a very supportive effect.

There would be a sense of collaborating with the staff to deal with problems together.

(Nichols, 1993: 66)

Nichols recommends the IIFAC three-stage model of informational care (1993: 83):

- *Initial information check* (what does the patient already know about the particular topic and what do they expect)
- *Information exchange* – giving information
- *Final Accuracy Check* – ask the patient to repeat back the information, repeating the first two stages if necessary.

A proviso is that a small proportion of patients prefer not to know, but this would probably be clear from the initial information check. Another strategy here is to provide the patient with a list of questions that they may wish to ask (Nichols, 1993; Ley and Llewelyn, 1995). Individual differences in style of communication could be added to this model, for example those discussed in Chapter 7.

Maguire's (1991) model is similar to the IFFAC model. He suggests the following sequence, and gives good examples of each step: checking the patient's awareness of what might be wrong; giving the bad news if the patient wishes to know (informational care); acknowledging their reaction (emotional care); eliciting all concerns, and then offering advice and information (informational care), including 'I don't know' if this is the most accurate answer, accompanied by emotional care (e.g. 'I guess that not knowing is hard for you'), and then focusing on what might help the patient to live with the uncertainty.

Research on genetic screening (e.g. Marteau, 1994) illustrates some of the complexities in informational care. In a study of predictive testing for Huntingdon's Chorea, Tibben, Vegter *et al.* (1990) found that 50 per cent of *non-carriers* found no immediate relief from discovering this and 20 per cent felt depressed. The researchers suggested that the patients had been living their lives as if they were carriers and that the apparently positive test result meant a loss of this significant part of their identity.

Emotional care

It is normal for patients to respond emotionally to serious illness, to feel anxious when threatened, angry when frustrated, sad and grieving about loss of a part of the body or a capacity. 'Emotional care' means expecting and valuing such responses rather than blocking or subduing them. As with informational care, this means routinely checking a patient's emotional state and offering to listen. A basic

Patient's name .... Date...............................

Patient's mood ....

Comments:

Patient's level of knowledge about X ....

How much does she or he want to know at the moment? ....

Actions?

Modified from Nichols (1993: 140)

Figure 1.3: Record of informational and emotional care.

guideline is that 'emotional care involves helping a person into an emotional response' (Nichols, 1993: 100) – though helping is used here in the sense of 'allowing' rather than 'actively encouraging'.

Generally, expressing emotions is part of preparing for a stressful event or adapting to it. For example, a patient is very anxious about an operation. He anticipates the worst outcomes, is tense, cannot concentrate and sleeps badly. This is a normal response to a threat. To say 'Don't worry' is not helpful, even though that may well be the intention. Rather, emotional care involves you and your patient recognizing the potential value of his anxiety in the form of increased energy to respond to the threat, and better preparation for various outcomes, including the worst. Emotional care is helping patients through this natural process by first forming a trusting and caring relationship and then inviting them to talk about their operation (or illness or disability) when they are ready, or being ready to listen if the invitation is not needed, or alternatively respecting a wish not to talk about it. Nichols (1993) also recommends keeping a record, e.g. about once a week completing a card like that in Figure 1.3. The section on mood could be a checklist, e.g. anxious, depressed, cheerful etc.

The ideal setting for informational and emotional care will usually be a quiet interview room with privacy and no interruptions. And the ideal 'frame of mind' is relaxed and focused on the patient's reactions. The patient's demeanour may be flat and inexpressive, especially early on, or very emotional, but the aim of emotional care is for the patient to feel accepted and be able to talk to you as freely or as little as he or she wishes. Finally, it may be helpful to recognize that listening *without saying much* is helpful in emotional care. Counselling is different: in most approaches, counsellors actively communicate their understanding of what is being said and implied, and counselling also has wider aims – to stimulate greater self-awareness, to challenge, e.g. blind spots, cognitive distortions, contradictions, etc., and to help clients set goals (see Figures 1.1 and 1.2).

People in 'difficult' states

In this section we make some suggestions rather than prescriptions. Much depends on each person's own style and personality, and there are different ways of being effective with different people who are angry, for example. Moreover, most of the suggestions have not yet been fully substantiated by research. Nevertheless, the practical idea here is to consider trying some of these suggestions or hints for action, and adapting them to suit yourself. Please bear in mind, though, that they underline the complexity of such 'difficult situations' rather than defining exactly what to do.

Another way of putting this point is that *meaning* is at the heart of communication – behaviour is more peripheral. 'Learning certain behavioural "skills" guarantees nothing about the meaning this behaviour will have . . . ' (Plum, 1981: 7). Intentions matter too, as does how the other person judges the behaviour. Plum cites Laing's (1969) discussion of the 'tea ceremony': 'It is not so easy for one person to give another a cup of tea, she might be trying to put me in a good mood . . . trying to get me to like her . . . wanting me as an ally . . . ' (p.106). Simply to give another person a cup of tea, and *only* to do that, is very difficult. In the same way, the most skilful act of listening can be seen as insensitive, intrusive or condescending. This is where qualities like 'sensitivity' and 'self-awareness', and skills such as 'timing' and 'tone' are vital. They imply that developing a skill requires a degree of talent or artistry that cannot be taught through a book or a short training course, but can be worked on as part of being a professional and as part of in-depth training.

For people in most 'difficult states', one or more of the three sets of skills discussed already, plus listening (Chapter 3) and assertiveness (Chapter 2) are most likely to be effective. For example, with someone who is angry, say calmly: 'Mr X, you're very angry, I'd like to talk about it with you' (emotional care plus an offer to listen), or 'Ms X I'd like you to move back. Will you tell me what you're angry about?' (assertive request plus emotional care plus an open question). For some situations additional factors are important, as indicated next.

Angry, violent or potentially violent

There are several guidelines and possible actions, such as:

- Be aware of any relevant irrational beliefs (discussed in Chapter 2) e.g. 'I must never run away', 'I should be able to help everyone'.

- Tell the client or patient where to sit and how long they may have to wait. (Anxiety, frustration, confusion and boredom can all lead to outbursts of aggression. Frustration and fear are linked closely to violent and aggressive behaviour.)

- Do not keep clients waiting. (Clients coming to counselling are usually anxious, especially on the first occasion when they may be uncertain about where to come, how to get there, what the building will be like, what to expect, or who you are.)

- Do not start a counselling session with a client who is under the influence of alcohol or drugs and unable to have a normal conversation.

- Arrange the chairs so that both you and your client can leave by the door quickly should this be necessary.

- It is advisable to avoid any form of physical contact with clients apart from a handshake offered by the client.

- Avoid seeing clients on your own when you are alone in the building or when no one is about.

- Do not leave any objects around the room which could be used as weapons.

- Make sure the door of the counselling room is not locked or jammed and that you know how to open it quickly.

- If you are working with a client of the opposite sex, try to ensure that someone of the same sex as the client is within calling range.

- If you see clients in the evening, make sure the corridor lights are on; inform someone of the starting and finishing time and the room in which you are counselling; and avoid seeing any men clients (if you are a woman).

- Clients seldom become aggressive towards you without warning. Be alert for signs; assess the situation; try to remain calm and confident. Be empathic – clearly and sincerely acknowledge the importance to the client of whatever has triggered the aggression.

(Adapted from Burns, 1993;
Breakwell, 1997 and Wykes, 1994 are other useful sources)

Loss

About 50 per cent of people do not experience intense anxiety, depression or grief after a serious loss, and continue to be psychologically well-adjusted (Wortman and Silver, 1989). Wortman and Silver

17

discuss several related myths about coping with loss, e.g. that distress and working through are necessary, and that recovery or resolution are inevitable. They stress the great variability of people's reactions to loss; on Wortman and Silver's review of the evidence, about 30 per cent of people feel depressed and distressed after a serious loss, 18 per cent are 'chronic grievers' and 2 per cent appear well-adjusted at first but are distressed a year later. See Chapters 2 and 4 of this book on Pennebaker's research, and Chapters 11 and 14 on applying models of loss to infertility and in rehabilitation counselling, respectively.

Withdrawn

The main options are for you to be silent too – most people will then speak – and/or a comment such as, 'I'm wondering why you haven't answered' or, 'You seem puzzled/anxious/upset etc.'

Too talkative

Try summaries, or remind the person of the contract, especially the amount of time. Interrupt, e.g., 'I'm sorry to interrupt you but can we return to . . . ' You may need to say something like, 'Mr X, I need to stop now. I have someone else to see. Can we arrange another time' or, 'We have five minutes left and I'd like to ask you . . . '

Making a complaint

Complaints can be seen as opportunities to create trust and goodwill. To use complaints in this way, speed of response and remembering that the patient is probably upset and disoriented, are crucial (Calnan, 1991). Informational and emotional care should prevent a lot of complaints. When they do not, Calnan's suggestions include treating every complaint with respect, however trivial it may seem; staying calm; dealing with a complaint on that day (or at least reporting progress); listening until the patient and you agree about 'the heart of the matter'; investigating; explaining in a straightforward way; apologising if appropriate; and thanking the patient. Calnan also recommends three steps in response to being accused of professional negligence or incompetence. In a different order from Calnan's they are:

1. Inform your manager and ask a colleague to take over the client's or patient's care.

2. Inform your administration.

3. Contact your professional insurers quickly. Send a brief statement and photocopies of relevant documents.

References

BAC (1996a) *Code of Ethics and Practice for Counsellors.* Rugby: BAC. Address: 1 Regent Place, Rugby, CV21 2PJ. Phone: 01788 578323.

BAC (1996b) *Recognition of Counsellor Training Courses* Rugby: BAC.

Bayne, R., Horton, I., Merry, T. and Noyes, E. (1994) *The Counsellor's Handbook. A Practical A–Z Guide to Professional and Clinical Practice.* London: Chapman & Hall.
   Brief entries on about 150 everyday aspects of counselling, e.g. beginnings, difficult clients, boundaries, sexual attraction, silence, supervision.

Bergin, A.E. and Garfield, S.L. (1994) (Eds) *Handbook of Psychotherapy and Behavior Change* 4th ed, New York : Wiley.
   The standard reference on counselling research which also suggests and documents current trends in counselling practice, e.g. towards integrative models and brief counselling.

Breakwell, G.M. (1997) *Coping with Aggressive Behaviour* Leicester : BPS Books.
   Reviews theories of aggression, methods for assessing dangerous situations and personal and organizational strategies for coping.

Broome, A. and Llewellyn, S. (1995) (Eds) *Health Psychology* 2nd ed. London : Chapman & Hall.

Burns, J. (1993) Working with potential violence. In R. Bayne and P. Nicolson (Eds) *Counselling and Psychology for Health Professionals* London: Chapman & Hall.

Calnan, J. (1991) Handling complaints. In R. Corney (Ed.) *Developing Communication and Counselling Skills in Medicine* London: Routledge.

Connor, M. (1994) *Training the Counsellor. An Integrative Model.* London: Routledge.

Curtis Jenkins, G. and Einzig, H. (1996) Counselling in primary care. In R. Bayne, I. Horton and J. Bimrose, (Eds) *New Directions in Counselling.* London: Routledge.

Davis, H. and Fallowfield, L. (1991) (Eds) *Counselling and Communication in Health Care.* Colchester: Wiley.

Dryden, W., Horton, I. and Mearns, D. (1995) *Issues in Professional Counsellor Training.* London: Cassell.

Egan, G. (1975) *The Skilled Helper. A Model for Systematic Helping and Interpersonal Relating* Monterey, CA: Brooks/Cole.
   Best-selling textbook, now in its 1994 5th edition, but we prefer the earlier, simpler versions.

Greenberg, L.S. and Safran, J.D. (1987) *Emotion in Psychotherapy* New York : Guilford Press.

Horton, I.E. (1993) Supervision. In R. Bayne, and P. Nicolson (Eds) *Counselling and Psychology for Health Professionals.* London: Chapman & Hall.

Horton, I.E. (1996) Towards the construction of a model of counselling: some issues. In R. Bayne, I. Horton and J. Bimrose (Eds), *New Directions in Counselling.* London: Routledge.

Houston, G. (1990) *Supervision and Counselling*. London: Rochester Foundation.

Inniss, S. and Bell, D. (1996) *Final Project Report for Therapeutic Counselling, Couple Counselling and Psychotherapy Competencies* (Report 39, May 1996). Welwyn: The Advice, Guidance, Counselling and Psychotherapy Lead Body.

Ivey, A.E., Ivey, M.B. and Simek-Morgan, L. (1997) *Counselling and Psychotherapy. A Multicultural Perspective*. 4th ed. London: Allyn & Bacon.

Lambert, M.J. and Bergin, A.E. (1994) The effectiveness of psychotherapy. In A.E. Bergin and S.L. Garfield (Eds) *Handbook of Psychotherapy and Behavior Change* 4th ed. New York: Wiley.

Laing, R.D. (1969) *Self and Others*. Harmondsworth: Penguin.

Langlands, A. (1996) Foreword. In *NHS Psychotherapy Services in England: Review of Strategic Policy*. Wetherby: Department of Health.

Ley, P. and Llewelyn, S. (1995) Improving patients' understanding, recall, satisfaction and compliance. In A. Broome and S. Llewelyn (Eds) *Health Psychology : Processes and Applications*. 2nd ed. London : Chapman & Hall.

Maguire, P. (1981) Doctor-patient skills. In Argyle, M. (Ed.) *Social Skills and Health* London: Methuen.

Maguire, P. (1991) Managing difficult communication tasks. In R. Corney (Ed.) *Developing Communications and Counselling Skills in Medicine* London: Routledge.

Marteau, T.M. (1994) Psychology and screening: Narrowing the gap between efficacy and effectiveness. *British Journal of Clinical Psychology, 33*, 1–10.

McLeod, J. (1993) *An Introduction to Counselling*. Buckingham: Open University Press.

Mellor-Clark, J. and Barkham, M. (1996) Evaluating counselling. In R. Bayne, I. Horton and J. Bimrose (Eds) *New Directions in Counselling*. London: Routledge. Breaks evaluation down into a series of questions, and illustrates the answers with a study of Relate.

Neimeyer, R.A. (1993) Constructivism and the problem of psychotherapy integration. *Journal of Psychotherapy Integration, 3*, 2, 133–157

NHS (1996) *Psychotherapy Services in England : Review of Strategic Policy*. Wetherby, Department of Health.

Nichols, K. (1993) *Psychological Care in Physical Illness* 2nd ed. London: Chapman & Hall.

Norcross, J.C. and Grencavage, L.M. (1990) Eclecticism and integration in counselling and psychotherapy: major themes and obstacles. In W. Dryden and J.C. Norcross (Eds) *Eclecticism and Integration in Counselling and Psychotherapy*. Loughton: Gale Centre Publications.

Nurse, G. (1980) Counselling and helping skills : how they can be learned. *Nursing Times*, April 24, 737–738.

Patterson, C.H. (1986) *Theories of Counselling and Psychotherapy*. New York: Harper & Row.

Plum, A. (1981) Communication as skill: a critique and alternative proposal. *Journal of Humanistic Psychology, 21* (4) 3–19.

Quinn, P. (1985) Mind treatment, *Nursing Times*, June 19, 38–40.

Shillitoe, R. (1994) *Counselling People with Diabetes* Leicester: BPS Books.

Thorne, B. (1992) Psychotherapy and counselling: the quest for differences. *Counselling 3* (4) 244–48.

Tibben, A., Vegter, V.D., Vlis M., Niermeijer, M.F., *et al.* (1990) Testing for Huntingdon's disease with support for all parties. *The Lancet, 335,* 553.

Wortman, C.B. and Silver, R.C. (1989) The myths of coping with loss. *Journal of Consulting and Clinical Psychology 57* (3) 349–357.

Wykes, T. (Ed.) (1994) *Violence and Health Care Professionals.* London: Chapman & Hall.

Chapter 2

Looking after yourself

Rowan Bayne

This chapter is about managing or coping with 'stress' – both everyday and psychotraumatic. 'Psychotrauma' is the term used by Buyssen (1996) to mean a reaction to a stressful incident which includes re-experiencing it, denial, and inappropriate arousal. I will assume that it is professionally responsible for health professionals to look after themselves, and I hope to show that it can be involving and enjoyable too. I suggest a practical three-stage model of coping with stress (Table 2:1) and focus on two strategies: writing and assertiveness. In an appendix there are notes on four other ways in which some people look after themselves: physical relaxation, massage, physical activity and social support.

Most of the chapter is about everyday stress. However, health professionals also face many traumatic incidents and several 'small' events can have the same effect cumulatively as a traumatic event. The final section therefore includes three sets of practical guidelines on responding to psychotraumatic stress: 'What you can do for yourself', 'When to call·in professional help', and 'Helping others'.

I chose writing as a coping strategy for several reasons : (a) it illustrates well the stages outlined in Table 2:1, (b) the evidence for its effectiveness is unusually good (although individual differences have not been studied yet), (c) it is not usually included in books on stress management, (d) there are no contra-indications yet, which there are for nearly all the other strategies, even physical relaxation, (e) it is very inexpensive, portable and private, and – sometimes most usefully – (f) it can be used to clarify motives for *not* looking after yourself. These reasons, apart from (c), also apply to assertiveness. In addition, assertiveness is primarily an action strategy whereas writing is mainly exploratory and analytic.

The chapter assumes sufficient motivation and a lack of serious

Table 2.1: Managing stress: three stages

Stage 1	Monitor your signs of too much or too little stress, especially *early* warnings
Stage 2	Choose one or more strategies
Stage 3	Try them out, monitoring the effects

'blocks' to looking after yourself; obviously this is not always so. Counselling and supervision are the usual ways of trying to improve motivation and tackle blocks, and these are discussed in Chapter 1. The sections in Chapter 7 on motives and on the limits of change may also be helpful sources of ideas and strategies.

There are numerous definitions of stress. One argument is that the term is now defined and used too broadly and is therefore obstructing useful questions. 'Strain' has been suggested for the effects of stress, and 'stressor' for the causes (O'Driscoll and Cooper, 1996). However, 'stress' is a meaningful term for most people. Bond's (1986) definition is 'the experience of unpleasant over or under stimulation, as defined by the individual in question, that actually or potentially leads to ill health' (p.2), which emphasises individual experience, and has a flavour of feeling threatened and strained to the extent of being overwhelmed. It also includes a statement about effects on health. Fontana's (1989) 'snappy' definition is more objective and detached : 'stress is a demand made upon the adaptive capacities of the mind and body' (p.3). Both definitions include the idea that stress can be good, neutral or bad.

Managing everyday stress: a model

This section outlines a three-stage model for managing stress: monitor, choose, act (Table 2.1). The first stage is observing and monitoring our own levels of stress and in particular knowing our earliest signs of too much or too little stress. One person speaks a little more abruptly than usual, another smokes more, a third develops a slight tic. These cues can show when a good level of stress (excitement, aliveness) is becoming too much (strain) or too little (boredom). They can be discovered or confirmed through observation, of varying degrees of formality. A model of inner self-awareness (Figure 2.1) makes this process more systematic. Ask, 'What am I thinking?', 'What am I sensing?, etc. We each tend to be more aware of some of these categories than of others, but we can increase our awareness and range through practice.

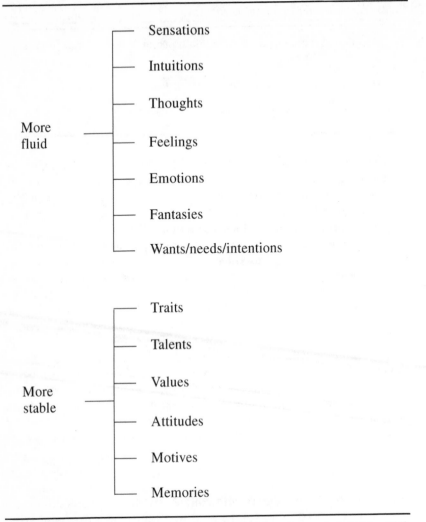

Figure 2.1: A model of inner self-awareness (modified from Bayne et al. 1994, p.135).

Early signs of stress can be elusive, but friends and colleagues may have useful observations to make, and another way to check them is by remembering a stressful time in detail. The early signs of stress are important for three main reasons. First, it is easier to notice them before getting caught up in feeling stressed (although it is also easier to dismiss them as trivial or momentary). Second, the external cause of our stress may be more apparent and it is then easier to respond to it directly. Third, it is easier and healthier to take action before stress takes hold.

Health professionals should be good at Stage 1. They know the symptoms of strain and that they may be normal reactions or symptoms of illness. They also know that tics, for example, are

Table 2.2: Some strategies for managing stress

---

1. Reduce effects of stress

    - relaxation
    - play/fun
    - massage
    - exercise (short-term)
    - meditation

2. Increase self-awareness (with a view to action)

    - talk/write
    - support groups
    - counselling
    - uncover, challenge and replace irrational beliefs
    - clarify values
    - develop other assertive qualities and skills

3. Discover situational causes (and consider dealing with them directly or changing your attitude towards them).

4. Build up physical and emotional resilience: diet, exercise (long-term), sleep etc.

---

probably just physical tension. On the other hand, they may also be less willing to take any notice, and, when they do notice, more likely to push them aside and concentrate on caring for others.

Stage 2 involves choosing one or more strategies. For example, I noticed that I was biting my lip shortly after a colleague had spoken to me. I checked through some strategies (e.g. Table 2.2) and decided to (1) relax physically, (2) talk to a friend about the situation and my reaction, and (3) look for an irrational belief. These were all immediate responses (1 and 2 more so). I found that my colleague was not (this time) the primary cause of my stress, and that an irrational belief (one of those in Table 5) was, or seemed so. What mattered most, though, was that I looked after myself by trying to clarify what had happened through observation and specific, realistic actions. There can be a subtle effect here: relatively minor changes leading to greater motivation, and then to more changes – the opposite of a spiral of decline.

Managing stress: strategies

Ideally, each strategy for managing or coping with stress would be rated as most likely to work for particular kinds of stress and for particular kinds of people, but the research has not yet been done. A later chapter, on psychological type, suggests some broad possibilities, but there is at the moment no firm specific evidence for or against these possibilities. It is therefore a matter of trying out strategies, perhaps using the kind of person you are as a guide to those to try first. Table 7.2, on the basic motives of the four temperaments in psychological type theory, illustrates this idea. Moreover, knowing one's psychological type may itself help to reduce stress.

A further complication in choosing strategies for coping with stress is that the same strategy may be beneficial in some circumstances and harmful in others. For example, denial and illusion are useful when a patient faces minor surgery: anxiety about the danger and possible complications is self-defeating, denial and a passive trusting approach are associated with a more rapid recovery (Lazarus and Lazarus, 1994). Conversely, denial is of course dangerous when faced with the symptoms of, say, a heart attack or cancer, or when convalescence is not taken seriously.

Writing

The effects of writing about stressful experiences have been studied by Pennebaker and his colleagues (eg Pennebaker; 1993, Pennebaker *et al.* 1990). Pennebaker *et al.* divided students who had just started their first year of university randomly into two groups. The experimental group was asked to write for 20 minutes on three consecutive days about their 'very deepest thoughts and feelings about coming to college'. The 'control' or comparison group wrote on what they had done since they woke up that day. Thus, in the first group, thoughts and feelings were emphasized, and in the second group, behaviour. The main finding was that students in the experimental group had a lower level of stress-related hormones in their blood and went to the health centre less in the next six months than those in the control group. The basic findings have been replicated several times, with some attention being given to explaining the positive effects on health of this form of writing. This area of research and counselling – more broadly called 'narrative therapy' (see Chapter 4) – is expanding rapidly. A basic assumption is that a defining characteristic of being human is 'telling stories'.

A strategy consistent with Pennebaker's research is illustrated below with a personal example. Writing in this way requires you to take your inner experience seriously, but, like the model in Table 2:1, it guards against becoming morbidly introspective or unduly passive by also emphasising action.

Steps 1 and 2

Choose an experience that matters to you, e.g. part of a conversation, interview or counselling session, or something you have seen, done or read.

Describe the experience in a sentence or two, or list key words. See if you can 'go into' and, to some extent, re-live the experience.

Longer run than usual on Monday. In the night pain in my knee woke me up, and yesterday it was stiff and I hobbled.

(End of steps 1 and 2).

Step 3

Write as freely as you can about your experience – not analysing, not concerned with literary merit, and for yourself only.

Felt despairing and angry: I'll have to stop running. Also annoyed that I'd just bought new running shoes, and disturbed by the strength of my reaction. I was flat and ill most of the day at work, and abrupt with some of my colleagues. During the day my knee eased. This morning it's near normal. Feel much more buoyant and constructive. I'm not crippled!

(End of step 3, reflection – at least on this occasion).

Step 4

Analyse your reactions and perhaps challenge them.

- be specific (cf. Figure 2:1)
- what is the evidence for any assertions, beliefs?
- is there a familiar feeling or pattern there?
- what assumptions are you making? (cf. Table 2:5)
- do your reactions tell you anything else about yourself, e.g. suggest important values?
- how realistic are you being?
- what other ways (however unlikely) are there of looking at what happened?

  I'm left wondering about my reaction to injury (and illness).

  1. *I believe it's awful and catastrophic not to be able to run.*

  2. *It's a recurring pattern. It may be related to lots of illness as a child, especially being scared I'd stop breathing.*

  3. *Everyone is ill or injured sometimes (especially good athletes!). It's normal.*

(End of step 4 – a more considered analysis. It is meant to contrast

27

with step 3, which is written more freely – indeed as freely as possible).

Step 5

Consider action.

   a. Is there any action you want to take now?

   b. Is there anything that you might do differently next time?

   Possible actions:

   1. *Look up knee injuries. Preventive measures?*

   2. *Ask Dave's advice.*

   3. *Make a special effort re 'flatness' next time: perhaps explain to other people, 'go into' my feelings, treat it like loss. Do 1 and 2 today.*

(End of step 5 – possible actions).

Comment on the example

The steps overlap but give some shape and sense of direction. Analysis is relatively neglected. The actions are feasible, but could be expressed more specifically.

Assertiveness

The various approaches to assertiveness and assertiveness training differ radically. Some books and trainers focus on skills and techniques and ignore self-awareness, while others do the opposite. One problem is the role of social and cultural context. For example, Western values tend to be for autonomy and individualism, while Eastern values tend to be for humility and community. However, a basic existential problem is relevant to people in all cultures: how much do I do what *I* want to do and how much what *others* want me to do.

   More than 20 definitions of assertiveness have been put forward (Rakos, 1991) but I think the variety is more apparent than real and that it is useful to distinguish between four levels of definition: general, assertive rights, styles of behaviour and skills. A general definition is 'being able to express and act on your rights as a person while respecting the same rights in other people'. There are several lists of rights, with substantial overlap between them. Table 2.3 (from Bayne *et al.*, 1994 p.7) is a composite from Bond (1986), Dickson (1987) and elsewhere. The unusual format is from Bond; its value is that it makes explicit the dual nature of assertiveness: respect for both self and others.

   One way of applying Table 2.3 to yourself is to consider the right

Table 2.3 *Assertive rights*

1. I have the right to be treated with respect	**and**	Others have the right to be treated with respect.
2. I have the right to express my thoughts, opinions and values	**and**	Others have the right to express their thoughts, opinions and values.
3. I have the right to express my feelings	**and**	Others have the right to express their feelings.
4. I have the right to say 'No' without feeling guilty	**and**	Others have the right to say 'No' without feeling guilty.
5. I have the right to be successful	**and**	Others have the right to be successful.
6. I have the right to make mistakes	**and**	Others have the right to make mistakes.
7. I have the right to change my mind	**and**	Others have the right to change their minds.
8. I have the right to say that I don't understand	**and**	Others have the right to say that they don't understand.
9. I have the right to ask for what I want	**and**	Others have the right to ask for what they want.
10. I have the right to decide for myself whether or not I am responsible for another person's problem	**and**	Others have the right to decide for themselves whether or not they are responsible for another person's problem.
11. I have the right to choose not to assert myself	**and**	Others have the right to choose not to assert themselves.

hand column first. Which do you find difficult to accept as rights for other people? Then consider the left hand column. Are there any rights you want to cross out? Any to add? I have found it particularly helpful to examine my part in a particular incident, taking each right in turn. I suggest trying something you feel very angry or upset about. Your strong reaction may be healthy but it may be because you are not accepting one of the rights of the other person.

The next level of definition of assertiveness is styles of behaviour. Most writers suggest three non-assertive styles: aggressive (or blaming), passive (or compliant), and manipulative (e.g. Dickson, 1987).

'Aggressive' can be defined as overtly ignoring one or more of the rights of others, e.g. through threats; 'manipulative' as indirectly ignoring others' rights, e.g. through 'emotional blackmail'; and 'passive' as ignoring your own rights. In some circumstances, aggression or passivity is the best style (Dickson, 1987) and in any case, no one is assertive all the time.

Finally, there are assertive skills. Again views differ, but some central skills are:

- saying no
- making requests
- giving and receiving compliments
- giving and receiving criticism
- developing and maintaining self-esteem.

The following outline of characteristics of saying 'no' skilfully is summarized from Dickson (1987).

The skill of saying 'no'

- Speak briefly, with a 'key phrase' if appropriate. The key phrase can be repeated if necessary, as in calm repetition (below), e.g. 'You may think it's silly *but I don't want to do it*'. It is important to find words that feel right to you.

- Speak clearly, directly and confidently (watch for inappropriate smiles and apologies).

- Notice your *first* reaction (as something to take into account, but not necessarily decisive).

- If unsure, ask for time and/or further details, e.g. 'I need to know more before I can decide'.

- *Calm repetition* may be useful (cf. Dickson's image of a tree swaying in a wind and returning to an upright position).

- Offer an alternative? e.g. 'I don't want to do X but I'd like very much to do Y'.

- Empathise? e.g. 'I guess you're disappointed but I really don't agree'

- Put in context? e.g. 'I like lots of things about our relationship and we've been friends a long time. I particularly like your liveliness. But I don't want to ... '

The skill of making requests is very similar to that of saying no e.g. being clear and direct, as in, 'I'd rather you didn't touch my arm'. An additional aspect is not to sabotage your request by expecting a

Table 2.4: Examples of the relationship between elements of self-awareness and self-disclosure

Awareness of:	Can be expressed as:
Thoughts	I think ... I wonder ... etc.
Sensations	I see ... I hear ... etc.
Emotions	I feel ... I'm ... etc.
Wants	I want to ... I'd like to ... etc.

rejection (or too confidently assuming acceptance!). Here is a final example: 'Can I say something to you that's important to me? ... I feel threatened (or upset or irritated, etc., whichever is true) when you touch my arm, and *I'd like you to stop doing it*' (key phrase). There are many good longer examples in Dickson (1987).

A framework for applying assertive skills

1. Choose the person and the issue carefully at first, i.e. if skills are new to you, choose relatively easy situations. Consider doing a 'risk analysis': potential costs? benefits?

2. Prepare what you want to say.

3. Rehearse, preferably with coaching from truthful, sensitive, constructive friends. Choosing words that feel right for you can be crucial and so can nonverbal aspects like stance, tone of voice and facial expression.

4. Choose the time. Check with the other person if appropriate, 'e.g., 'I want to ask you something. Is it a good time or can we meet later?'

5. Try it.

6. Analyse constructively what happened, looking out for irrational beliefs (this is discussed in the next section).

Assertiveness depends, in part, on self-awareness (Figure 2.1). Table 2.4 illustrates some of the links between the two. The more elements of our 'self' that we are aware of, the greater our choice of things to say. More subtly, increased self-awareness seems likely to mean a more sturdy sense of self, and perhaps also a more positive sense of self.

Irrational beliefs and assertiveness

This section focuses on an aspect of self-awareness which can be an obstacle to being assertive: irrational beliefs. The list in Table 2.5 is a

Table 2.5: Examples of irrational beliefs

- I must be liked by everyone

- I must be perfect in all that I do

- if I make a mistake, I'm bad and should be punished

- when things are not the way I want them to be, it is horrible and catastrophic

- we have very little control over what happens to us

- if something may be dangerous, harmful or distressing then it is important to think about it constantly

- it is easier to run away from difficulties than to face them

- we are the products of our upbringing and can do little to change who we are

- we should be concerned and upset by the problems of other people

- there is always a correct answer to a problem

- anger is always bad and destructive and should be curbed

- it is better to give than to receive.

sample of what may be some of the most common irrational beliefs (see, e.g. Ellis, 1962). Ellis argues that anyone who treats one or more of these beliefs (or variations) as a guide is likely to be upset and unhappy as a result. They overlap considerably with the rights listed in Table 2.3.

Good clues to irrational beliefs are the words 'must', 'always' and 'should'. They can, sometimes with considerable patience and several attempts, be changed as follows.

1. Examine the belief. Dispute it, e.g. Why is it awful? What is the evidence for it? And against? How good is the evidence? What is the effect of this belief on me? Do I want this effect to continue?

2. Write a more realistic version. For example, a more realistic version (rationally) of 'I must be liked by everyone' is 'No one is liked by everyone. Some people won't like me'.

3. Repeat the new belief to yourself as often as necessary, and try to behave as if it is true.

Assertiveness and sexual attraction

Sexuality, and power masquerading as sexuality, are problems in some health care settings (Buyssen, 1996). Sexual relationships between counsellors and clients are unethical because of the effects on some clients (Russell, 1993, 1996) and so that clients and potential clients feel safe and are not deterred. Is this true for health professionals and patients? What about ex-patients and ex-clients? Russell (1993) suggested, on the basis of models of loss and grief, a 6-month period before ex-clients (not counsellors) make contact socially, and Bond (1993) that counsellors should be able to demonstrate that they have acted ethically and that an absolute ban ignores clients' right to act autonomously. On the other hand, as he points out, some counselling organizations argue that there will always be a power imbalance and that therefore relationships with ex-clients are always unethical. Either way, assertive skills are obviously relevant to both attraction and harassment.

Managing psychotraumatic stress

Working in health care settings inevitably means being involved in disturbing and horrifying events, e.g. seeing and treating serious injuries, patients or clients suffering severe emotional or physical pain, violence or the threat of violence, mistakes, or an accumulation of smaller incidents. Reactions can often be coped with in the same way as everyday stress, but sometimes they become psychotraumatic – defined by Buyssen (1996) and others as

1. re-experiencing (e.g. flashbacks);
2. denial/absence of emotion when not actually re-experiencing and feeling overwhelmed by the incident, and also avoiding related situations;
3. inappropriate arousal (e.g. being constantly alert and afraid).

Each of these three elements can be the main one for a particular person and post-traumatic stress disorder (PTSD) is diagnosed when they last more than a month. However, strategies for coping are generally the same for all three levels of reaction – stress, psychotrauma, PTSD – with the obvious provisos that earlier is better and that professional help is more likely to be needed for psychotrauma and PTSD. The main general principle for coping with psychotraumatic stress is to 'work through' it rather than pressing on, or coping in silence. Buyssen (1996) includes three checklists on aspects of 'working through', which I have condensed as follows:

What you can do for yourself:

- Try to focus on what happened.
- Allow time for the natural healing process.
- Alternate confrontation with distraction.
- Talk (and/or write) about what happened.
- Ask for and accept support.
- Expect some people to be more understanding than others.
- Resume work as soon as possible, but stay in the background.
- Be more careful than usual.

When to call in professional help:

- when your emotions are too much, and you feel chronically tense and empty
- when symptoms do not disappear, e.g. lack of appetite, night-mares
- when one or more of the three main elements of psychotrauma – re-experiencing, denial and inappropriate arousal – persists
- when, after a month, you are still not able to enjoy anything.

Helping others:

- Keep in contact.
- Let the other person talk: they may well need to go over the event several times.
- Occasionally say what you understand the other person to be saying.
- Be patient, both with the person and with the process of recovering.
- Offer to do the things with them that you normally do with them.

The rest of the original checklist is mainly 'don'ts', but if you do the above, and not much else, you will avoid these anyway.

In Buyssen's final chapter he discusses what organizations can do to support staff, when often they do nothing: after all, it is said, nurses are trained to help each other and if they are not able to withstand disturbing incidents perhaps they should change jobs. Buyssen argues that debriefings, when they are available, often lack the necessary depth, and that the vital policies are: routinely to provide basic information about traumatic events and their after-effects, to establish support teams (for trauma support, *not* for complaints or problems), to select and train the teams carefully, and to support the teams themselves.

Conclusion

The underlying logic of this chapter is that looking after ourselves is a priority, partly because we are then more likely to be effective in our work (and to be able to work for more years!). I realize it is easy to believe this but still get 'caught up' or 'sucked in' – vivid metaphors. But it is not inevitable. Looking after ourselves means keeping watch on our physical and emotional state, recognizing that there are more people to see and things to do than anyone could possibly manage, and taking action accordingly.

Appendix 1: Four strategies

This appendix contains brief notes on four strategies for managing or coping with stress. Evidence is cited and examples of when a strategy is contra-indicated are given where possible, but mainly it is a matter of trying them out. Combinations of strategies are also worth trying, e.g. hot bath plus or followed by writing.

1. Physical relaxation

Physical relaxation is an obvious way of coping with stress, both immediately and preventively. Two 10-minute sessions of progressive relaxation a day seem to have a beneficial and cumulative effect (Seligman, 1995). However, sometimes attempting to relax is itself stressful (Lazarus and Mayne, 1990 – see contra-indications below). Instructions/guidelines are widely available but several factors can make a difference, e.g. some people prefer a well-lit room, others a dark one, some respond best to several 2- or 3-minute sessions, and so on (Lazarus and Mayne, 1990; cf. Rosenthal (1993) on guided imagery, visualization, pets, etc.)

Some contra-indications and risks:

- Fear of losing control
- Very competitive
- Requires considerable patience and persistence (Cf. Table 7.2)
- May lead to avoiding causes or to an unhelpfully passive state.

2. Massage

Massage is quite common in intensive care units, oncology wards, hospices and other health care settings (Vickers, 1996). However, there are problems with assessing the competence of practitioners and with deciding which kind of massage is suitable for which patients, and for how long. Vickers carefully reviews research, practice and professional issues, and concludes that typical, gentle massage techniques (i.e. not deep pressure) are relatively safe.

Examples of contra-indications (from Vickers, 1996: 263):

- acute infectious disease
- unstable pregnancy
- any condition in which skin or bones are weak
- burns, broken skin, fungal infection.

3. *Physical activity*

The current main recommendation is to accumulate about 30 minutes' 'low intensity' activity per day, (at the level of walking fairly briskly – rather than getting sweaty and out of breath) (Wimbush, 1994). In practice, the strategy is to become more active *gradually and comfortably*, with more than 30 minutes a day or more rigorous exercise giving a reserve of fitness and more protection against some illnesses (Wimbush, 1994; Seligman, 1995). For a safer form of sit-ups, called sit-backs, see Bayne (1997).

A contra-indication and risk:

- injury.

4. *Social support*

Social support gives a sense of belonging, coherence and involvement. Low levels of social support are related to increased risk of several illnesses. It is not exactly clear what support is or how it protects, but it is powerful: for example, in two studies it was found to reduce complications and halve the length of labour in childbirth, and to double average survival time in sufferers from metastatic cancer (discussed in Totman, 1990). The support in the two studies consisted of conversation with an allocated untrained person and a weekly 90-minute group meeting, respectively.

Support groups seem to be most effective when they concentrate on specific difficulties at work rather than personal emotional problems (Llewelyn and Payne, 1995). Bond (1986) provides excellent guidelines for setting up and running support groups, distinguishes several kinds of support (e.g. listening, giving information) and discusses pitfalls in giving and receiving support. If you set up a peer support group rather than one with an expert leader, Nichols and Jenkinson (1991) is another useful resource.

Some contra-indications and risks:

- asking for the wrong kind of support, or the wrong person, or at the wrong time
- badly given support
- lack of limit-setting/boundaries.

References

Bayne, R. (1997) Survival. In I. Horton with V. Varma (Eds) *The Needs of Counsellors and Psychotherapists*. London: Sage.

Bayne, R., Horton, I., Merry, T. and Noyes, E. (1994) *The Counsellor's Handbook. A practical A–Z guide to professional and clinical practice.* London: Chapman & Hall.

Bond, M. (1986) *Stress and Self-awareness : A Guide for Nurses.* London: Heinemann. Notable for its non-patronizing tone and thoughtful discussions of contra-indicators. A new edition would be very welcome (10+ years is a long time in this area) but for me it is still the best book on stress so far, for other occupational groups too.

Bond, T. (1993) *Standards and Ethics for Counselling in Action,* London: Sage.

Buyssen, H (1996) *Traumatic Experiences of Nurses: When your Profession becomes a Nightmare.* London: Jessica Kingsley.

Dickson, A. (1987) *A Woman in Your Own Right.* London: Quartet.
The best applied book on assertiveness, for men too.

Ellis, A. (1962) *Reason and Emotion in Psychotherapy.* New York : Lyle Stuart

Fontana, D. (1989) *Managing Stress.* Leicester: BPS Books and Routledge.

Lazarus, A.A. and Mayne, T.J. (1990) Relaxation : some limitations, side effects, and proposed solutions. *Psychotherapy 27* 261–6.

Lazarus, R. and Lazarus, B.N. (1994) *Passion and Reason. Making Sense of Our Emotions.* Oxford: Oxford University Press.

Llewelyn, S. & Payne, S. (1995) Caring: the costs to nurses and families. In Broome, A. and Llewelyn, S. (Eds). *Health Psychology: Processes and Applications.* 2nd ed. London : Chapman & Hall.

Nichols, K.A. and Jenkinson, J. (1991) *Leading a Support Group.* London: Chapman & Hall.

O'Driscoll, M and Cooper, C.L. (1996) Sources and management of excessive job stress and burnout. In P. Warr (Ed.) *Psychology at Work,* 4th ed. Harmondsworth: Penguin.

Pennebaker, J.W. (1993) Putting stress into words: health, linguistic and therapeutic implications. *Behaviour Research and Therapy 31* 539–48.

Pennebaker, J.W., Colder, M. and Sharp, L.K. (1990) Accelerating the coping process. *Journal of Personality and Social Psychology 58* 528–37.

Rakos, R.F. (1991) *Assertive Behaviour: Theory, Research and Training.* London: Routledge.
A very careful and detailed analysis.

Rosenthal, T.L. (1993) To soothe the savage breast. *Behaviour Research and Therapy, 31* (5) 439–62.
Reviews methods – some familiar, some strange – for 'unwinding'.

Russell, J. (1993) *Out of Bounds, Sexual Exploitation in Counselling and Therapy.* London: Sage.

Russell, J. (1996) Sexual exploitation in counselling, in R. Bayne, I. Horton. and J. Bimrose. (Eds) *New Directions in Counselling.* London: Routledge.

Seligman, M.E.P. (1995) *What You Can Change and What You Can't*, New York: Ballantine Books.

Totman, R. (1990) *Mind, Stress and Health*. London: Souvenir Press.

Vickers, A. (1996) *Massage and Aromatherapy. A Guide for Health Professionals*. London: Chapman & Hall.

Wimbush, E. (1994) A moderate approach to promoting physical activity: the evidence and implications. *Health Education Journal 53* 322–26.

PART 2

GENERAL SKILLS

Chapter 3

University of Nottingham
School of Nursing & Midwifery
Derbyshire Royal Infirmary
London Road
DERBY DE1 2QY

Listening: some basic qualities and skills

Rowan Bayne and Verena Tschudin

Health professionals spend much of their time listening to patients, patients' relatives and colleagues. When listening to patients, important information has to be heard to make an accurate diagnosis or to decide what treatments to follow or change. This sometimes means that medical and nursing staff ask specific questions, and therefore get answers which may not be what the patient wants to say. As Clare (1991: 17) puts it: 'Some symptoms can be embarrassing and the patient may find that having buoyed himself (sic) up to unburden himself, he actually cannot give a full account of what ails him without a good deal of encouragement and understanding . . . '

It is more difficult to listen to what people feel or mean rather than to their factual information. Patients may want to talk not only about embarrassing physical symptoms, but also about such things as relationship problems, fears about the future, worries over past mistakes, beliefs that may be ridiculed, admissions of ignorance and whether they are being told the whole truth about their condition or illness. Perhaps the patient does not want to burden the doctor or nurse, and yet needs them to know. Moreover, although it takes time and emotional energy to hear them, it may be that because of this effort now, very real savings are made in terms of less medication, fewer wasted visits to GPs and clinics, and more effective use of referrals.

In this chapter we briefly review some ideas about personal qualities associated with listening well and related skills – challenging, goal-setting, interviewing, reporting and negotiating – and a framework of four questions for helping. Finally, we touch on ways of improving listening qualities and skills.

Basic qualities of listening

The first quality that anyone needs who wants to help another person, or hear what needs to be said, is *attentiveness.* This is a stance that conveys to the patient or client that only she or he counts right now. It is an openness to the other that encourages trust to develop and in which both persons can be honest. Ideally this means that the two persons are not interrupted and that they can speak easily with each other. Being attentive means being present in mind as well as body. It also means being aware of feelings, memories and conflicts stirred within ourselves as we are with another person, and noticing any blocks and reasons why we may not be attentive or willing to be attentive, and, quite differently, it means observing nonverbal communication well, especially patients' posture, expression, voice tone and gestures. Most health professionals are skilled at observing physical symptoms but, in concentrating on these, may overlook the language of the body concerned with feelings, memories, hopes and fears. By paying attention to a patient's nonverbal communication we may understand more quickly and fully what matters to them and how they are feeling.

Posture, use of space and furniture communicate qualities such as status, which Clare (1991) sees as the major barrier to good communication. It is not only that there may be a difference in stance – the professional standing up and the patient lying down – but it is the difference between a professional expert and a lay person, a healthy and an ill person, a giver and a receiver, a person referred to by profession (doctor, nurse) and a person not so known. A patient waits for the doctor. The doctor has information about patients that patients do not (normally) have about themselves. These differences make for stereotypes, prejudices and values that can make communication problematic from the start.

Being *non-judgemental* of the other person is also essential. Codes and policies urge professionals to respect their patients' views (GMC, 1995) and not to judge them on grounds of ethnicity, beliefs, personal attributes, the nature of their health problem or any other factor (UKCC, 1992). But it happens. For example, sometimes a judgement is made, almost automatically, on the basis of a name before the patient is even seen. However, being non-judgemental does not mean that making judgments is wrong, but must entail working to become more aware of this part of our selves and how it affects relationships and communication. Being with another person 'means that for the time being, you lay aside your own views and values in order to enter another's world without prejudice' (Rogers, 1980: 143).

Another quality of someone who listens is being *hopeful*. Hopefulness is more than optimism, reassurance or enthusiasm. It is a deep belief in the other person. Negativity, dark moods and setbacks are not brushed aside, but acknowledged. Being hopeful means that we believe that this is not all there is to a person or a situation. It means using or awakening imagination. It also means being *supportive:* standing by someone, believing in the person, encouraging them and also challenging them, but always with the aim of helping, never condemning (Tschudin, 1994).

Perhaps the most important quality is *empathy*, described by Rogers (1980) in detail and from many different points of view. He called the following passage an 'attempt' to describe it:

> To be with another in this way means that for the time being, you lay aside your own views and values in order to enter another's world without prejudice. In some sense it means that you lay aside your self; this can only be done by persons who are secure enough in themselves that they know they will not get lost in what may turn out to be the strange or bizarre world of the other, and that they can comfortably return to their own world when they wish.
>
> (1980: 143)

Empathy is a difficult state and process to define precisely, let alone to research well. See, for example, Mearns and Thorne (1988), Bayne *et al.* (1994), Marangoni, Garcia, Ickes and Teng (1995), Merry (1995), Duan and Hill (1996). Psychological type theory (Chapter 7 of this book) implies a multi-faceted conception and practice of empathy, with different emphases reflecting the different 'types' of the author or practitioner. For example, counsellors with a preference for 'thinking' and 'judging' tend to have a more active conception and reported practice than those who prefer 'feeling' and 'perceiving', and sensing types focus more on empathy as an immediate state, while intuitive types are concerned more with the *process* of empathy and with patterns and possibilities (Churchill and Bayne, submitted for publication). The theory suggests that all the elements are important at different times.

Listening and related skills

All the skills of communication are also skills of counselling, and vice versa. Skills such as listening, paraphrasing, challenging and goal-setting help patients and clients to be clearer about their thoughts and feelings, find what matters most and least to them, move forward emotionally and thus, in time, feel more comfortable. Skills needed particularly in health care also include giving information (discussed in Chapter 1), interviewing, reporting and negotiating.

The skill of *paraphrasing* consists of two parts: a simple reflection of a) the words spoken, and b) what may be unspoken but implied. As an example:

> Client: I have been thinking about what they are going to do when I go into hospital.
>
> a. You've been thinking about the operation
>
> b. You sound as if you are scared about whether your operation will be successful or not.

The simple reflection of the words spoken in the first response can be particularly useful at the beginning of an interaction, to check that the listener understood the client correctly. It shows that the listener is listening at a relatively straightforward level. The patient may then say more, e.g. that she is looking for information about the operation, or on what the anaesthetist's success rates are. In order to respond adequately, it is important to have understood the patient's need and feelings (emotions). In the second response, the helper implies that he or she notices that the client is scared (as well as worried). Bayne *et al.* (1994) discuss paraphrasing in detail.

In order to *challenge* a client well, the listener needs to be specific and clear; tackle only one point at a time; stay supportive; encourage the client or patient to be self-challenging; and above all, build on success (Tschudin, 1994). What needs to be challenged are irrational fears and blind spots, the mental blocks and the various restraints that we put in our way. Challenges are invitations to change. The idea of them is to help clients move where they need to go rather than push them to where you (the counsellor) think they ought to be, and they are more likely to be effective if you have *earned the right* to challenge by first being empathic and developing a trusting relationship.

Challenging often takes little more than an observation and a willingness to share your sense of what may be going on for the other person. For example, Liz had a mastectomy just three days ago. Her consultant had told her that her tumour had been very small and that her prognosis was very good. Having talked with her fellow patients, Liz found that most of the other women had lumpectomies, but her consultant was considered to be of the 'old school' and still performed mastectomies. A conversation with her physiotherapist, Jane, whom she instinctively trusted, was therefore important. During this conversation Jane challenged Liz: 'You say that you are feeling fine but you look angry. You mentioned several times that you are not angry with the consultant, but I wonder whether this is really true as you seem so tense'. This challenge was only the start for the release of much anger towards several men in Liz's life. Jane was able to help her sensitively before contacting the breast care specialist, with whom Liz talked further on several occasions.

The skill of *goal setting* is sometimes necessary to help a client to move forward. Empathy (communicated mainly through skilful para-phrasing) and challenging can lead to deeper understanding or to seeing things differently, but that in itself is not always enough. Putting understanding into practice is the next, sometimes the most difficult, step. Having goals can focus the client's attention and action, mobilize energy and effort and motivate the search for strategies to accomplish them.

Goals have to be realistic and neither too ambitious nor too undemanding. They also have to be specific. Wanting to live more comfortably with a chronic illness is a general goal, and to achieve this intermediate goals may be necessary. The helper's skill here is not to provide the goal, but to help the patient to find his or her own goal, and to keep the focus on searching for and implementing adequate goals. Thus, this skill consists of focusing, shaping, clarifying, consid-ering new perspectives, and generating options.

The skills of *giving information* (see also Chapter 1) seem very basic to daily living. In health care, where information is essential to giving informed consent, the need for clear, honest and adequate information is paramount. How much or how little information is given may be a matter of trust between the professional and the client, but the need for information also changes with the state of illness. Someone with a broken finger will probably need less information and debate than someone following a mastectomy. But when the broken finger is on the hand of a professional violinist, different information is necessary than would be the case for a teacher. Perhaps the main thing to stress is that we should not make assumptions about people's knowledge, nor about their capacity to absorb information when it is given in emotionally charged situations. 'Bad' news so judged by professionals may not be 'bad' to patients, and conversely seemingly minor information can transform someone's life.

The skills of listening and paraphrasing are also basic to the skills of *interviewing*. This term is here understood to apply to interviewing patients and clients for purposes of establishing a basis for treatment and care. In Clare's view 'an open-ended interviewing style is most likely to create the type of clinical relationship desired' (1991: 18). Most interviewing starts with some specific questions like the age and occupation of the client and it is tempting to go on in this style even when the questions refer to completely different material. A series of closed questions is less likely to lead to real understanding (Bayne *et al.*, 1994). It too readily feels like an interrogation and results in a passive role for the interviewee.

When an interview has taken place, *reporting* on it may be the next step, either orally or in writing. Handing on to colleagues the information gained means that a team can care for and treat a person. It is important that the relevant information is handed on and that it is clear to all concerned. However, it is important also to respect the patient's or client's right to confidentiality. Much information is handed on in the form of abbreviations, and this needs to be done in such a way that there is no ambiguity. Schultz (1997: 231) draws particular attention to the many different ways in which not-for-resuscitation codes are documented, leading at best to confusion and at worst to death.

Patients and clients not only have a right but also a need to receive reports of investigations and treatments. Important here is that what may be 'bad' news to a health professional, may not be 'bad' to a patient, and what is seemingly 'good' to a professional may be shattering to a client. Having heard the client's story in the first instance may make it much easier to convey news in the most appropriate way for them (see Chapters 1 and 7).

Negotiating is more than a skill for winning. Many situations are not clearcut, and treatments or care plans need to be negotiated between doctors and patients, between doctors and doctors, or doctors and other health professionals. It may also mean negotiating with managers for provisions for care. Honey (1988) lists a number of negotiating skills for reaching agreement when there are two or more different starting points. Focusing on interests rather than on positions means that alternatives can be considered, and the most appropriate option selected. Exploring proposals rather than counter-proposing allows the pros and cons of each proposal to be seen for what they are. Attacking the problem rather than the person is essential if negotiations are to be constructive. By sticking to the facts rather than exaggerating, the emotional temperature is kept at a reasonable level. When disagreements have to be voiced, making them constructive by giving the explanation first enables the other person to react to the explanation rather than to the disagreement. Being open about thoughts and feelings is not naive but contributes to openness. We make assumptions very easily and they are often wrong; by asking questions, paraphrasing and being empathic, we are less likely to fall into traps. Summarizing the discussion makes the decisions explicit, assuring as good an agreement as possible.

Four questions for listening

The following is a set of questions that one of the authors has used both in practice and in teaching (especially nurses) for a number of years. These questions can be applied to most situations and problems and are suggested as guides only, not as a fixed model. The questions are:

- What is happening?
- What is the meaning of it?
- What is your goal?
- How are you going to do it? (Tschudin, 1995: 56)

Listening is usually considered to be paraphrasing rather than questioning. However, to have a model in the form of a set of questions has several advantages. The questions are simple and can be remembered easily. They keep the focus on the client. They are open questions, seeking a 'story' rather than a one-word answer, and they help the listener to concentrate on the client or patient. They also make clients work to find the answers within themselves rather than having them suggested.

The proposed questions are by no means exclusive. Indeed, the particular questions need never be asked at all in this form as long as the session develops in the general directions in which the questions point. The questions can also be useful for professionals to evaluate their own part in a conversation. They are as relevant for very short one-off interactions as for long-term counselling, and as helpful for parts and segments of interactions as for complete sessions with clients, patients, colleagues and friends.

What is happening? This is perhaps the most useful question in any type of helping. It is the basic question in any process, research, review or enquiry. Surprisingly, it is perhaps also the question asked least often. Most people, when faced with a problem of any kind, try to give an answer or solution, rather than consider what the problem is about.

When we ask questions that explore 'what is happening?' we are asking for a story. This is where the problem starts: most health professionals do not readily have time to hear stories, especially if they start way back in the past. Various tactics can be used to curtail such stories, including asking the next question in this model at strategic moments, or re-focusing on the present. But perhaps the story *needs* to be told. Very often it is in the telling of the story that clients finds an answer, solution or goal for themselves.

In more complex situations it may be necessary to ask many people 'what is happening?' In some situations this question needs to be asked of everyone involved: the patient or client first of all, and also friends, family, nurses, doctors, social workers and everyone around a patient. This is particularly the case in complex family circumstances, in acute settings in intensive care, and about any situation that remains unclear. This question may need to be asked again as a situation changes. However, when this question has been exhaustively asked and thoroughly answered, then the next three questions may be found to have been answered too.

What is the meaning of it? This question points to the reason for telling the story. It is not only the meaning of the story itself that matters, but the meaning of an illness, accident or relationship, making connections, and becoming aware of values, needs and desires. These may need to be refocused and restructured. This question (or a variation of it) points to the deeper layers of life and living, where the inner essence of a person is addressed, and where religious and spiritual values may be relevant. Many people have difficulties with these aspects, and helpers may be hesitant or unsure of how to help others with them. A useful principle is that even asking this question awkwardly is more likely to be helpful than avoiding it.

What is your goal? When an insight has been reached, it needs to be externalized in some way, otherwise it may be lost. Understanding is helpful only if it also helps us to change our attitudes, behaviour, or both. It is sometimes easy to say, 'Now all I have to do is . . . ' but it probably needs to be made more concrete, otherwise it may become just a pious wish. For example, a patient who admits to feeling overwhelmed in the presence of a consultant may aim to have enough courage at the next meeting to ask for more information regarding her prognosis. Making the goal more concrete by preparing two or three specific questions will make it more likely to be achieved.

How are you going to do it? When a goal has been seen as a possible way for moving forward, it needs to be put into practice, but there can be a world of difference between saying 'I have to write a letter' and actually writing the letter, or between 'I need to be assertive' and being assertive. Therefore this question anchors the process by asking the client to be specific as to how this is going to be carried out.

If possible, a review and evaluation should also take place. This can easily involve using the same set of questions again, perhaps in the past tense.

Improving listening qualities and skills

Counselling and communication skills are interactive skills and are therefore ideally learned in interactive settings, such as courses and workshops. Maguire (1981) has shown that medical students trained in history-taking make more accurate diagnoses. Horton and Bayne (1996) suggest some ways of using tape-recordings to improve listening and challenging qualities and skills. Many people consider themselves to be good listeners, but when confronted with themselves on tape, a different reality comes to light. The fact that they have gone so far probably means that this is an incentive to learn more, rather than a cause for disillusionment. When video or audio recording is not possible, reflective diaries may be helpful.

Everyone who uses counselling skills with clients and patients should have a supervisor with whom cases and situations can be discussed on a regular basis (see Chapter 1). Strategies and skills can be reviewed and perhaps also tried out in this safe environment. More important than any form of explicit learning is, however, an awareness of self that leads to a willingness to be challenged and to change. Listening to ourselves, reflecting on our ways of being, and negotiating with ourselves are fundamental to communicating effectively with others.

References

Bayne, R., Horton, I., Merry, T. and Noyes, E. (1994) *The Counsellor's Handbook; A Practical A–Z Guide to Professional and Clinical Practice.* London: Chapman & Hall.

Churchill, S. and Bayne, R. (Submitted) Psychological type and different conceptions of empathy.

Clare, A. (1991) Developing communication and interviewing skills, In R. Corney (Ed.) *Developing Counselling and Communication Skills in Medicine.* London: Routledge.

Duan, C. and Hill, C.E. (1996) The current state of empathy research. *Journal of Counselling Psychology* 43 (3) 261–74.
Reviews theoretical confusions and methodological weaknesses in empathy research. Argues that empathy needs to be studied more, and distinguishes between different kinds or aspects of empathy.

GMC (1995) *Duties of a Doctor.* London: General Medical Council.

Honey, P. (1988) *Improve Your People Skills.* London: Institute of Personnel Management.

Horton, I. and Bayne, R. (1996) Audio-tape recordings in counsellor education and training. In S. Palmer, S. Dainow and P. Milner. (Eds) *Counselling. The BAC Counselling Reader.* London: Sage.
On practical and ethical issues, e.g. how to introduce the idea of tape recording to a client, and who owns the recording.

Maguire, P. (1981) Doctor-patient skills. In M. Argyle (Ed.) *Social Skills and Health.* London: Methuen.

Marangoni, C., Garcia, S., Ickes, W. and Teng, G. (1995) Empathic accuracy in a clinically relevant setting *Journal of Personality and Social Psychology* 68 (5) 854–69.
Incisive review of previous research, and a good example.

Mearns, D. and Thorne, B. (1988) *Person-centred Counselling in Action*. London: Sage.

Discusses in depth the person-centred attitudes of empathy, unconditional positive regard and congruence.

Merry, T. (1995) *Invitation to Person Centred Psychology* London: Whurr.

Rogers, C. (1980) *A Way of Being*. Boston, MA: Houghton Mifflin Co.

A wide-ranging collection of articles, e.g. on growing older, empathy in everyday life as well as in counselling and education. Rogers' last book.

Schultz, L. (1997) Not for resuscitation : two decades of challenge for nursing ethics and practice. *Nursing Ethics 4* (3) 227–38.

Tschudin, V. (1994) *Counselling; A Primer for Nurses, Workbook*. London: Bailliere Tindall.

Tschudin, V. (1995) *Counselling Skills for Nurses*. 4th edn. London: Bailliere Tindall.

This is a basic book used by many professionals in health care, not only nurses.

UKCC (1992) *Code of Professional Conduct*. London: United Kingdom Central Council.

Chapter 4

Listening to stories about illness and health: applying the lessons of narrative psychology

John McLeod

In the main, health professionals are trained to adopt a scientific, objective perspective on the ailments and complaints presented by patients. The goal of assessment and diagnosis is to identify symptoms that will lead to the classification of a disease and the subsequent formulation of a suitable form of treatment. Behind the questions asked by the health professional lies a highly complex, schematic model of how the organism functions. It is the possession of this kind of deeply-structured expert knowledge that allows doctors, nurses and other health workers to frame and test hypotheses regarding the illness process and prognosis in patients.

Patients, by contrast, do not have at their disposal the same powerful biological models of health and illness. Nevertheless, anyone who is ill shares with their doctor or nurse a need to explain and understand what is happening to their body. With non-professional, lay people, the form of understanding of accounting for illness that is most often employed is the *story*. People tell stories about their health and illness. The sense of 'what made me unwell', 'how I feel today' or 'how I got better' is communicated to others through stories.

Role and development of the narrative approach

The aim of this chapter is to highlight some of the ways in which an awareness of storytelling can be a valuable asset in the field of health care. Essentially, paying attention to the stories told by patients has the potential to improve collaboration between health professionals and their patients (through enabling better communication and mutual understanding), and to reduce the psychological impact of the illness. Telling the story can also have direct effects on health status (Pennebaker, 1988, 1993a,b).

One of the most significant developments of the last two decades in psychology, and in the social sciences in general, has been an increasing appreciation of the role of narrative and storytelling in everyday life. Increasingly, it is being recognized that the way that most people make sense of their lives, in most circumstances, is to narrate stories about events. We let each other know about our experiences by capturing the meaning of these experiences in stories. More than that, we are surrounded by stories – in news media, novels, films, and television – that express moral dilemmas, solutions, and ways of feeling and behaving. The work of Bruner (1986, 1990), Sarbin (1986), McAdams (1985, 1993) and Howard (1991) has led to the establishment of a 'narrative psychology'. This movement has also had an increasing impact on the practice of counselling and psychotherapy (see, for example, White and Epston, 1990; McLeod, 1997) as practitioners of psychological therapies have discovered the value of working with the stories their clients tell about their troubles. From a narrative perspective, therapy becomes an opportunity to review and 're-author' problem stories.

For the purpose of applying narrative ideas to issues of illness and health, it is useful to simplify narrative theory by concentrating on three principal themes. First, a story represents a way of *structuring* information about events. At one level, events are given narrative structured through the *sequential* nature of storytelling. A story conveys a sequence of actions or occurrences: what happened, what happened next, and so on. However, a story that comprises merely a series of 'things that happened' is not very interesting: 'good' stories achieve more of a dramatic climax. There are several models of story structure, of which the best-known is derived from the work of the sociolinguist William Labov (Labov and Waletzky, 1967). This model proposes that 'well-formed' stories begin with an 'abstract' or summary of what the story is about, then the 'orientation', which locates the narrative in a particular time and place. The story proceeds through one or more action sequences that lead to a resolution and then finally a 'coda', which brings the speaker back to the present moment. Throughout the narrative, but particularly towards the end, there are 'evaluation' statements'. Labov's model of story structure captures many of the functions that a story fulfils: describing action, expressing a sense of judgement or evaluation, and positioning the speaker in relation to his or her audience.

The second main theme in understanding narrative concerns *self-presentation*. A story communicates information about the storyteller, about how he or she perceives the world, how he or she feels about things, what he or she believes to be right or wrong. In Bruner's words, a story is set in a 'landscape of subjectivity'. A story carries messages about the sense of self of the teller. Finally, a story is a *performance*; it is something that is to a greater or lesser extent co-constructed between teller and audience. The story that is told will reflect the quality of the relationship between teller and listener. More than this, as a performance the story has an effect on those who hear it. Part of the meaning of any story depends on the answer to questions such as, 'Why is it being told now?' or 'What does it mean that it is told in *that* way?'.

These three key dimensions of stories – structure, self-presentation and performance – provide a scaffolding from which the meaning of stories of illness and health can be deconstructed and understood. Counselling and communication in health care settings usually centre around the construction of illness narratives. One of the key characteristics of health care institutions is that they privilege the stories told by professional experts, to the extent that users and patients can experience themselves as silenced, as unable to tell their story.

Stories about illness and health: achieving coherence and continuity

When one person tells another about an episode of ill-health, he or she is doing more than merely chronicling a series of visits to the doctor, days off work, medical procedures, and so on. Drawing on the ideas introduced earlier, an illness narrative can be seen as a way of conveying a sense of 'who I am' to the listener or audience. One of the qualities of illness narratives that has been noted by several researchers is that the experience of being ill represents a *disruption* in the life-narrative of the person. Most people are able, at least in principle, to talk about the story of their life in terms of a continuous narrative that stretches from birth through to the present and then into various possible futures. At one level this life-narrative can be simple and schematic: 'I grew up in London, went to college, trained as a teacher, got a job, got married, had two kids . . . ' Clearly, the teller can build layer upon layer of complexity on top of this core life-narrative, depending on the circumstances and audience. Illness, or at least serious or chronic illness, cuts across this story. The person's life-narrative has taken an unexpected turn, they have 'lost the plot'. And yet, living outside of a coherent life-story is a frightening experience. The person who is ill works hard to re-create a unified life-story into which the illness can be placed.

A powerful example of this kind of narrative process can be found in the account of her cancer experience written by Jackie Stacey (1996). On learning of her diagnosis, she started to read everything she could about her illness, until:

> a story began to take shape. First, the cancer was named ... the narrative that emerged gradually organized physical sensations into a temporal sequence with a causative effect.
>
> (pp. 6–7)

Stacey expresses the sense of crisis surrounding the collapse of her previous life-narrative:

> the past must now be re-imagined and re-scripted. Life, it has turned out, was not what it appeared to be. The present is not the imagined future it once was ... as for the future, it is suddenly compressed into the most frightening of time scales, previously unimaginable.
>
> (p. 7)

In constructing a 're-imagined' life-narrative, Stacey noted that she was aware of the expectation of many of those around her that she construct a 'heroic' story, an account of medical triumph over tragedy.

Another useful study of illness narratives is offered by Williams (1984), who interviewed people suffering from rheumatoid arthritis. One of the case studies he presents is that of Bill, an ex-soldier who had worked as a machine operator in a paperworks. Bill has given a great deal of thought to the issue of how he came to have arthritis: 'how the *hell* have I come to be like this?' His explanatory account, around which he builds his illness narrative, centres on exposure to toxic circumstances in the print shop. By contrast, Gill, a schoolteacher living in a prosperous area, tells an arthritis story that highlights a series of stressful life events in the year preceding the onset of the disease, while Betty, a shop worker, narrates a story of her arthritis that locates its genesis in the working of God's will. Williams interprets these stories as expressions of the distinctive ways that individuals perceive the social world within which they live. The particular causal factors selected by Bill, Gill and Betty are 'important reference points in the interface between self and society' (p. 198). Williams asserts that:

> narrative reconstruction is an attempt to reconstitute and repair ruptures between body, self and society by linking-up and interpreting different parts of biography in order to realign present and past and self with society.
>
> (p. 197)

The illness narrative that a patient and his or her family construct is therefore created out of the key themes in his or her biography. Bill, for example, had had a life centred around resistance to, and mistrust of, authority. Betty's life was given order and meaning by her religious faith. The illness, when it arrives, has to be made to fit into these pre-existing narrative structures.

Kleinman (1988) has brought together a comprehensive account of the process of constructing stories of illness and sickness. Building on studies carried out in many different cultures, he argues that:

> patients order their experience of illness – what it means to them, and to significant others – as personal narratives. The illness narrative is a story the patient tells, and significant others retell, to give coherence to the distinctive events and long-term course of suffering. The plot lines, core metaphors, and rhetorical devices that structure the illness narrative are drawn from cultural and personal models for arranging experience in meaningful ways and for effectively communicating these meanings. Over the long course of a chronic disorder, these model texts shape and even create experience. The personal narrative does not merely reflect illness experience, but rather it contributes to the experience of symptoms and suffering. To fully appreciate the sick person's and the family's experience, the clinician must first piece together the illness narrative . . .
>
> (p. 49)

Kleinman emphasizes the role of narrative in structuring and ordering the experience of suffering. The story becomes a means of living with the uncertainty of illness.

Running through the work of Stacey, Williams, Kleinman and others into how people 'narrativize' their illnesses are themes of *coherence* and *continuity*. In terms of psychological and existential needs, people who are ill seek to re-establish a life-narrative that will allow them to make sense of what has happened, that will re-connect past, present and future. The process that occurs is similar to the experience of any kind of trauma. Wigren (1994) has shown how therapy with people suffering from post-traumatic stress disorder needs to include the opportunity for the client to tell his or her story. The traumatic event represents an experience that is hard to assimilate into the on-going life-narrative of the person, partly because it has had the effect of 'shattering' the assumptions of safety and trust around which that story has been constructed, and partly because elements of the trauma story are so painful that they are just not told; they cannot be put into words.

An example of what it can be like to have lost the thread of life story, and to be at a stage of being unable to piece together an alternative version, is captured in an interview which Kleinman (1988) carried out with an unmarried 25-year-old woman who had a large part of her colon surgically removed, and who was learning to live with a colostomy. She told Kleinman that:

> I feel so embarrassed by this – this thing. It seems so unnatural, so dirty. I can't get used to the smell of it. I'm scared of soiling myself. Then I'd be so ashamed I couldn't look at anyone else. I've met four or five colostomy patients. They seem to be doing so well. But none was my age and unmarried. Who would want a wife like this? How can I go out and not feel unable to look people in the eyes and tell them the truth? Once I do, who would want to develop a friendship, I mean a close one? How can I even consider showing my body to someone else, having sex? Now they tell me the colitis is gone, together with my bowel; but what is this I'm left with? It's a disaster for me. I feel terrible, like a monster. I see my folks. They cry; they feel so bad for me. They can't talk about the future. What future?
>
> (p. 163)

This passage expresses directly the experience of a patient who has lost a crucial component of her life-story: friendship, dating, marriage. She cannot, at this point, find any way of creating a story through which she can live in normal society. She sees herself as a 'monster'.

The power of the dominant narrative

A multiplicity of stories can be told about almost any event, reflecting the different perspectives that people may wish to take in relation to that event. For example, someone who is ill in hospital may put on a 'brave face' and tell a hopeful story to visitors, sharing their stories of fear and pain only with their spouse or close family members. However, it is not the case that all possible stories have an equal likelihood of being told. We live in a social world in which some stories and voices are privileged and others are silenced. The story that is told depends, in many situations, on the power and authority of the teller in relation to his or her audience.

As mentioned earlier, the account of her cancer experience written by Stacey (1996) refers to the pressure she felt to frame her story in 'heroic' terms. She wrote of finding herself enmeshed in the 'masculine hero narratives of science':

> stories of surviving cancer fit easily into ... patterns of a journey from chaos to control. They combine the masculine heroics of such narratives with the feminine suffering and sacrifice of melodramas ... There is the meta-narrative of the fight against cancer in general, accompanied by the micro-narratives of the emotional episodes along the way.
>
> (p. 14)

The point being made here is that the way that people tend to talk about the experience of cancer (e.g. as a 'fight' or 'battle') can be seen as a particular kind of story-line (a heroic good-triumphs-over-evil narrative). Stacey suggests that this type of dominant cultural narrative serves to suppress other stories that might be told. She writes:

> what of those who declined rapidly, who cried with fear and terror in the face of death, who continue to be haunted by the threat of the cancer returning . . . for whom there is no 'hope' . . . (who) discovered new depths of loneliness or depression, or felt betrayed and abandoned by those they relied upon?
>
> (p. 19)

It seemed clear to Stacey that it was important to 'rescue' these submerged, non-heroic cancer stories, that it was necessary for her or for anyone else suffering this disease to have the opportunity to tell her own story, in its fullness and in her own way. Although she could see that heroic stories served a purpose in helping to offer a positive direction and purpose to those in despair, it was also essential to find ways of articulating and expressing the stories of 'fear and terror in the face of death', as a means of gaining support and comfort in some very bad times.

One of the most significant developments in counselling and psychotherapy in recent years has been the 'narrative therapy' of White and Epston (1990). They hold the view that in any culture or social group, there exist 'dominant stories' – narratives that are widely held to be valid and true. These stories are perpetuated through all of the cultural media available to members of that group, such as everyday gossip, books, religious teaching, film and so on. There is, as a result, strong pressure on any member of the group to live 'within' that story, to frame his or her experience in terms of the dominant narrative. However, the experience of individuals sometimes falls outside of the dominant story. There are times when it can be difficult or impossible to reconcile what 'did happen' with the story of what 'should happen'. White and Epston use the term 'unique outcome' to describe these occasions when the complex lived experience of a person clashes with the dominant cultural story.

People seek therapy, according to White and Epston, because they find themselves stuck in a dominant narrative that does not do justice to their experience; that does not 'fit' any more. Their main therapeutic strategy is to work with the person to achieve two goals. The first is to 'externalize' the dominant narrative. The intention here is to help the person to see that the dominant story is only one way of describing and accounting for what goes on. It is as though the person is able to put some distance between himself or herself and a story-line which, up to then, had served to define their sense of who they were. The second goal of therapy is to identify 'unique outcome' moments, and to build meaning around them to the stage where they can become 'alternative stories'. Ultimately, the person is then more able to become something like the 'author' of their own personal story, rather than living out a story that has been 'authorized' by (invisible) others: 'as persons become separated from their stories, they are able to experience a sense of personal agency ... a capacity to intervene in their own lives and relationships' (White and Epston, 1990: 6).

The ideas of White and Epston can be applied to the kind of situation recounted by Stacey (1996). For example, a person receiving treatment for cancer may tell nothing but 'heroic' stories of how he will 'win the battle'. Initially, his family may support and encourage this story-line, because it may appear to be the only option. As the disease progresses, however, the person's inability or unwillingness to talk about his vulnerable and difficult experiences, his 'stories of fear and terror in the face of death', may become a barrier between him and those who love him. White and Epston would approach this situation by inviting the patient to find a name for the dominant story, and then mapping all the ways in which the story affected his life. The person might come to talk about his 'heroism' and the times when 'heroism' was useful for him, and other times when it prevented him from saying what he felt. He might be able to talk about the experiences in his life that made him able to create 'heroism'. His family members could be put on the alert for appearances of 'heroism'. All this sets the scene for the discovery of 'unique outcomes', perhaps by inquiring about 'the times when you don't feel the need to be heroic'.

This is a highly simplified example, and it would be wrong to imply that the process of helping people to open up a space for what White and Epston call 'the performance of new stories' is a simple or straightforward matter. It requires sensitivity, time and courage. But the key issue is that the story told by a person who is ill may not be the only story that he or she is able to tell. Behind the dominant story are other, hidden, stories which, if brought to light, can greatly assist the ill person and their carers to negotiate the experience of the illness.

It would be wrong to assume, following White and Epston, that 'dominant stories' and 'unique outcome' stories are always to be found in separate, neat narrative packages. Although a person with cancer may at one moment tell a story that is saturated in 'heroism' and then at a later time recount an alternative version of his chemotherapy that is equally suffused in vulnerability, it is more likely that these two (or more) plot-lines will be intertwined in almost every story he tells. One way of making sense of this phenomenon is to make use of the concept of *voices*: different facets of the 'landscape of subjectivity' of the storyteller are expressed through contrasting or competing voices within a story. Penn and Frankfurt (1994) provide some valuable examples of the use of 'voice' in counselling situations.

The concept of voice has also been used by Mishler (1984) in a study of the dynamics of medical interviews. On close analysis of the way that patients told the story of their illness in the context of a consultation with a doctor, Mishler was able to see that what the patient said could be regarded as a struggle between the 'voice of medicine' and the 'voice of the lifeworld'. The former constituted a biological, scientific way of understanding illness, centred on symptoms, while the latter expressed the significance and meaning of the ailment in the everyday life of the patient. Both voices existed within the patient's story. During some parts of an interview, the patient might be drawn by the physician's questioning toward speaking in the 'voice of medicine'. At other parts of the same interview, the doctor would be pulled into the patient's narration of a lifeworld. In the lifeworld, the patient is a protagonist, engaged in purposeful, motivated action. Within stories told through the voice of medicine, by contrast, it is the *body* that is the protagonist: the disease is the active agent.

It is vitally important for health professionals to listen to the voice of the lifeworld, as a means of making it possible to develop a collaborative approach with the patient. Clark and Mishler (1992) offer a sensitive reading of two contrasting doctor-patient consultations, one in which the patient was allowed and encouraged to expand on his personal story, and one where the doctor kept interrupting the patient's story. The doctor who worked *with* the patient, and who was willing to enter the lifeworld, proved to be much more effective at eliciting clinically useful information. The doctor who controlled the consultation through his use of the 'voice of medicine' appeared to leave the patient upset and confused.

Katz and Shotter (1996) suggest some ways in which health professionals may encourage the expression of a patient's personal voice. They give as an example the segment of doctor–patient dialogue summarized in Table 4.1. The patient was a woman from Haiti, and the consultation took place in a primary care clinic in Boston, Mass. Most of what is said in this section of transcript represents the gathering of routine clinical information. However, this interaction took place in the presence of a cross-cultural facilitator, employed by the clinic to mediate between patients and doctors. The facilitator urged the doctor to explore what the patient meant by her statement 'it's not like it is back home'. As the patient then began to tell her personal story, her demeanour changed: before, she had appeared depressed and disconnected, now she became 'energized and present' (p. 923). The emergence of this new voice transformed the way that this doctor was able to experience this patient. Katz and Shotter (1996) suggest that, for health professionals, the secret of gaining access to voices and areas of experience that are usually suppressed in ordinary patient-professional encounters is to be open to being 'moved' or

Table 4.1: A fragment of a conversation between a doctor and a patient

---

The doctor began by asking the patient:

'How old are you?'

'33.'

'What brought you to the primary care clinic?'

'Oh, two months ago, I was coughing, deep in my stomach ... '

'In your chest?'

'Yes.'

'Who did you see then?'

'Oh, I will find the letter the doctor gave me.'

'How is it now?'

'It's better, but I still feel something in my chest.'

'Congested? Do you cough up phlegm? What colour was it?'

The doctor asked where she was living.

'River Park. I live on the top floor with friends from church living down-stairs.'

'Do you work?'

'Yes, as a nurse's aide in a nursing home ... It's not like it is back home. It's hard to work there. I'm working too hard.'

The doctor continued, and asked, 'What else?'

'Pain from my period which I have two times a month, or every three weeks.'

'Anything else?' asked the doctor.

'I had a TB test ... '

'arrested' by momentary occurrences in what patients do or say.

Training in any of the health professions, such as medicine, nursing, midwifery or physiotherapy, can be viewed as comprising not only a process of learning about theories and procedures, but also as exposure to a period of intensive socialization into a set of professional norms and world-view. Becoming a health professional involves learning the 'dominant narrative' of that profession. Practising as a professional healthcare worker involves continual reinforcement of that narrative in conversations with colleagues, reading professional journals, and participating in continuing education. At times it can become far from easy for those who are immersed in the 'voice of medicine' to appreciate the idiosyncratic and apparently irrational stories that lay people tell about their illnesses. In an effort to counteract this tendency, many medical and nursing schools are attempting to integrate a sensitivity to the patient's story into the training curriculum. The Katz and Shotter (1996) paper, cited earlier, is part of this movement. Marshall and O'Keefe (1995) offer an example of how narrative sensitivity can be built into medical training.

The therapeutic value of storytelling

The value for health professionals of listening to stories about illness and health has been presented, so far, largely in terms of improving the quality of patient-carer communication. It is worth also giving brief mention to some evidence that suggests that storytelling can have a direct effect on health status. This evidence is derived from the work of James Pennebaker and his colleagues. Pennebaker has carried out a number of experiments in which people who have suffered a difficult and stressful life event (e.g. loss of a job, moving home) have been asked to write about their feelings about this experience for a set amount of time (e.g. 10 minutes) each day (Pennebaker, 1988, 1993a,b; Pennebaker, Kiecolt-Glaser and Glaser, 1988). In this research it has been found that, in comparison with subjects in a control condition, at follow-up the people who had 'put their stress into words' reported fewer visits to their doctor, and were healthier on a variety of other measures of physical and psychological well-being.

Pennebaker argues that there is a basic human need to disclose difficult experiences, and that the act of holding back and *not* talking about problems uses up physiological energy and lowers resistance to disease. The core ideas in Pennebaker's model are outlined in Table 4.2. The practice of asking clients to write about difficult experiences is being used increasingly by counsellors and psychotherapists (see, for example, Lange, 1996). The findings reported by Pennebaker are consistent with the results of studies that show that social support is an important aspect of recovery from illness. While it is necessary that social support can be associated with practical assistance concerning finances/money, mobility and diet, it is also clear that people with social support are more likely to have someone in their life to whom they can tell their story, or with whom they can construct a meaningful 'illness narrative'. The popularity and effectiveness of self-help groups for people with health problems can also be explained in this way.

Although most of the studies carried out by Pennebaker involved

Table 4.2: Pennebaker's model of the link between the process of disclosing
traumatic experience and health

---

1. Inhibiting ongoing thoughts, feelings or behaviour is associated with physiological work. Short-term inhibition is manifested in increased autonomic nervous system activity. Long-term inhibition serves as a low-level cumulative biological stressor that can cause or exacerbate a variety of health problems, ranging from colds and flu to heart disease and cancer.

2. Active inhibition is associated with deleterious changes in information processing. In holding back significant thoughts and feelings associated with an event, individuals do not process the event fully, and are left with ruminations, dreams and other intrusive cognitive symptoms.

3. Confronting traumatic memories can help to negate the effects of inhibition, by reducing the physiological work put into inhibition, and by enabling individuals to understand and assimilate the event.

---

people writing about their experiences, there were also studies in which people were asked to tell their story orally to another person. For example, Pennebaker, Barger and Tiebout (1989) found that when Holocaust survivors told their story, the stress levels of the teller (as measured by their galvanic skin conductance) went down, while the stress of the listener was significantly raised. This experiment offers a simple but convincing demonstration of the fact that listening to stories of illness and trauma can be distressing and stressful for the audience. The implication for health professionals who allow their patients to disclose stories of the 'lifeworld' is that they themselves then need somewhere where they in turn can share these stories. As Nichols (1991) has argued, health professionals can allow their patients to open up only when they themselves feel sufficiently supported to allow this process to take place.

Conclusion: the importance of the story space in health care

This chapter has introduced some of the issues and possibilities that flow from taking patients' stories seriously. People who are ill are often in a period of transition, struggling to make the link between their pre-illness life-narrative and the story of who they are now. Achieving a coherent narrative can help to give the person a sense of control and mastery over his or her condition, and can facilitate the process of establishing a viable role within their social group. Telling the story is a way of being known. The growing theoretical and research literature in narrative psychology suggests ways of assisting people to tell their stories in creative and health-enhancing ways. Allowing space for telling the story, and creating opportunities for the experience of being heard and understood, are part of effective health care.

References

Bruner, J. (1986) *Actual Minds, Possible Worlds*. Cambridge, Mass: Harvard University Press.

Bruner, J. (1990) *Acts of Meaning*. Cambridge, Mass: Harvard University Press.

Clark, J.A. and Mishler, E.G. (1992) Attending to patients' stories: reframing the clinical task, *Sociology of Health and Illness*, 14 (3): 344–72.

Howard, G.S. (1991) Culture tales: a narrative approach to thinking, cross-cultural psychology and psychotherapy, *American Psychologist*, 46: 187–97.
A clear and accessible description of a narrative approach to psychology.

Katz, A.M. and Shotter, J. (1996) Hearing the patient's 'voice': toward a social poetics in diagnostic interviews, *Social Science and Medicine*, 43 (6): 919–31.

Kleinman, A. (1988) *The Illness Narratives: Suffering, Healing and the Human Condition*. New York: Basic Books.
This book is highly recommended as essential reading for anyone interested in a humanistic, patient-centred approach to health care.

Labov, W. and Waletzky, J. (1967) Narrative analysis: oral versions of personal experience. In J. Helm (Ed.) *Essays on the Verbal and Visual Arts*, Seattle: University of Washington Press.

Lange, A. (1996) Using writing assignments with families managing legacies of extreme traumas, *Journal of Family Therapy*, 18: 375–88.

Marshall, P.A. and O'Keefe, J.P. (1995) Medical students' first-person narratives of a patient's story of AIDS, *Social Science and Medicine*, 40 (1): 67–76.

McAdams, D.P. (1985) *Power, Intimacy, and the Life Story: Personological Inquiries into Identity*. New York: Guilford Press.

McAdams, D.P. (1993) *The Stories We Live By: Personal Myths and the Making of the Self*. New York: William Murrow.

McLeod, J. (1997) *Narrative and Psychotherapy*. London: Sage.

Mishler, E.G. (1984) *The Discourse of Medicine: Dialectics of Medical Interviews*. Norwood, NJ: Ablex.

Nichols, K.A. (1991) Counselling and renal failure. In H. Davis and L. Fallowfield (Eds) *Counselling and Communication in Health Care*, Chichester: Wiley.

Penn, P. and Frankfurt, M. (1994) Creating a participant text: writing, multiple voices, narrative multiplicity, *Family Process*, 33: 217–32.

Pennebaker, J.W. (1988) Confiding traumatic experiences and health. In S. Fisher and J. Reason (Eds) *Handbook of Life Stress, Cognition and Health*, Chichester: Wiley.

Pennebaker, J.W. (1993a) Putting stress into words: health, linguistic and therapeutic implications, *Behaviour Research and Therapy*, 31: 539–48.

Pennebaker, J.W. (1993b) Social mechanisms of constraint. In D.W. Wegner and J.W. Pennebaker (Eds) *Handbook of Mental Control*. Englewood Cliffs, NJ: Prentice-Hall.

Pennebaker, J.W., Barger, S.D. and Tiebout, J. (1989) Disclosure of traumas among Holocaust survivors, *Psychosomatic Medicine*, 51: 577–89.

Pennebaker, J.W., Kiecolt-Glaser, J.K. and Glaser, R. (1988) Disclosure of traumas and immune function: health implications for psychotherapy, *Journal of Consulting and Clinical Psychology, 56*: 239–45.

Sarbin, T.R. (1986) The narrative as a root metaphor for psychology. In T.R. Sarbin (Ed.) *Narrative psychology: the storied nature of human conduct*, New York: Praeger.

One of the clearest statements of the nature and scope of a 'narrative psychology'.

Stacey, J. (1996) Conquering heroes: the politics of cancer narratives. In P. Duncker and V. Wilson (Eds) *Cancer: Through the Eyes of Ten Women*, London: Pandora.

A powerful piece of writing, which combines personal experience and social science in a very effective manner. The other chapters in the book are equally worth reading.

White, M. and Epston, D. (1990) *Narrative Means to Therapeutic Ends*, New York: Norton.

The highly influential book that stimulated interest in narrative approaches to counselling and psychotherapy.

Wigren, J. (1994) Narrative completion in the treatment of trauma, *Psychotherapy, 31*: 415–23.

Williams, G. (1984) The genesis of chronic illness: narrative re-construction, *Sociology of Health and Illness, 6* (2): 175–200.

An early classic in the area of applying narrative ideas to health problems. Beautifully written.

Chapter 5

Mental illness and communication

Jim Monach

Health professionals play a vital role in protecting and extending the capacity for full citizenship among those who suffer from a mental illness. The exercise of rights as a citizen requires effective communication. This chapter will address core generic communication qualities and skills in the specific context of mental illness, some blocks to effective communication, and some of the specific contributions of talking treatments to the conditions of hearing voices and delusions.

Why is communication important in mental illness?

The essence of mental illness is a disturbance of thinking and/or feeling. While this is usually (but not always) evidenced in speech or action, the diagnosis and treatment of mental illness has to be rooted in understanding the inner world of the presenting patient. Only sensitive and effective communication skills can ensure the validity or reliability of the diagnostic process or the effectiveness of subsequent treatment. The blood test and the x-ray are of little use clinically, the key diagnostic tool is therefore the skill of the health professional in communicating effectively with the person in distress (Chamberlin, 1988).

The claims made in the 1970s by 'existential psychiatry' that schizophrenia could be caused by distortions of communication within families (Laing and Esterson, 1970) have since been found to have no foundation. Unfortunately, they caused much distress to relatives and much misplaced therapeutic effort. The positive legacy of these theories has been to focus attention on the dangers of distorted communication patterns (such as the double bind) in generating distress and possibly other forms of mental illness and personality disturbance (Laing, 1972). They also helped to create the climate in which the emotional quality of close relationships came to be studied carefully, leading to family interventions with schizophrenia (Barrowclough and Tarrier, 1994).

A further significant issue is the prevalence of mental disorder. About six million people a year receive treatment in the UK for some form of mental distress: as many as for heart disease, and thrice the numbers suffering from cancer. Estimates of 1:3 or 1:4 are accepted as representing the rate of psychiatric 'caseness' among general practice consultations. Those with physical disease are especially vulnerable to psychiatric illness; the reverse is also true (Goldberg et al., 1994). Perhaps only half of these cases will be identified as 'mentally ill' by their GP (Goldberg and Huxley, 1992). Training in communication skills is known to improve significantly the ability to recognize mental illness among a GP's patients (Goldberg et al., 1980) which in general has been found to improve outcome for the patient concerned, independent of the treatment provided (Goldberg and Huxley, 1992). All health professionals need to have the skills to promote the recognition and appropriate treatment of mental illness.

Since the signs and symptoms of mental disorder rely heavily on discriminating normal from abnormal aspects of feeling and thinking, effective communication is essential. All communication takes place in a context of time, place, culture, age, class, and so on. Attempting to interpret communication without reference to such issues will lead to misinterpretations and misunderstandings. There can be no 'normal' without careful consideration of these referents. The writings of transcultural psychiatry warn of the consequences of trying to understand significant communication without a proper understanding of the cultural context of the transaction; personal distress, religious experience and grief are described in that individual's own cultural context (Littlewood and Lipsedge, 1989). The American Navajo saying puts it graphically: 'never judge a man until you have walked a moon in his moccasins'. Few psychiatric symptoms are exclusive to abnormal mental states. Indeed, it has been demonstrated that *ordinary* thinking processes lie behind the maintenance of abnormal thought (Brett-Jones et al., 1987). (The interested reader will find a detailed discussion of the evidence against a categorical model of mental illness in Goldberg and Huxley (1992)).

Even in the case of delusions there are numerous cultural, bacteriological, toxicological and physiological possibilities to explore before it is safe to consider the possibility of psychosis; and then there is the unexplained phenomenon of long-term voice-hearing with neither apparent psychiatric nor medical explanation (Romme and Escher, 1993). We may all at times feel preoccupied, sad, distressed, distracted, anxious or restless without having a mental illness; all those who have a mental illness may also exhibit such feelings without their being significant parts of their 'illness'. There is ample evidence that psychiatric professionals are quick to pathologize normal behaviour, which reinforces the warning that the 'normal are not detectably sane' (Rosenhan, 1996). Reliable and skilled communication in the context of psychiatric knowledge and knowledge of the patient has to disentangle these problems.

What constitutes effective communication?

There are a number of features of effective communication that are of special importance in work with those who are mentally ill. These are not unique, as has been emphasized already. Given the impact that mental illness has on key aspects of interpersonal relationships, it does make them even more important. The first three qualities discussed below are readily recognizable as the 'Rogerian Trinity'. Sheppard (1993) found that these qualities were strongly related to measurements of patient satisfaction. In summarizing the evidence for the effectiveness of psychotherapy, Lambert and Bergin (1994) emphasize the significance of the qualities of the therapist, rather than the theoretical model of psychotherapy used, in predicting outcome; empathy was especially valued by patients and related to successful therapy in several studies reviewed. Although Carl Rogers seems to believe that these qualities are both necessary *and* sufficient conditions for therapeutic change, the view emerging in overviews of recent research is that these qualities are necessary but *not* sufficient.

Empathy

Empathy is the characteristic emphasized by virtually all commentators on effective helping relationships, since Carl Rogers: the ability to understand accurately what another person's world looks and feels like from their point of view and to convey this understanding in a relationship; what Huxley (1963) called the 'attempt to penetrate the metaphysical aloneness of the other'. Essentially, we can never succeed in this attempt: we are all 'I's' and can never fully know another 'I', but to try is vital in the therapeutic relationship. Empathy is not of course the same as showing concern or compassion for suffering, which is 'sympathy', although the term is sometimes used in this erroneous way. The distinction might also be made that empathy is to feel 'with' someone, while sympathy is to feel 'for' someone. Egan's (e.g. 1975) skills-based approach to counselling is very helpful in developing an understanding of 'accurate empathy' and a competence in its use.

> *Client:* I wake up feeling so depressed, so sad and desperate . . . every morning.

> *Counsellor:* That must make it very hard to get going, even to get out of bed.

Tilbury (1993) suggests that empathy has several functions: it helps us to assess what is not normal for that individual; it permits an understanding of the other's internal world; it can be therapeutic in itself for the individual who rarely experiences such a quality in a relationship; and it can foster the relationship. The expression 'I know how you feel' has, of course, no place in professional helping, being either naive, arrogant or impertinent; if used, it rather indicates a *failure* to empathize. How can one begin to know, taking Hart's example, what it is like to suffer the continual background of a voice saying 'you are useless' and 'you might as well be dead'? We can gain insight from listening to our clients, from reading personal accounts like Linda Hart's (1995) and even through having a similar experience ourselves, but her experience will remain unique – *her* voice speaking to aspects of *her* experience with *her* father and *her* relationship with him, and his expectations of *her* – which even another voice-hearer cannot know fully. Recent reports of failed community care which have ended in tragedy have often emphasized failure by the professionals to get to know the inner life of the sufferer, thus offering the opportunity to assess risk realistically.

Acceptance

Rogers called this quality 'unconditional positive regard'. It implies respect for the other as a person of value and unique worth, irrespective of what she or he might do, or has done. It expects of the worker and promises clients that they will be accepted for themselves, while in no sense suggesting acceptance or approval of all that they might do or say. There are no conditions attached to such a relationship. Truax and Carkhuff's (1967) preferred variant of this is 'non-possessive warmth'; this is valuable for emphasizing that while the relationship is one of warmth and concern, it should not invade the private space of the client. A psychiatric survivor wrote of her psychotherapy that she doubted it had any value 'without a feeling of being liked and understood' (Reynolds 1996). An important aspect of this is that the worker focuses on the person, not on the problem: in the words of an old patient who died in Ashludie Hospital, Dundee, Scotland 'so open your eyes, nurses, open and see / not a crabbit old woman, look closer – see ME!'

(An accepting response to a client with schizophrenia after he smashed up his bedroom:)

Client: 'I am sorry that I upset my parents so much, but I can't help it when things get on top of me.'

Counsellor: ' . . . do you think that's why we need to keep meeting? – to find ways of avoiding you feeling so upset that things like that happen; to prevent you losing your temper with them?'

Genuineness

Also described as 'congruence', the quality of being a real person with the client. Such a characteristic requires that the health professional does not adopt a pose and is as spontaneous and non-defensive as the situation allows. This does not advocate divulging endless details of their own lives or troubles; rather that they are able to share some common experiences where it is judged that this will, in some way, free clients to accept certain things about their own situation or feelings that would otherwise be felt abnormal or idiosyncratic. This area is clearly one of those where professional experience and supervision are crucial if the health professional is to be able to distinguish where such self-revelations are likely to be helpful to the client, clarifying an issue or problem, rather than self-indulgent or diversionary.

In psychoevolutionary terms, Gilbert (1992) sees high attachment security as a key protective factor against depression; certain knowledge that close attachment relationships are reliable and will be there when needed. This is a quality of relationships that will be effective in helping the depressed patient: genuineness is an important contributory element.

(In responding to a client experiencing hallucinations that urine was coming through the ceiling:)

Counsellor: 'No, I can't see any urine, but seeing it must be very upsetting for you.'

This makes the distinction between their reality and your own, which can lay the foundations for work that might help them come to see this experience as an hallucination also, without the rejecting and humiliating experience of being told they are imagining things. The therapist can accept another's reality without colluding with a delusion. Some workers may be tempted to 'agree' with someone's delusions as a means of pacifying them or gaining their co-operation, e.g. in an admission to hospital. It is possible, and much better, to take the line suggested that acknowledges the client's reality without implicating the worker in pretending to share it.

Experience suggests that a client suffering delusions, especially paranoid ones, will find an interested but cool and slightly detached approach more acceptable than one that is very warm or effusive, and thus too personally involved. This might seem to offer the danger of smothering or becoming absorbed into the client's confusing world. An unhelpful answer in the above situation might be:

'How terrible for you; you must be so confused and miserable!'

Practical help

This might not appear to rank as an aspect of communication. The literature, however, suggests that it should be seen as one of the ways in which the effective helping relationship is created, given credibility and sustained. This may be so especially for those who are harder to reach through the distress or deficits caused by their mental illness. In the early 1970s, when social work was becoming professionalized, absorbing the ideas of the social sciences, considerable controversy was caused when a social worker wrote an article about his work entitled 'Why I give them money'. This was considered by his superiors to hark back to an older, less professional time of practical welfare and earned him temporary suspension and a rebuke. While money or other practical assistance might not be the panacea, it has become clear that it is highly valued by clients of the mental health services, as others. The literature of service user views emphasizes the importance of practical assistance with the problems of daily living. The top three priorities of service users in one survey (Shepherd *et al.*, 1994) were assistance with housing, financial problems and physical health matters; while professionals and carers rated professional support, treatments and monitoring as most important.

Services are just beginning to relearn the lesson of Samuel Tuke writing in 1813, 'Of all the methods by which the patients might be induced to restrain themselves, regular employment is perhaps the most generally efficacious' (Warner, 1994: 245). This lesson has not been lost on the radical 'psichiatria democratica' reforms in Italy, where such practical interventions are seen as the prerequisite for more conventional therapeutic work.

The 'closure' of San Giovanni Hospital in Trieste was accompanied by the opening, in the old ward blocks, of a cafe-bar, radio station, print workshop, community gardening enterprise and toy-making shop. Not only is such practical assistance a vital part of full communication, it can also facilitate communication over difficult areas of 'inner life' which the client might otherwise find it difficult to share, especially in the false situation of the counselling room. The value of sharing an activity in order to give the client the opening to share personal information, if wished, has long been a significant element in working with adolescents, which is of equal value in this area. Activity is itself an important aspect of communication and it can provide an opening for other important communications.

A serene mind

It might seem a counsel of perfection, but there is ample evidence that those who are troubled communicate most effectively with those who can leave their own troubles outside the interview room. 'Begin with a serene mind' is the Zen-inspired way of describing this requirement (Brandon, 1982). This is not advocating the therapist as a *tabula rasa* in the manner of traditional psychoanalysis, where the specific purpose is to facilitate the exposure of the transference and counter-transference processes; rather it is reminding us that the needs of the patient *in front of us* must be paramount in the professional helping relationship. Heller (1996) in the aptly titled 'Doing being human' reminds us how difficult this might be in the midst of a very heavy practice, 'we all need support, encouragement and continuing reflective training' (p.365). Worker stress will inhibit therapeutic relationships: one cannot truly be with one's client, focusing attention on their issues, when preoccupied with the difficulties of managing an over-large workload, or fearing redundancy, or dreading management or public reaction if one of the worker's many volatile clients really does act out some awful threat. These scenarios are all too familiar to those working in community mental health. Personal support is therefore crucial to engaging with the client therapeutically. This principle does not conflict with the injunction to genuineness; sharing personal information must be like Wordsworth's description of poetry, 'emotion recollected in tranquillity' (1979).

Confidentiality

The etymology of this word is significant: it is not possible for any of us to have *confidence,* trust, in a relationship if we cannot believe that *confidences*, personal information, will not be treated with respect and kept private, unless permission is given otherwise. Not every personal detail will be sensitive, of course. However, all of us who work in teams will sooner or later come across the client who wants information kept secret from one or more members of the team. In many cases this can be respected, in a few it cannot, e.g. where the information relates to hostile or aggressive feelings that might be acted out. In the same way, it is not uncommon for a delusional patient to include family members in his or her delusional system; and if these involve feelings of persecution or injunctions to harm then such confidences cannot be kept. In most of these situations the patient can be told, without destroying trust, that this sort of information will need to be shared with those who might be at risk. Much will depend on the worker being honest and open about the limitations to the guarantee of confidentiality, and tackling situations directly. The patient will often then agree that the information in question needs to be shared, and will approve the names of those who 'need to know'. If agreement is not possible the worker has the opportunity to explain why the confidence cannot be maintained absolutely, and that breaching the general guarantee in one instance does not make *all* confidences unsafe.

Interviewing in a suitable manner

The Mental Health Act, 1983, took the unique step of requiring that where a person suffering from a mental disorder might require compulsory admission to hospital in order to safeguard their own health or safety, or that of other people, the assessment interview should be conducted 'in a suitable manner'. The Mental Health Act Code defines this in terms that fit the requirements of good communication to be observed by mental health professionals wherever circumstances permit:

> making arrangements to overcome any communication difficulties such as not having a shared language, there being significant cultural difference or the client having impaired hearing or a speaking difficulty;
>
> the client being conscious and not incapacitated by alcohol or drugs (prescribed or illicit); ensuring that an actual interview takes place i.e. face-to-face discussion with the client, and not via a third party or through a closed door or window if it can be avoided.
>
> Summarized from Jones, R. (1996)
> *Mental Health Act Manual 6-018*, p. 574

These requirements may seem basic, but are easily neglected in the distressing, perplexing and sometimes intimidating context of acute mental distress.

Advocacy

Much has been said and written in recent years on the potential value for disempowered mental patients of having an advocacy service available. Advocacy arose in the context of normalization theories in the field of learning disabilities. Beresford and Croft (1993) discuss the different forms of advocacy thoroughly: *citizen* – unpaid, non-professional advocacy for the individual unable to represent his or her own interests fully through disability; *legal* – pursuit and defence of rights using skilled lawyers; *professional* – committed representation of the client's interests by a professional, sometimes acting within the role of case or care manager; *self* – people speaking for their own rights and interests. The last usage, it should be noted, may not be acceptable to all user and self-help groups, who may see this as suggesting some 'permission' from professionals to use one's own skills and competence in this way (Chamberlin, 1988). In practice, the term 'advocacy' is often used in a fairly loose way, combining elements of each of these ideal types. A survey of mental health service users in Barnet, U.K., found that the following characteristics were most valued in an advocate: empathy, good communication skills, knowledge of mental health issues, strength of character to be able to stand up to professionals and to be on the side of the client at all times. An ex-user of services was seen as the most suitable, and a relative as the least suitable person to be an advocate. Mental health services are increasingly regarding the availability of good advocacy as an essential counter-balance to the disempowerment, in communication especially, experienced by those with mental health problems.

What blocks effective communication?

If it is true, as Leff and Isaacs (1990) state, that 'a psychiatrist usually makes up his mind about the diagnosis within five minutes of first seeing the patient' there is all the more need to question the adequacy of the communication that has preceded diagnosis and treatment, and where any blocks might have occurred.

Power and the 'sick role'

Power differentials in the medical encounter confound equal and adequate communication. The medical clinic might be considered in these terms a 'laboratory of power' (Silverman, 1987). Clearly, the patient is the weaker in this situation and unless the clinician takes responsibility for monitoring the effect of this differential it might distort communication significantly, whether through deference, intimidation or fear. One in-patient coming out of a consultation with his psychiatrist said: '

What's the point? I can't understand a word he said! I just said I was fine.'

There are situations in mental health practice where power is an unavoidable aspect of professional relationships, especially those that involve the Mental Health Act. Whether risk to the self or others is feared, mental illness might then require the use of statutory restrictions on the freedom of the patient. There is no evidence that this makes it impossible for the worker invoking such powers subsequently to communicate effectively or work therapeutically with that person. The key lies in the open and honest acknowledgement of what was done, and why, in the worker's judgement, it had to be done. Only if the transaction is denied or avoided are problems to be expected. Linda Hart (1995) demonstrates both positive and negative ways of handling such situations.

> Christine came in . . . her attitude made me instantly angry and I jumped up and ran down the corridor towards the stairs . . . then Christine, in her 'hoity-toity' voice announced that I was being sectioned under Section 3 of the Mental Health Act. I felt deep despair. The nurse Trudy explained . . . her explanation sounded perfectly reasonable and if she had put this to me instead of Christine I wouldn't have tried to run off the ward . . . I felt totally powerless.

Becoming the identified patient in a situation might lead to a radical re-evaluation of that person's position (Radley, 1994). This might have four significant consequences: the sick person may be exempted from social expectations and roles 'I can't go to work – I'm sick'; she or he might be ascribed a lower level of personal responsibility, 'it's not my fault, I'm sick'; it is necessary to behave as if sick to be accepted as such, 'I'm agoraphobic; even on good days I can't risk going out in case I panic'; appropriate, qualified help should be sought 'you have to see a doctor, you're ill'. While the last of these consequences might match seeking counselling (at least if the expectations of those significant to the patient endorse it) the others tend to militate against the fundamental premise of counselling – that it is possible for clients to take ownership of their own problems with the guidance of the counsellor and, through mobilizing innate strengths, solve them. Change means assuming and accepting responsibility for oneself.

Ethnic difference

The history of Western psychiatry is blotted by examples of practice that was culturally specific and which therefore ignored the significant differences that need to be understood. Rack (1982), Littlewood and Lipsedge (1989) and Fernando (1991) provide differing, but complementary discussions of the challenges of psychiatric practice across cultures. The point has already been emphasized that the assessment tools of mental health practice are language, perceptions, beliefs and attitudes. It is therefore inevitable that problems will arise unless the most careful efforts are made to avoid misinterpretation of difference as pathology. The classic cases in the British context are the overdiagnosis of schizophrenia among African-Caribbean men, and misdiagnosis of distress among Asian women, in which it is argued that certain ethnic groups develop specific ways of reacting to mental distress which are misunderstood and therefore misdiagnozed by Western modes of medical nosology represented by conventional psychiatry. To give just one example: which behaviour is normal in the following scenario? A woman's husband dies tragically, at a young age, leaving her to cope alone with young children. Should she confine her tears to when she is alone, weep decorously at the funeral, receiving praise if 'she doesn't give way', 'keeps a stiff upper lip' and 'stays strong for her children'? Or should she weep uncontrollably, especially in front of her relatives, bewail her fate, perhaps tear her clothes, refuse to be consoled? Objectively there is only right or wrong in the cultural context; there is little doubt how white British society would evaluate these (admittedly stereotyped) alternatives; equally there is little doubt that British psychiatry (as Rack demonstrated) can easily make the error of seeing the latter not as evidence of appropriate behaviour for a Punjabi woman, especially if highly dependent on her husband and his family, but as excessive grief requiring psychiatric treatment.

The over-representation of African-Caribbean men in the forensic parts of the mental health services suggests to many commentators something more sinister than cultural mistakes; rather an institutionalized negative evaluation of such men, high expectations of their being violent, low expectations of change and lack of interest in providing the more complex, interpersonal treatments; in short, racism (Sashidharan 1986). Ensuring effective communication across ethnic boundaries is therefore subject to the very significant barriers of cultural misinterpretation and racist stereotyping.

Other 'cultural' barriers

The less obvious barriers, perhaps, are gender, disability, age and class. The sobering realities are that psychiatry has often been more ready to ascribe pathology to those outside the accepted social milieu of the assessors, who are predominantly white, male, heterosexual and middle class. Socially determined patterns of behaviour will also affect diagnostic practice: women are more likely to be diagnosed and treated as depressed and anxious as they will more readily communicate such feelings to their doctors. Men are more likely to be investigated for heart disease or have their drinking investigated as they will present physical symptoms more immediately, and drinking excessively is still seen as a masculine trait. Busfield (1996) discusses the extent to which gender influences psychiatric assessment and practice, independent of behaviour or distress.

There are striking research experiments reported in the psychological literature of interviews: for example, when disabled men were interviewed by a researcher, once feigning disability, sitting in a wheelchair and once 'undisguised', the interactions were significantly different in their length, verbal and physical spontaneity, eye contact, and even the amount the interviewee smiled. In particular, the interviewee presented in more stereotyped ways in the latter condition than in the former, and was less positive about the encounter. For both assessor and assessed the disability can overshadow all other aspects of the presentation, and confuse the communication (Comer and Piliavin, 1970). This evidence resonates with the negative reception that those who have a history of mental illness report when trying to get work (Birch, 1983).

This mechanism of perceived difference unconsciously releasing cultural stereotypes seems also to affect other groups. Elderly people, it seems, are under-diagnosed for depression especially, and are less likely to be offered talking treatments for any mental distress. Social class seems to operate in similar ways: lower class being more associated with reliance on drug therapy, more readiness to diagnose neurotic illness in response to unexplained physical complaints, less optimistic approaches to prognosis (Pilgrim and Rogers, 1993). Prejudice is a part of these interactions, but the degree of shared identity seems to have a direct and significant impact on the content and therefore on the quality of communication.

Language

Service user and carer research indicates the extent of dissatisfaction with the way in which professionals talk to them about mental health issues (Rogers, Pilgrim and Lacey, 1993). It might be suggested that one of the 'non-specific' reasons for the apparent success of psychosocial interventions with people with schizophrenia, and their families, is the extent to which attention is paid to getting this aspect of professional relationships right (Birchwood and Tarrier, 1994). In a service user survey, one said, 'When I asked him what's wrong with me, this doctor said, "you're slightly schizophrenic" whatever that means'. Jargon, technical terms, acronyms for legislation or services and so forth have no place in working with the mentally ill, unless the worker knows that the communication is clear and understood. Therefore the question should not be, 'have you ever had delusions or hallucinations?' but, 'have you ever heard voices that no one else heard, or seen something which others couldn't see?' It may not be simply the words we use, but also the strong messages that come across that communication is acceptable only in the theoretical terms of the therapist. Thus:

communication was a problem – and I had always thought I was an excellent communicator. June complained that I was never prepared to express myself in a way that was clear to her ... perhaps I did leave a lot out, but there didn't seem any point in explaining things that I already knew about ... (I felt) crushed by negative interpretations.

(Reynolds in Read and Reynolds, 1996: 165)

Stigma comes in all sorts of guises: professionals need to be aware of it in themselves as well as in others.

Psychiatric illness

The nature of the illness itself is of course an important factor which has to be remembered in talking and working psychotherapeutically. A defining characteristic of psychosis is often said to be the impairment of insight into the condition. This should not, however, be overstated; which of us enjoys perfect self-knowledge? Robert Burns urged, 'O wad some pow'r the giftie gie us / To see oursels as others see us!' The functional psychoses, such as schizophrenia and manic-depression, do cloud perceptions of reality. Where there are delusions, significant areas of discourse might be distorted, such as the nature of family relationships, or the content of some conversations. This is not the same as invalidating accounts of all family interactions or all conversations. Psychiatric labels are notoriously 'sticky' (that is, they persist and easily generalize). Good communication and effective counselling demand that the professional knows the individual and his or her social setting well enough to disentangle reality from fantasy or delusion. While the form of a communication might be delusional there might be important meaning within it. An elderly Hungarian refugee I knew in the 1960s, and naively helped to rehouse near a TV transmitter mast covered in red warning lights, thought this was Communist Party HQ. This terrified her; a lonely isolated woman who fled from the Russian invasion of her homeland, losing everything in the process. Had I known to attend to the meaning and not just the form of her delusions further distress could have been avoided.

Studies of psychiatric patients have demonstrated the extent of untreated communication difficulties (e.g. Emerson and Enderby, 1996). Those who work with people with schizophrenia will testify to the enormous distress associated with the realization of lost potential for ordinary life and relationships that so often follows, hence perhaps the enormously increased rate of suicide. *Accepting Voices* (Romme and Escher, 1993) and *Speaking our Minds* (Read and Reynolds 1996) both provide eloquent testimony to the continuing degree of understanding of other views of psychotic experience even during very florid episodes. Hannah Green (1964) in her evocative autobiographical novel *I Never Promised You a Rose Garden* writes of 'fading amid the clamour' of her voices but crying out for help while the 'ice-cold doctor' makes no answer but writes his notes.

Rowe (1988), in a book which many sufferers find very helpful, describes depression as 'a prison where you are both the suffering prisoner and the cruel jailer'. Her argument is that we become depressed when we hold firmly six opinions about ourselves and our world: 'I am worthless and unacceptable to myself and others'; 'I must hate, fear and envy others'; 'life is terrible and death is worse'; 'the past and future are alike, bad'; 'I must not get angry'; 'I must never forgive anyone, least of all myself'. These opinions are related to the cognitive approach to depression, which takes the view that it is not events themselves, but the beliefs we hold about these events that affect our mental health. In particular, it is because in some cases we come to have automatic thoughts that put a depressive spin on experiences, that we become, and stay, depressed. It is the therapist's task to challenge these automatic thoughts (Blackburn and Davidson, 1990). The depressed person may find it very difficult to engage in therapy that asks for a view of the future or optimism; the feeling that things are bad and will never improve is often a core feature of clinical depression. Similarly, having very low self-esteem may make any relationship hard to begin or sustain, let alone one intended to bring about change.

Among key characteristics of bipolar disorder (or manic-depression) is that of impulsiveness or recklessness. The therapist might have the important role to play of advising caution in taking decisions: it is not unusual for such a person to give away money and property impulsively or take potentially ruinous financial decisions. The same characteristic might imbue counselling and distort the process of communication, through a readiness to accept differing views of the situation, or decide on courses of action which are then equally impulsively changed or rejected. Distractibility and excitability may also be features of these conditions; an inability to concentrate or pursue a consistent line of thought is obviously inimical to the process of counselling.

However, Lambert and Bergin (1994) conclude that the effectiveness of psychotherapies, mainly with depression and neurotic disorders, equals or exceeds that of drug treatment which might otherwise have been used for the condition being treated.

Stigma

The work of Scheff and Goffman is still fresh and valuable in helping us to understand the difficulties faced by those who are mentally ill in receiving good quality, appropriate services and fair treatment in the community (see Heller *et al.*, 1996. Part 1). The evidence is clear that the general public still often equates mental illness with a propensity for violence. This has been made the more noticeable in the frequent struggles to get local communities to accept resettled patients from closing psychiatric hospitals, and in the publicity surrounding episodes of unusual violence that have lead to high-profile trials and enquiries (Muijen, 1996). Those who try to obtain employment after a period of mental illness testify to the futility of being open and expecting to get work (Birch, 1983).

Another aspect of this stigma is the poor expectations that workers themselves have of mental patients. One study which looked at mental health social workers found a depressing lack of optimism or expectation that anything significant could be achieved from working with a caseload of people with severe and enduring mental illness (Fisher, Newton and Sainsbury, 1984). Another example lies in the unanticipated move of community psychiatric nurses away from working with psychotic patients (Wooff, 1992). It may be this continuing professional stigma that has in part forced the Department of Health in the UK to issue strong guidance to health authorities to prioritize this group of patients (e.g. Department of Health, 1995).

Psychotropic drugs

Drugs are the first line of treatment in conventional Western psychiatry. A survey of psychiatric patients revealed that 98.6 per cent had received psychotropic medication for their problems: this is one aspect of psychiatric services that has received heavy criticism (Rogers, Pilgrim and Lacey, 1993). These drugs are demonstrably efficacious in the treatment of psychiatric symptoms, but they are rarely curative in the sense that without other, especially social, interventions of any kind the problem will permanently remit. At the same time, they carry significant side-effect profiles in many cases. One concern to be noted in this discussion is that effective communication or counselling might be inhibited by concomitant treatment with these drugs. Anxiolytics, such as the benzodiazepines, have a sedative action, slowing and possibly blunting reactions. Antipsychotics, such as the phenothiazines, are described by patients as leaving them 'living in a fog', lacking in emotional vitality, causing memory impairment and confusion. Antidepressants, especially (but not exclusively) the older tricyclic drugs, may cause agitation, sedation and confusion (Lacey, 1991). No claim is being made that all patients receiving these drugs experience such problems, only that working with someone who is a current psychiatric patient requires the awareness that their ability to use talking therapy may be impaired by the medication they are taking.

Another aspect of medication that is important in this context is 'non-compliance'. As Ley (1988) indicates, between 20 per cent and 70 per cent of all drugs prescribed are not taken as advised. He discusses in detail some of the research evidence on why this happens and how it might be avoided. The concept of 'non-compliance' is misleading in the flavour it often has in the literature of meaning 'a failure entirely located in the patient to follow the expert advice of the doctor'. This is as inadequate an understanding as when those working in the field of addiction talk glibly about a lack of motivation for change. Compliance, like motivation, is in substantial part the result of a communication process. The patient complies (takes the drug, follows the diet etc.) when it has been successfully explained and fully understood why the advantages of doing so will outweigh the costs of change, and has come to believe that following the advice is, in every sense, in her or his interests, and what she or he, *not* the doctor alone, wants. Prescribing drugs without careful attention to the effectiveness of the communication between prescriber and patient is unlikely to be satisfactory.

Specialized communication issues

In recent years a number of avenues have been profitably explored which offer more focused and specialist ways of responding to the specific problems raised by mental illness processes, and finding ways whereby communication and counselling of various kinds can play a direct therapeutic role. For much of the modern history of psychiatry, the twin tracks of physical and psychological treatment have run alongside each other, with greater or lesser degrees of cross-fertilization and mutual respect. Too rarely have these themes been viewed as having complementary functions; drugs have been castigated as the 'chemical cosh', psychotherapy as 'psychobabble' and psychogenetics as the 'new eugenics'. None of these polarities encourages effective interdisciplinary communication. There are, however, a number of specialized approaches to communication that have proven value.

Accepting voices

Hearing voices or auditory hallucinations has long been accepted as characteristic of serious mental illness and, in some circumstances, may be regarded as symptomatic of schizophrenia – in many respects the archetypal mental illness. Although historical, religious and literary sources are full of instances of voice-hearing in which there is no other suggestion of mental illness, psychiatry itself has, arguably, been slow to acknowledge the dangers of according excessive diagnostic status to voice hearing *per se*. The work of Romme and Escher (1993) and the Hearing Voices Network have publicized both the extent of non-psychotic voice-hearing in the 'normal' population (where normal excludes both the psychotic and those with strong mystical or religious beliefs) and the ways in which self-help approaches can assist those finding their voices (of whatever origin) troublesome.

Romme (1996) emphasizes the importance of taking the voice-hearer seriously, whether or not there is also a serious mental illness process. The significant factor is whether (among other things) the voice-hearer finds the experience painful and wants to end, or at least control, these voices. It is the role of the professional to understand as much as possible about the voices; their gender, what they say, when they are most active, their tone, when they are hostile and when friendly, and so on. There is no place in this approach for a psychiatrist simply recording in case records 'hears voices'. Managing the anxiety generated by voice-hearing will be a first step; a voice-hearers' self-help group can play a vital role in this. It will then be important to establish the situations, people, and emotions particularly associated with the onset or intensification of voice hearing – the triggers. Romme attaches great importance to attending to the *content* of what the voices say, not simply their existence or form, as traditional psychiatry might.

Another significant feature of working with voice-hearers is being receptive to both the worker's own, and the voice-hearer's, emotions. If the voices are critical, it is appropriate and understandable for the voice hearer to show irritation; and for the helper to show his or her empathy with somebody who is subject to continuous disembodied criticism. Where voices encourage the hearer to avoid and not deal with an important situation or set of emotions, it might be appropriate to confront the voice-hearer. Romme believes that a psychotic reaction could result from such a confrontation, but that this might be therapeutic: clearly it should be considered only in the context of a strong and very well-informed relationship. Finally, Romme argues that the helper will need to acknowledge painful experiences that underlie the voices, and which might lead to significant problems: Linda Hart (1995) describes how the voice she hears is that of the father who committed suicide and urges her to do the same. Without anyone to acknowledge this aspect of her voices, Hart follows her father's urgings. Social autonomy is seen as especially important, as voice-hearing is a 'penetrating experience' which, together with the stigma of hearing voices. leads all too easily to isolation. Finally,

Romme repeats the necessity of the trusting relationship within which such therapeutic work needs to happen.

Psychological therapy for delusions

The original work in this area was done in direct psychological, mainly behavioural, management of auditory hallucinations. These interventions included operant procedures using classical conditioning approaches; systematic desensitisation, usually in association with relaxation training; thought-stopping, involving the patient and the therapist in actively intervening to interrupt delusional thoughts; management of sensory input to reduce external stimulation thought to exacerbate delusional material or alternatively counter-stimulation; self-monitoring of hallucinatory experiences by diary or record; aversion therapy using electric shock or white noise, whether self- or therapist-administered; ear-plug therapy in which the client wears one ear-plug (this relates to a theory of the origin of hallucinations in defective communication between hemispheres of the brain); first-person singular therapy, in which the client is encouraged to re-attribute the origin of voices from an external agency to describing the process as 'talking to myself', and distraction using alternative sound sources, e.g. radio-cassette.

Slade and Bentall (1988) review in detail the evidence for the effectiveness of these interventions. In summary, they all appear to have some merit on a case-by-case basis, but should be used only in the context of a very careful assessment of the individual's experience. Much of the research evidence is case-study based and does not support their general application. It does underline the importance of understanding the lived experience of the individual who suffers delusions as the only way to construct a relevant programme of intervention.

Cognitive approaches

Cognitive behaviour therapy had its origins in the treatment of depression and the belief stated by Hamlet that 'there is nothing, either good or bad, but thinking makes it so'. Individuals respond to situations depending on what they think, believe or feel about them: problems arise through the faulty cognitions people reach about certain situations, and the automatic thoughts or inference chains that are triggered. These are technical terms, explained well by Slade and Bentall (1988). Gilbert (1992) puts it well in saying that the process is not so much one of teaching or retraining but:

> engaging with a person their internal constructions and meaning-making processes and helping them to explore alternatives, to treat beliefs

as hypotheses and to test out new ideas; to understand the relationship between thoughts, feelings and behaviours and to acquire new skills.

Cognitive approaches to serious mental illness have lagged behind their introduction in other areas of mental distress, perhaps for the usual reasons of 'difference' and 'otherness' mentioned already. Chadwick, Birchwood and Trower (1996) discuss in detail the implementation of this approach. It starts with the classic ABC assessment. What are the *Activating* or precipitating events of relevance to these experiences – 'does something always happen immediately before you hear these voices, which occurs only then?' What *Beliefs* does she or he have about these events (images, thoughts, inferences, assumptions) and what did you think was happening then? Where were the voices coming from? What are the *Consequences* of such experiences (emotional or behavioural) what did the voice make you feel? What did you do to get on with the day despite these voices?

A great deal of productive research is now going into finding ways of helping clients, by using these methods, to deal with what are often very distressing experiences for them and those around them.

Expressed emotion and family interventions

The term 'expressed emotion', or simply EE, had its experimental origin in the work of Brown *et al.* (1958) evaluating the re-adjustment in the community of long-stay, male hospital patients with schizophrenia. This research suggested that patients who returned to their families adapted less well than those who were discharged to residential care. Over time this was refined to suggest that the emotional climate or expressed emotion within the home was a crucial factor in determining early relapse: relapse was likely to be earlier where the parents were highly critical or hostile or emotionally over-involved, especially in the absence of maintenance medication. This association has also been found in relation to staff of community facilities (Moore and Kuipers, 1992). A great deal of research has been generated by these insights and there has been lively debate about its aetiological and clinical significance.

A parallel development has been that of the stress-vulnerability model of schizophrenia with its emphasis on the reactivity of the psychotic person (as with all others) to environmental and personal stressors in the context of a certain level of ability to cope with such stress. These approaches have informed the psychosocial interventions, particularly those encouraging work with families (Birchwood and Tarrier, 1994) and are firmly based on improving communication between professionals and sufferers from serious mental illness and their families (Barrowclough and Tarrier, 1994). Key components include careful assessment of symptomatology, social functioning and patient strengths; education about the mental illness, its history, diagnosis, symptomatology, aetiology, medication, prognosis and management; assessment of stress and coping responses and the teaching of effective management strategies; setting goals for improved social functioning and relationship patterns. Much of this work involves families, but the approaches are by no means specific to them. The core components of detailed assessment, beginning with the client's own understanding of the problems, active engagement, working on agreed targets and goals for change and improvement within a therapeutic relationship, reflect the characteristics of the helping relationship fundamental to all therapeutic work applicable to work with individuals and groups.

Conclusion

Both the core skills of effective inter-professional communication and specialized approaches are essential when working with people who have mental health problems. In this arena, where disorders of communication may be central to the service user's experience, helping professionals have to be keenly aware of the need to optimize their communication skills.

References

Barrowclough, C. and Tarrier, N. (1994) Interventions with families. In M. Birchwood and N. Tarrier (Eds) *Psychological Management of Schizophrenia.* Chichester: Wiley.

Beresford, P. and Croft, S. (1993) *Citizen Involvement: a Practical Guide for Change.* Basingstoke: BASW/Macmillan.
A practical discussion of how to maximize user involvement in services.

Birch, A. (1983) *What Chance Have We Got: Occupation and Employment after Mental Illness – Patients' Views.* Manchester: Manchester Mind.

Birchwood, M. and Tarrier, N. (1994) *Psychological Management of Schizophrenia.* Chichester: Wiley.
Summarizes the theoretical and practice base for psychosocial interventions in serious mental illness.

Blackburn, I.M. and Davidson, K. (1990) *Cognitive Therapy for Depression and Anxiety.* Oxford: Blackwell Scientific.
Valuable beginner's handbook on the use of CT.

Brandon, D. (1982) *The Trick of Being Ordinary.* London: MIND.

Brett-Jones, J., Garety, P.A., and Hemsley, D.R. (1987) Measuring delusional experiences: a method and its application. *British Journal of Clinical Psychology*, 26, 257–65.

Brown, G.W., Carstairs, G.M. and Topping, G. (1958) Post-hospital adjustment of chronic mental patients. *Lancet, ii*, 685–9.

Busfield, J. (1996) *Men, Women and Madness*. London: Macmillan.

Chadwick, P., Birchwood, M. and Trower, P. (1996) *Cognitive Therapy for Delusions Voices and Paranoia*. Chichester: Wiley.
The authoritative guide to this subject for the academic and practitioner.

Chamberlin, J. (1988) *On Our Own: Patient Controlled Alternatives to the Mental Health System*. London: MIND.
The classic case for user-defined needs and user-controlled services.

Comer, R.J. and Piliavin, J.A. (1970) The effects of physical deviance upon face-to-face interaction: the other side. *Journal of Personality and Social Psychology*. 23 (1) 33–39.

Department of Health (1995) *Building Bridges: a Guide to Arrangements for Inter-Agency Working for the Care and Protection of Severely Mentally Ill People*. London: Department of Health.

Egan, G. (1975) *The Skilled Helper: A model of systematic helping and interpersonal relating*. Belmont, California: Brooks/Cole.
One of the most helpful, practical approaches to counselling, valuable at the beginner and experienced practitioner levels.

Emerson, J. and Enderby, P (1996) Prevalence of speech and language disorders in a mental illness unit. *European Journal of Disorders of Communication, 31 (3)* 221–36.

Fernando, S. (1991) *Mental Health, Race and Culture*. London: Macmillan/MIND.
Clear statement of the racism and cultural blindness of mental health services and how they need to change.

Fisher, M., Newton, C. and Sainsbury, E.E. (1984) *Mental Health Social Work Observed*. London: George Allen and Unwin.

Gilbert, P. (1992) *Depression: the Evolution of Powerlessness*. Hove: Lawrence Erlbaum.

Goldberg, D., Benjamin, S. and Creed, F. (1994) *Psychiatry in Medical Practice*, 2nd edn. London: Routledge.

Goldberg, D. and Huxley, P. (1992) *Common Mental Disorders: a Bio-Social Model*. London: Routledge.

Goldberg, D., Steele, J., Smith, C. and Spivey, L. (1980) Training family doctors to recognise psychiatric illness with increased accuracy. *Lancet 2*, 521–23.

Green, H. (1964) *I Never Promised You a Rose Garden*. London: Pan.

Hart, L. (1995) *Phone At Nine Just to Say You're Alive*. London: Douglas Eliot Press.
Powerful evocation of one woman's journey through madness.

Heller, T. (1996) Doing being human. In T. Heller *et al.* (Ed.) *Mental Health Matters*. London: Open University Press/Macmillan.

Heller, T., Reynolds, J., Gomm, R., Muston, R. and Pattison, S. (Eds) (1996) *Mental Health Matters*. London: Open University Press/Macmillan.
Comprehensive, stimulating coverage of the most important perspectives on mental illness and mental health services; theory, policy and practice.

Huxley, A. (1963) *The Doors of Perception*. New York: Harper & Row.

Jones, R. (1996) *Mental Health Act Manual*, 5th ed. London: Sweet and Maxwell.
The authoritative guide to mental health and related legislation.

Lacey, R. (1991) *The Mind Complete Guide to Psychiatric Drugs*. London: Ebury Press.
Accessible and comprehensive guide for the lay person.

Laing, R.D. (1972) *Knots*. London: Penguin.

Laing, R.D. and Esterson, A. (1970) *Sanity, Madness and the Family*. London: Penguin.

Lambert, M.J. and Bergin, A.E. (1994) The effectiveness of psychotherapy. In A.E. Bergin and S.L. Garfield (Eds) *Handbook of Psychotherapy and Behavior Change*. 4th ed. New York: Wiley.
An authoritative summary of the relevant research and its implications.

Leff, J.P. and Isaacs, A.D. (1990) *Psychiatric Examination in Clinical Practice*. London: Blackwell Scientific.

Ley, P. (1988) *Communicating with Patients*. London: Chapman & Hall.

Littlewood, R. and Lipsedge, M. (1989) *Aliens and Alienists: Ethnic Minorities and Psychiatry*. 2nd ed. London: Unwin Hyman.
The most comprehensive treatment of this material.

Moore, E. and Kuipers, L. (1992) Behavioural correlates of expressed emotion in staff-patient interactions. *Social Psychiatry and Psychiatric Epidemiology*, *27(6)* 298–303.

Muijen, M. (1996) Scare in the community: Britain in moral panic. In Heller *et al.* (Eds) *Mental Health Matters* London : Open University Press/Macmillan.

Pilgrim, D. and Rogers, A. (1993) *A Sociology of Mental Health and Illness*. Buckingham: Open University Press.
Valuable summary of some of the socio-political factors involved in understanding the mental health services.

Rack, P. (1982) *Race Culture and Mental Disorder*. London: Tavistock.

Radley, A. (1994) *Making Sense of Illness*. London: Sage.

Read, J. and Reynolds, J. (Eds) (1996) *Speaking our Minds: an Anthology*. London: Open University Press/Macmillan.
Balanced and readable collection of service users' experiences.

Reynolds, J. (1996) Building relationships. In J. Read and J. Reynolds (Eds) *Speaking our Minds: an Anthology*. London: Open University Press/Macmillan.

Rogers, A., Pilgrim, D. and Lacey, R. (1993) *Experiencing Psychiatry*. London: Mind/Macmillan.

Romme, E. (1996) Rehabilitating voice hearers. In Heller, T. *et al.* (Eds) *Mental Health Matters* London : Open University Press/Macmillan.

Romme, E. and Escher, S. (1993) *Accepting Voices*. London: MIND.

Rosenhan, D.L. (1996) On being sane in insane places. In Heller, T. *et al.* (Eds) *Mental Health Matters*. London : Open University Press/Macmillan.

Rowe, D. (1988) *Depression: the Way out of Your Prison.* London: Routledge.
A user-friendly guide to understanding and self-talking therapy.

Sashidharan, S.P. (1986) Ideology and politics in transcultural psychiatry. In J.L. Cox (Ed.) *Transcultural Psychiatry.* London: Croom Helm.

Shepherd, G., Murray, A. and Muijen, M. (1994) *Relative Values: The Differing Views of Users, Family Carers, and Professionals on Services for People with Schizophrenia in the Community.* London: Sainsbury Centre for Mental Health.

Sheppard, M. (1993) Client satisfaction, extended intervention and interpersonal skills in community mental health. *Journal of Advanced Nursing, 18 (2)* 246–59.

Silverman, D. (1987) *Communication and Medical Practice: Social Relations in the Clinic.* London: Sage.

Slade, P.D. and Bentall, R.P. (1988) *Sensory Deception: a Scientific Analysis of Hallucination.* London: Croom Helm.

Tilbury, D. (1993) *Working with Mental Illness.* London: BASW/Macmillan.

Truax, C.B. and Carkhuff, R.R. (1967) *Toward Effective Counselling and Psychotherapy.* New York: Aldine.

Warner, R. (1994) *Recovery from Schizophrenia.* London: Routledge.
Detailed review of understandings of schizophrenia and methods of intervention.

Wooff, K. (1992) Service organisation and planning. In M. Birchwood and N. Tarrier (Eds) *Innovations in the Psychological Management of Schizophrenia.* Chichester: Wiley.

Wordsworth, W. in Owen, W.J.B. (1979) (Ed.) *Preface to the Lyrical Ballads.* London: Greenwood Press.

Chapter 6

Increasing multicultural competence

Jenny Bimrose

Effective communication between individuals in every health care setting is a desirable goal, whether this occurs within a counselling relationship or in exchanges not recognized formally as counselling. In this chapter I examine the potential of 'multicultural counselling' for increasing this effectiveness. The meaning of multicultural counselling and how it differs from more established approaches are discussed first. Then the need for this relatively new approach to counselling is considered. Finally, some exercises that I have found most useful for increasing the multicultural competence of counsellors in training are presented.

The meaning of multicultural counselling

'Multiculturalism' is a term usually associated with policy and prac-tice related to ethnic difference. For example, 'multicultural education' often refers to attempts to make the process and content of education more relevant for groups of students representing varied ethnic backgrounds. In its application to counselling practice, the meaning of 'multicultural' has expanded and now includes gender, sexual prefer-ence, disability, social class, and so on. For example, Pedersen (1991) argues that 'culture' in this context should be defined to include 'demographic variables (e.g. age, sex, place of residence), status variables (e.g. social, educational, economic), and affiliations (formal and informal), as well as ethnographic variables such as nationality, ethnicity, language, and religion' (1991: 7). This inclusive definition clearly has potential application to all communication and counselling relationships – not just to those involving ethnic difference.

The need for multicultural counselling

The origins of this approach to counselling have been traced back to the racial civil rights movement in the United States in the 1950s, 1960s and 1970s (Helms, 1994; Ridley, 1995; Sue *et al.*, 1996). Since it was concerned with the equal and fair treatment of all citizens in every sphere of society, the movement stimulated research into the use of counselling services by ethnic minority groups, among many other issues. The findings are disturbing. For example, Pine's literature review (1972) revealed that minority groups reported counselling to be a 'waste of time' and that 'counsellors do not accept, respect, and understand cultural differences; that counsellors are arrogant and contemptuous; and that counsellors don't know how to deal with their own hangups' (p.35). Sue and Sue (1990) summarize the findings of other research carried out in the 1970s which revealed that not only did minority groups under-use mental health services, but that minority clients terminated counselling/therapy at a rate of approximately 50 per cent compared with a termination rate of less than 30 per cent for white clients (p.7).

If, as such evidence suggests, ethnic minority groups are less than enthusiastic about counselling services in mental health services, what could be the explanation? The most compelling and widely accepted explanation is that counselling practice is an ethnocentric activity. Many authors, for example, Pedersen (1983), d'Ardenne and Mahtani (1989), LaFromboise and Foster (1989), Ivey *et al.* (1997), Ridley, (1995), Lago and Thompson (1996), Sue *et al.* (1996) have argued that mainstream counselling and psychotherapy approaches are white, middle class activities that operate with many distinctive values and assumptions. They are ethnocentric or 'culturally encapsulated' (Wrenn, 1985), holding at their centre a notion of normality derived from white culture, which is irrelevant to them and has the potential for alienating them.

This explanation of why ethnically different clients find mainstream counselling unhelpful also has relevance to other client differences such as gender, sexual preference and disability. The discussion of 'culture' quickly broadened to include a wide range of these factors. The central message is clear: since the majority of mainstream counselling approaches have originated from, and been developed by, a distinctive group sharing not only key characteristics (i.e. ethnicity, gender, socio-economic status) but also associated core values, caution needs to be exercised when applying these approaches to those clients who do not belong to this distinctive group.

The views of the counsellor (or communicator) are also relevant when examining the need for multicultural counselling. Bimrose and Bayne (1995) conducted a postal survey of practising counsellors who were ex-students. One question in the survey asked respondents to indicate whether, in counselling situations, they had ever experienced discomfort with a client who was different from them in a particular respect. Of the respondents, 57 per cent referred to discomfort based on gender, 46 per cent to discomfort based on ethnicity, 42 per cent to discomfort based on disability, 17 per cent to discomfort based on sexuality and 46 per cent to discomfort based on other factors (e.g. social class, age and sexual preference). It was then asked whether there was a more accurate expression than 'discomfort'? Responses included anxiety, disquiet, confusion, embarrassment, unease and irritation. Only 7 per cent of the sample reported themselves free from discomfort when dealing with client difference. Not only, therefore, have certain groups of clients questioned the usefulness of main-stream counselling approaches – some counsellors also feel uncomfort-able when applying these approaches in certain situations.

A new approach to counselling?

Because a multicultural approach to counselling is relatively new, the implications for practice are still being developed, with competing views of just how practice needs to change. The emerging consensus suggests that, while maintaining the integrity of the distinctive new approach, multicultural counselling should strive to select and build on the best of current counselling practice. Arguing for a distinct new approach, Pedersen (1991) suggests that 'we are moving toward a generic theory of multiculturalism as a "fourth force" position, complementary to the other three forces of psychodynamic, behavioural and humanistic explanations of human behaviour', and claims that 'a multicultural perspective has changed the way we look at counselling across fields and theories' (p.6). Similarly, Ivey et al. (1997) argue that traditional counselling theories are responding to mounting criticisms, particularly from 'women and those of non-European background', by incorporating a 'broader view of counseling and therapy' (p.7).

So what is the current stage of development of multicultural counselling? Bimrose (1996) argues that certain benchmarks now exist that signal the arrival and acceptance of this new approach as more than just a passing trend. For example, more critiques of multicultural approaches are being published on a regular basis; pressure is building around the need for more training in this area for both student and qualified counsellors; and research effort is increasingly being focused on producing methods for measuring and evaluating multicultural competence. These and other indicators seem to endorse the view that multicultural counselling is here to stay.

One particular weakness in the way that multicultural counselling has developed is the lack of a unifying theoretical framework. Sue *et al.* (1996) have attempted to redress this weakness by publishing a theory of multicultural counselling which they claim is a 'metatheory of counselling and psychotherapy' (p.23). They outline six key propositions, including the need for counselling practice to focus on larger social units and systems (as well as on individuals); and the need to take more account of the contexts in which counselling takes place, and for practice to accommodate goals from diverse cultures as alternatives to traditional goals (e.g. self-actualization). Also included are the need to incorporate models of healing other than Western models into counselling practice and to acknowledge more explicitly the crucial role of cultural values in attitude formation.

As a unifying framework, this has both merits and weaknesses. It represents an important attempt to integrate disparate research findings and different strands of thinking into a more coherent form. The framework usefully draws attention to the structures and systems which (arguably) create the need for this counselling support. Problems are highlighted that may result from an uncritical application of ethnocentric counselling approaches together with the potential value of incorporating alternative healing methods with established orthodoxy.

There are also considerable weaknesses. The key propositions of this new theory are so broad that they may be regarded by some as unwieldy. The implications of the theory for practice remain somewhat obscure. Perhaps most importantly, rigorous testing of the validity of the theory is still to be undertaken.

Increasing multicultural competence

A review of the literature reveals a wealth of material – some of which is underpinned by research and some which is not – to guide the practitioner in his or her search for new practice frameworks. Given the relatively early stage of development of multicultural counselling, it is largely left to practitioners to sift through this material and select for themselves material that suits their particular philosophical beliefs and practical needs. What follows is a selection of skills, techniques and strategies that I have found to appeal to counsellors in training. These are presented within the framework developed by Sue and Sue (1990), who identified the competencies required by the culturally skilled counsellor as being: awareness of own assumptions, values and biases; understanding the world view of the culturally different client; developing appropriate intervention strategies and techniques.

The framework was refined by Sue *et al.* (1995), who proposed a 'conceptual framework for cross-cultural competencies' (p633): a three by three matrix in which it is claimed most cross-cultural skills can either be organized or developed. The broad characteristics of cross-cultural competencies are identical to those specified in 1990:

- counsellor awareness of own assumptions, values, and biases;
- understanding the world-view of the culturally different client; and
- developing appropriate intervention strategies and techniques.

Each of these characteristics is also described as sharing three dimensions: beliefs and attitudes; knowledge; and skills.

For simplicity, the original framework (1990) identifying awareness, knowledge and understanding, and skills and strategies, will be used to present and discuss exercises that can be used to increase and/or develop multicultural competence.

Awareness

Many writers in the area of multicultural counselling advocate the need for all practitioners to embark on a continual process of cultural self-awareness. In a training context, I have found that a three-stage process that moves the focus from the individual to society and then beyond to 'world-view' values to be an effective method of contributing to this process. This approach is designed both to increase an awareness of the extent to which personal value systems reflect the dominant system of societal values and an awareness of alternative value systems.

The first task is to think about yourself; the second to identify the values of the dominant culture in which you practise counselling or communication; and the third to examine alternative value-orientations. Various exercises and schema have been developed to assist with this type of self-examination. At the level of individual awareness, Locke (1992: 2) suggests that the counsellor should ask the following questions:

- What is my cultural heritage? What was the culture of my parents and my grandparents?
- With what cultural group(s) do I identify?
- What is the cultural relevance of my name?
- What values, beliefs, opinions and attitudes do I hold that are consistent with the dominant culture? Which are inconsistent? How did I learn these?

- How did I decide to become a counsellor? What cultural standards were involved in the process? What do I understand to be the relationship between culture and counselling?
- What unique abilities, aspirations, expectations, and limitations do I have that might influence my relations with culturally diverse individuals?

It is usually most effective to compare your answers to these questions with other people's. All the questions have value, although the second question often has the greatest impact, perhaps because it highlights the extent to which the cultural conventions surrounding the 'naming system' of the dominant society are taken for granted by acculturated members of that society. It illustrates the ways in which 'naming systems' differ one from another, and how, for example, they can define and reinforce gender relations.

The next exercise is an attempt to specify the dominant values of the societal context in which you counsel. This can clarify the extent to which you have absorbed these values. Katz, quoted in Sue and Sue (1990: 148), suggests that the main components of white culture are: rugged individualism; competition; action orientation; communication; time; holidays; history; protestant work ethic; progress and future orientation; emphasis on scientific management; status and power; family structure; aesthetics; and religion (see Appendix 1 for brief definitions).

One way of using this framework is to consider the extent to which you agree or disagree that these are, indeed, the main components of white culture. Should any be excluded? Any added? Then decide which of these values and beliefs overlap with your own. Have you rejected any of these dominant values? Have you replaced them with other values?

The final stage in this process is to become familiar with value systems that are different from our own. Ibrahim, quoted in Sue and Sue (1990: 138), outlines the main characteristics of three different value-orientation models. For each of these three models, values relating to the following four dimensions are described: time focus, human activity, social relations, and the relationship between people and nature. These value models can be used to increase your own self-awareness in various ways. For example, take each of the four dimensions and try to describe your own personal values against each, using Table 6.1. What is your time focus (e.g., do you tend to focus on the past, the present or the future?); what type of human activity or 'state of being' do you value most (e.g. doing, being or becoming?); how do you view social relations (e.g. hierarchically, relationally or individualistically?); and finally, how would you define the relationship of people to nature (e.g. subjugation, harmony or mastery?).

Table 6.1: Summary of your personal value model

Dimension	Summary of your personal value model
Time focus	
Human activity	
Social relations	
People/nature	

Once you have tried to describe your own value model in this way, compare it with the following summary of Ibrahim's three models, which suggest coherence across the four dimensions:

1. For the first model, the time focus is on the past, which is all important; we should learn from history. Human activity should focus on being; it's enough to just be. Social relations are conceptualized as linear and vertical; there are natural followers and leaders in society. The people/nature relationship emphasizes subjugation to nature; life and destiny are largely determined by external forces (God, genetics, fate, etc.)

2. In contrast, the time focus of the second model stresses the present and the importance of living for today; the future is not a concern. Human activity is expressed as 'being and in-becoming', meaning that the purpose of life is to develop the inner self. Social relations emphasize the importance of consulting with friends and families when problems arise (collateral, relational). The people/nature relationship advocates harmony with nature; people should strive to co-exist in harmony with nature.

3. The third value model focuses on the future and stresses the need for planning; making sacrifices today will ensure a better tomorrow. Human activity focuses on 'doing'; being active and working hard ensures that efforts will be rewarded. Social relations stress individual autonomy and individualism; it is assumed that everyone controls his or her own destiny. The people/nature relationship advocates mastery over nature; the challenge is to conquer and control nature.

To what extent does your personal value system correspond with one of these three value models? If there are differences, how might you explain these? Do these value systems correspond – in your view – to ethnic difference? Have they any relevance for value systems that differ along gender lines? Perhaps you are able to discern differences that link to membership of various social class groups?

Knowledge and understanding

Increased multicultural awareness needs to be complemented by more in-depth knowledge and understanding of client and patient difference. Numerous exercises have been designed to help with this. Here are two that I have found particularly effective in training.

Locke (1992: 5) has developed a framework for gaining knowledge and understanding of cultural difference which consists of 10 elements: the degree of acculturation; poverty and economic concerns; history of oppression; language and the arts; racism and prejudice; socio-political factors; child-rearing practices; religious practices; family structure and dynamics; cultural values and attitudes. (For brief definitions, see Appendix 2.) Various methods can be used to research the information indicated by these 10 elements. For example, questions can be generated that are then used as the basis for a semi-structured interview with an individual who is a member of the group under study, or to guide an informal discussion with a group or representatives. This is the first exercise. A particular strength of Locke's approach is the way in which it acknowledges that differences existing within cultural groups may be greater than the differences between the dominant culture and other cultures.

The second exercise for gaining knowledge and understanding of difference is a role play adapted from a conference workshop run by Jackson (1995). The exercise is for three people, and takes about two hours plus some individual research time. It has two main purposes: first, to develop empathic understanding through your attempt to discover what it feels like to be a person from a different background; second, to begin to identify some practice guidelines.

To prepare for the role play, select someone from a culturally different group that you would like to understand 'culturally' better (defining 'different' in terms of social class, gender, sexual orientation, ethnicity, disability, etc.). Research the person's background as thoroughly as time and resources permit. Locke's model provides an excellent framework.

The exercise itself involves working in your training group for approximately one-and-a-half hours. During this time each member of the group will in turn perform tasks related to the three roles of client, counsellor and observer.

Client: for approximately half an hour you have an opportunity to be a person from a group that is culturally different from your own. Come prepared to present a problem or concern to a counsellor or health professional who would like to help you. Identify some realistic concern that the person you have chosen actually has or might reasonably be expected to have.

Counsellor: you will be asked by a 'client' to help resolve some difficulty that will be presented to you. If you wish, you may ask your 'observer' for ideas and suggestions on how to proceed.

Observer: you will be available to the counsellor or health professional to offer ideas and suggestions. After the role play, you will lead the feedback session, which should identify the most helpful statements or actions performed by the counsellor.

Suggested guidelines:

* Introductions: as client, introduce yourself to your two colleagues (the name of your person along with relevant cultural informa- tion). (2/3 minutes in total)

* Role play: conduct a brief counselling session in which the client presents a concern and the counsellor attempts to be as helpful as possible. (approximately 10 minutes)

* Feedback: review the session with the purpose of identifying the most helpful actions. All three members of the training group should contribute their observations. (approximately 10 minutes)

Finally, after you have each completed all three role plays, observa- tions should be pooled so that the most useful practices can be identified.

Skills

Ivey *et al.* (1997) and Ivey (1994) suggest that culturally appropriate nonverbal behaviour is crucial to successful counselling outcomes. Ivey advocates that all practising counsellors 'begin a lifetime of study of nonverbal communication patterns and their variations' (1994: 75). Various categories of nonverbal behaviour are identified and some cultural implications for each category are discussed (p.29). For example:

Eye contact: cultural differences abound regarding the use of eye contact during communication. Thus, direct eye contact is considered a sign of interest in European/North American middle-class cultures, although most people in those cultures usually maintain more eye contact while listening and less while talking. However, African- Americans in the United States tend to have the reverse pattern; i.e. looking more when talking and slightly less when listening. Among some American Indian groups, eye contact by the young is a sign of disrespect. Some cultural groups (e.g. American Indian, Inuit or

Aboriginal Australian groups) generally avoid eye contact, especially when talking about serious subjects.

Body Language: A comfortable conversational distance for North Americans is slightly more than arm's length and the British prefer even greater distance. Many Hispanic people often prefer half that distance and those from the Middle East may talk practically 'eyeball to eyeball'.

Vocal Tracking: this relates to staying with your client's topic. In the same way that people make sudden changes in nonverbal communication, so they may change topics when they are not comfortable. Cultural differences exist here, as with many other types of non-verbal communication. For example, direct tracking is most appropriate during middle-class North American communication. In contrast, some Asian cultures consider this type of direct verbal follow-up rude and intrusive.

To develop your own skills of non-verbal communication, try observing two 'culturally different' people talking. This might be at work, or you could use a suitable television interview. Watch how patterns of eye contact develop. Note the 'body language' of the two participants. Exactly what behaviours communicate attention? Interest? Boredom? Irritation? Or try a role play with a friend. For example, if you normally keep eye contact, you could communicate with someone without eye contact. Or you could sit either closer or farther away than you usually do. Try doing both. How did you feel? Ask the other person how they felt. Can you adopt different styles of non verbal communication and still listen effectively?

Conclusion

In health care settings, conventional wisdom suggests that treatments that have been developed from rigorous scientific tests can (indeed, should) be applied by medical and health professionals to all patients exhibiting common symptoms. Until recently, this approach has also generally applied to counselling. It has been accepted practice for prospective counsellors to choose an approach, undertake training in the relevant techniques and skills to become competent in this approach, and then apply the approach to all their clients.

A multicultural approach to counselling and communication challenges this conventional wisdom. Central to this alternative approach is acceptance of the principle that patients and clients differ in their needs and ability to respond according to certain stable characteristics.

Multicultural competence can be developed through increased awareness of one's own cultural identity, understanding the consequences of
these characteristics, and by the ability to use the relevant skills
creatively.

Appendix 1: Katz's (1985) Components of White Culture

Adapted from Sue and Sue (1990: 148)

Rugged individualism: the individual is the main focus in society.
Independence is a desirable goal and being an autonomous individual is the ideal. Control is a key value.

Competition: the desire to 'win' is overwhelming. The categories
'winners' and 'losers' dominate perceptions of 'players' in society.

Action orientation: this relates to the pervasive pressure exerted on
individuals to be 'proactive'. It's desirable to take control and
resolve situations; to adopt a pragmatic approach to life.

Communication: standard English is the norm for both written and
verbal communication. During verbal exchanges, direct eye contact
is expected, as are limited physical contact and carefully controlled
emotions.

Time: time is regarded as a commodity, and is used to organise and
structure activities.

Holidays: are based on the Christian religion (Christmas, Easter, etc.)
and white history.

History: is selective – relates to Europe, romanticizes war and
emphasises white (male) leaders.

Protestant work ethic: this describes the dominant value system which
promotes instrumentality and deferred gratification.

Progress and future orientation: linked to the protestant work ethic and
promoting the belief that planning and progress are both highly
desirable.

Emphasis on scientific management: being rational, objective and logical
are highly valued. Measurement of output and success using quanti-
tative methods.

Status and power: material possessions provide the key measure of
success. Other indicators of success include academic credentials,
titles, and positions. Ownership (of goods, space, property, etc.) provides an important measure of success.

Family structure: the nuclear family is the social ideal. This promotes the idea of the man as main breadwinner with the female cast in a caring and largely subordinate role.

Aesthetics: European cultures dominate music and the arts. Beauty is modelled on being blond, blue-eyed, thin and young for women. For men, physical prowess, material resources and status are highly desirable.

Religion: Christianity dominates.

Appendix 2: Locke's ten elements for increasing multicultural understanding.

Adapted from Locke (1992: 5–11)

- Acculturation: cultural groups vary in the way they have embraced the dominant culture.

  - Bicultural: function as effectively in the dominant culture as in their own, whilst maintaining elements of their own culture;
  - Traditional: retain many cultural traits from their original culture whilst rejecting much of the dominant culture;
  - Marginal: little real contact with traits of either original or dominant culture;
  - Acculturated: assumed the traits of the dominant culture.

- Poverty and economic concerns: many minority ethnic groups suffer disproportionately from poverty and deprivation. A clear understanding of the extent and causes of this poverty is fundamental to effective helping.

- History of oppression: similarly, it is important to understand the way in which significant and defining events from the past have an impact on the present.

- Language and the arts: 'Standard English' is the dominant method of communication and has become one measure by which members of culturally different groups can be judged. Nonverbal communication is also important and health professionals need to understand how culture affects communication.

- Racism and prejudice: all people are prejudiced. Prejudice may be personal, institutional, or cultural. The following matrix provides one way of making sense of prejudice/racism along two dimensions: overt versus covert, and intentional versus unintentional. This matrix identifies four types of prejudice/racism:

- **overt intentional**: openly expressing beliefs in the inferiority of culturally diverse groups;
- **overt unintentional**: counselling culturally diverse clients toward lower socioeconomic status jobs/careers;
- **covert intentional**: expecting culturally diverse individuals to communicate non-verbally in the same way as members of the dominant culture;
- **covert unintentional**: explicitly identifying particular cultures when certain behaviours are described.

- Sociopolitical factors: many items in this category overlap with other areas (e.g. family structure, child-rearing practices), but others are different. Holidays, the roles of social organizations and how friendship is determined are examples of social factors that are often unique to particular cultural groups. Political factors include the degree of self-determination of the cultural group (for example, involvement in political processes at local, regional and national levels may result from restrictions imposed by the dominant culture and/or confidence in the political system).

- Child-rearing practices: since the family is the primary socialization agent of a culture, the study of child rearing processes can provide insights into a culture's structure and core values. For example, how kinship networks operate, how sex roles are socialized, how respect is taught, who is respected, the children's obligations to parents and of parents to children, etc.

- Religious practices: religion helps a cultural group determine relationships with other peoples and with the universe since it represents an organized system of the belief in a god, gods, or other supernatural beings. In some cultural groups religion and local politics are closely tied.

- Family structure and dynamics: the family, as the basic unit of a culture helps us to understand various key aspects of the way that culture organizes itself in kinship patterns. For example, who holds authority in families, the impact of marriage outside the cultural group, the nature of relationships among members of the family, and how lineage is determined.

- Cultural values and attitudes: an examination of cultural values and attitudes is crucial for understanding difference. Locke proposes five categories:

  - *Time*: is the orientation based on the past, the present, or the future?
  - *Human relations*: are individuals, collateral relationships, or lineal relationships valued most?
  - *Human activity*: is the focus on doing, being, or becoming?

- *Human nature*: at birth, are people considered basically good, bad, neutral, or mixed?
- *Supernatural*: is the relationship with the supernatural one of control, subordination, or harmony?

References

d'Ardenne, P. and Mahtani, A. (1989) *Transcultural Counselling in Action*, London: Sage.

Bimrose, J. (1996) Multiculturalism, in Bayne, R., Horton, I. and Bimrose, J. (Eds) *New Directions in Counselling*. London: Routledge.

Bimrose, J. and Bayne, R. (1995) The multicultural framework in counsellor training, *British Journal of Guidance and Counselling*, 23, (2): 259–65.

Helms, J.E. (1994) How multiculturalism obscures racial factors in the therapy process: comment on Ridley *et al.* (1994), Sodowsky *et al.* (1994), Ottavi *et al.* (1994), and Thompson *et al.*(1994), *Journal of Counselling Psychology*, 41 (2): 162–6.

Ivey, A.E., Ivey, M.B. and Simek-Morgan, L. (1997) *Counselling and Psychotherapy: a Multicultural Perspective*, 4th ed. Boston, Mass: Allyn & Bacon. A useful introductory text to multicultural counselling which combines a discussion of theory with skill exercises.

Ivey, A.E. (1994) *Intentional Interviewing and Counseling: Facilitating client development in a multicultural society*, 3rd ed. California: Brooks Cole Publishing. A well-structured practical guide to skill development.

Jackson, M. A. (1995) *Innovative Counselor Training: multicultural and multimedia (component: Practice in Cross-cultural career counseling)*, Fifth National Conference of the National Career Development Association, San Francisco, July.

LaFromboise, T.D. and Foster, S.L. (1989) Ethics in multicultural counselling, in Pedersen, P.B., Draguns, J. G., Lonner, W.J. and Trimble, J. E. (Eds) *Counselling Across Cultures*, 3rd ed. Honolulu: University of Hawaii Press.

Lago, C. and Thompson, J. (1996) *Race, Culture & Counselling* Buckingham: Open University Press.

Locke, D.C. (1992) *Increasing Multicultural Understanding: a comprehensive model*, Newbury Park, California: Sage.

Pedersen, P. (1983) The cultural complexity of counselling, *International Journal for the Advancement of Counselling* 6: 177–92.

Pedersen, P. (1991) Multiculturalism as a generic framework, *Journal of Counselling & Development*, 70 (1): 6–12.

Pine, G.J. (1972) Counselling minority groups: a review of the literature, *Counselling and Values*, 17: 35–44.

Ridley, C.R. (1995) *Overcoming Unintentional Racism in Counseling and Therapy: a practitioner's guide to intentional intervention*, Thousand Oaks, California: Sage.

Sue, D.W. and Sue, D. (1990) *Counselling the Culturally Different: Theory and Practice*, New York: Wiley.
A seminal text in the development of skills and approaches for ethnic difference.

Sue, D.W., Arrendondon, P. and McDavis, R.J., (1995) Multicultural counseling competencies and standards: a call to the profession, in Ponterotto, J.G., Casas, J.M., Suzuki, L.A. and Alexander, C. M. (Eds), *Handbook of Multicultural Counseling*, Thousand Oaks, California: Sage.

Sue, D.W., Ivey, A.I. and Pederson, P.B. (1996) *A Theory of Multicultural Counseling & Therapy*, Pacific Grove:Brooks/Cole.

Wrenn, C. G. (1985) The culturally encapsulated counsellor revisited, in Pedersen, P. (Ed.) *Handbook of Cross-Cultural Counselling and Therapy*, Westport, CT: Greenwood.

Chapter 7

Psychological type (the Myers-Briggs)

Rowan Bayne

This chapter focuses on one factor that affects counselling and communication: 'psychological type' as used in Myers' theory (Myers, 1980; Bayne, 1995). This approach has a very positive and constructive tone: the terms used are intended to help people both value themselves more and also see people of the other 15 psychological types as different rather than weird, deliberately awkward or incompetent. Thus it may help medical and health practitioners to understand better their relationships with patients, patients' relatives and colleagues, and it suggests strategies to try out to improve those relationships.

The chapter is in five sections:

1. The first section is concerned with some relatively specific behaviours, which are part of the elaborated version of the Myers-Briggs Type Indicator (MBTI), the questionnaire that Myers developed to apply her theory.
2. Next, a simplified variation of type theory called temperament theory is related to stress. Temperament theory suggests that distinguishing between just four kinds of people can be useful for some purposes, although it obviously loses in richness of understanding what it gains in ease of use. The basic motives of each temperament are outlined and related to stress. Understanding what people of each temperament find stressful can help in both preventing stress and coping with it, and therefore in improving quality of communication.
3. This section is concerned with the basic or standard level of type theory. The central terms of 'preference' and 'type' are defined and

the preferences are related to communication. I could have started with these concepts but I wanted to lead into them via relatively specific behaviours and the four temperaments.

4. The idea that people who have radically different personalities to one's own can still be happy, fulfilled and effective can in itself be useful. However, Myers' ideas are most useful when other people's temperaments and preferences are observed accurately, and in this section I suggest some strategies for improving accuracy.

5. Finally, personality theories propose answers to several questions, for example

- How can we best describe a person?
- Are there 'basic' characteristics of personality?
- How influential are situations (in influencing behaviour)?
- How does personality develop?
- How much can personality change?

In the last section I touch on type theory's answer to the last two of these questions and its implications for counselling.

Personality and communication

As a starting point, you may like to reflect on your own ways of describing individual differences in personality. Exercise 1 can be a revealing way of doing this, as can analysing references or 'case' notes you have written, or observing yourself talking about other people.

Exercise 7.1: Kinds of people

Think of three people – patients, colleagues, friends – and some of the ways in which two of them are similar to each other and different from the third.

For example, I think of X and Y who usually mingle easily and warmly on social occasions and before meetings, and Z who does not, and who would far rather talk to one person she already knows well about something they both know about. You may like to rate yourself on 'mingling' (Exercise 7.2, p. 105).

One objection to using the term 'mingling' in this way is that comfort and frequency may not go together: some people mingle comfortably but do it rarely, others (probably because of their work) do so uncomfortably and often. Another complication is that behaviour and experience may be out of harmony with each other: James, for example, might appear effortlessly gracious as he greets new patients, but actually be making considerable effort. However, despite these

Exercise 7.2: Self-rating on mingling

| Mingles uncomfortably and as rarely as possible | | | M I X E D | | | Mingles comfortably and often |
| 1 | 2 | 3 | 4 | 5 | 6 | 7 |

and other complications, mingling is probably a genuine individual difference and one that matters in communication. For example, health professionals who mingle well (6 or 7 on the scale) enjoy making contact with a series of new people, and tend to stimulate patients who are more self-contained (1 or 2 on the scale) to respond more freely than usual. They may therefore gather information relevant to a patient's illness relatively quickly and fully.

An obvious question about individual differences in personality and style of communicating is which characteristics are the most important. Each personality theory, whether formal and appearing in psychology textbooks, or our own personal theory, suggests an answer. In practice, there may be various answers, depending on the follow-up question: important for what? For example, 'mingling' is a fairly specific behaviour, central in a few tasks and careers but peripheral or irrelevant in most.

Five other examples of quite specific individual differences that are directly relevant to professional communication are listed in Exercise 3 and Table 7.1. As with 'mingling', the notions of comfort and frequency apply, and the pairs of characteristics are opposites. All the characteristics – both ends of each scale – are also valued in Myers' theory: each of them is both comfortable and effective for some people, however extraordinary and unlikely this may seem to others. Again, you may wish to place yourself and others (tentatively) on the scales.

It can be difficult to cope with someone who is opposite to you on one or more of these behaviours or qualities. However, if at least one of you recognizes that both ways of behaving are valid, the difficulty can be transformed into a difference that is useful and complementary. For example, if a 'concrete' person and an 'abstract' person (as defined in Table 7.1) can work together on an information leaflet, the leaflet is likely to be more effective with a wider variety of people than if either of them had worked on it alone, or only with people like themselves.

A second application is to take individual differences into account when giving information, e.g. 'concrete' patients are more likely to want detailed, factual information about their illness and *not* speculations or predictions, especially not at first, while 'abstract' patients

Exercise 7.3: Five of the subscales*

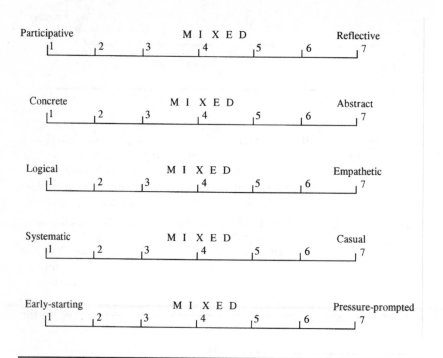

* for definitions, see Table 7.1, p. 107

may want or need facts at some point but are more likely to want first to know about options and possibilities. They are also most likely to be open to trying new or unorthodox treatments.

Four temperaments

Keirsey and Bates (1978) proposed the four temperaments summarized in Figure 7.1 and, more formally, in Table 7.2. Each person can be seen as a mixture of the temperaments, with one temperament dominant and giving an overall 'flavour'. Everyone needs some excitement (SP) and some stability (SJ) but is one of these motives *more* characteristic of a particular person? Thus, the four temperaments are properly used as a step towards understanding individuality, and not as a pigeon-hole or box.

You may like to use the stick figures in Figure 7.1 for a *provisional* assessment of the temperaments of yourself and others. Information later in this chapter can be used to check the accuracy of these assessments, as can detailed descriptions in other sources (e.g. Keirsey and

Table 7.1: Brief descriptions of five individual differences (subscales)

Participative/reflective	Prefer to communicate through talking and doing vs. prefer written communications, especially for complex material.
Concrete/abstract	Prefer to be realistic, cautious and factual vs. prefer to make 'mental leaps' and to 'read between the lines'.
Logical/empathetic	Prefer to be logical, analytic and reasonable vs. give priority to feelings and values.
Systematic/casual	Prefer to be neat and orderly, with efficient schedules vs. prefer to be easy-going and to welcome diversions.
Early starting/ pressure-prompted	Prefer to avoid the stress of deadlines by starting early vs. work best when a deadline is close.

Adapted from Kummerow and Quenk (1992) but some of the terms in the table are recent (so far unpublished) replacements. Kummerow and Quenk use Auditory/visual for Participative/reflective, Affective for Empathetic, and Stress avoider/polyactive for Early starter/pressure-prompted. The search for the most accurate, least distorting, words to describe personality characteristics continues.

Bates, 1978; Myers, 1980; Kroeger and Thuesen, 1988; Hirsh and Kummerow, 1990; Bayne, 1995). You can ask other people too; obviously, it helps if they know you well. The Myers-Briggs or MBTI plus skilled feedback is probably the most accurate method of assessing temperament and psychological type for most people (Bayne, 1995; Carr, 1997).

Table 7.2: Temperament and basic motives

SP	Excitement; solving practical problems; freedom; fun; variety.
SJ	Being responsible and useful; stability; planning in detail
NT	Developing new methods, theories and models; competence; analysing and criticizing.
NF	Supporting others; harmony; self-development.

University of Nottingham
School of Nursing & Midwifery
Derbyshire Royal Infirmary
London Road
DERBY DE1 2QY

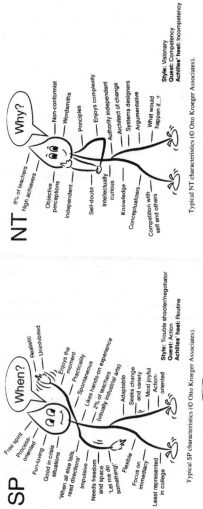

SP

Free spirit
Process-oriented
Fun-loving
Good in crisis situations
'When all else fails, read directions'
Impulsive
Needs freedom and space
'Let me do something!'
Flexible
Focus on immediacy
Least represented in college

When?

Realistic
Uninhibited
Enjoys the moment
Practicality
Spontaneous
Likes hands-on experience
2% of teachers (usually industrial arts)
Adaptable
Seeks change and variety
Most joyful
Action-oriented

Style: Trouble shooter/negotiator
Quest: Action
Achilles' heel: Routine

Typical SP characteristics (© Otto Kroeger Associates).

NT

8% of teachers
High achievers
Objective perceptions
Independent
Self-doubt
Intellectually curious
Knowledge
Conceptualizers
Competition with self and others

Why?

Non-conformist
Wordsmiths
Principles
Enjoys complexity
Authority independent
Architect of change
Systems designers
Argumentative
What would happen if...?

Style: Visionary
Quest: Competency
Achilles' heel: Incompetency

Typical NT characteristics (© Otto Kroeger Associates).

SJ

Loyal to system
Duty
Super-dependable
Resists change
Preserves traditions
Precise
'Don't fix what isn't broken'
56% of teachers

What?

Procedures
Decisive
Stability
'Should' 'Should not'
Social responsibility
Structure
Orderly
Authority dependent

Style: Stabilizer/traditionalist
Quest: Belonging
Achilles' heel: Disarray/disorganization

Typical SJ characteristics (© Otto Kroeger Associates).

NF

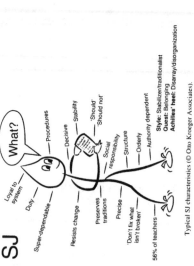

32% of teachers
Seductive
Interpersonal skills
Supportive of others
Sympathetic
Relationships
Possibilities for people
Interaction
Co-operation

Who?

Vivid imagination
Mysterious
Hypersensitive to conflict
Search for self
FOR YOU
Autonomy
Needs encouragement and recognition
Integrity
Gives strokes freely
'Becoming'

Style: Catalyst
Quest: Identity
Achilles' heel: Guilt

Typical NF characteristics (© Otto Kroeger Associates).

Figure 7.1: The four temperaments: From Bayne (1995).

Table 7.3: The temperaments, what is most likely to be stressful, and typical reactions

SP	Not much happening. Lack of freedom. *Reaction:* Frivolity, flight.
SJ	Ambiguity. Changes of plan. Lack of control. *Reaction:* Redefine objectives, more effort.
NT	Repetitive things. Bureaucracy. *Reaction:* Fight, conform rebelliously, pedantic debate.
NF	Conflict. Saying no. Criticism. *Reaction:* Self-sacrifice, hysteria, depression, cynicism.

From Bayne (1995), adapted from unpublished material by Valerie Stewart, and from Keirsey and Bates (1978)

Temperament and stress

The ideas about personality and stress in Table 7.3 are broadly consistent with type theory and the evidence for it, but they are yet to be tested rigorously in their own right. As far as managing stress is concerned, the implication is to try to be and behave most of the time in ways that fit your temperament. Conversely, temperament and type theory both assume that people who do not behave like their types most of the time become 'frustrated, inferior copies of other people' (Myers, 1980: 189). A more gentle version of this idea is that they are less happy and effective than they would be behaving as their true types.

The preferences

In Myers' theory of psychological type the central concepts are 'preference' and 'type'. Preference can be defined as 'feeling most natural and comfortable with'. Thus, behaving in the opposite way to your preference occurs, but usually less frequently and with more effort, as discussed in the first section of this chapter. The meaning of each of the preferences (Table 7.4) is briefly indicated by the characteristics in Tables 7.5 and 7.6, which are behaviours that tend to be associated with the preferences, rather than definitions of them.

Each psychological type includes one from each of the four pairs of preferences, e.g. ENTP or ESTJ, and there are 16 possible combinations, and therefore 16 types. In this chapter I have concentrated on the more immediately applicable temperaments and preferences rather

Table 7.4: The four pairs of preferences

Extraversion (E)	or	Introversion (I)
Sensing (S)	or	Intuition (N)
Thinking (T)	or	Feeling (F)
Judging (J)	or	Perceiving (P)

than the richer, more speculative levels of each type: 'type dynamics' and 'type development'.

Table 7.6 is a more detailed version of Table 7.5. It suggests which aspects of counselling are likely to be most comfortable for people of each type, and therefore most used by them, and which are likely to need more effort and practice. The implications for how health professionals might communicate differently with each patient or client follow directly from the behaviours listed. For example, a counsellor who prefers introversion can consider being more active with an extraverted client. To some extent this happens anyway (Thorne, 1987) but greater awareness should make an appropriate and comfortable degree of flexibility more likely, and critical judgments less likely.

Table 7.6 fits well with the integrative three-stage model of counselling outlined in Chapter 1: the skills associated with each preference are the most relevant at different stages, most notably I, S, F and P (all the Stages), N and T (Stage 2) and E and J (Stage 3). Thus, type theory proposes that people of all the psychological types can be effective counsellors, in their different styles. Further, it states an approach to developing as a communicator and counsellor: develop the strengths associated with your type first, and add the opposite strengths, in a subsidiary way, later. Tables 7.7 and 7.8 illustrate this principle in relation to writing (letters, memos, leaflets, reports etc.) For discussions of type applied to learning styles see Lawrence (1997), to

Table 7.5: Some general characteristics associated with the preferences

E	More outgoing and active . . . More reflective and reserved	I
S	More practical and interested in facts and details . . . More interested in possibilities and an overview	N
T	More logical and reasoned . . . More agreeable and appreciative	F
J	More planning and coming to conclusions . . . More easy-going and flexible	P

Table 7.6: Behaviour associated with the preferences (adapted from Bayne 1995)

People who prefer:	Tend to:
Extraversion	be more active
	be less comfortable with reflection
	be optimistic and energetic
Introversion	be more at ease with silence
	be less comfortable with action
	be more private
Sensing	be concrete and detailed
	like a 'practical' approach
	not see many options
	be uncomfortable with novelty
Intuition	take a broad view
	jump around from topic to topic
	see unrealistic options
	see lots of options
	overlook facts
	like novelty and imaginative approaches
Thinking	avoid emotions, feelings and values in early conversations
	need rationales and logic
	be critical and sceptical
	want to be admired for their competence
	be competitive
Feeling	focus on values and networks of values
	need to care (e.g. about a value, a person or an ideal)
	be 'good' clients or patients
	want to be appreciated
Judging	fear losing control
	find sudden change stressful
	need structure
	need to achieve
	work hard and tolerate discomfort
Perceiving	avoid decisions
	need flexiblity
	avoid discomfort

Table 7.7: The preferences and writing: likely strengths of your own preferences

E	Discussing the topic before writing. Fluency and breadth.
I	Immersion in the topic, and depth.
S	Details and concrete examples.
N	Themes and variety of perspective.
T	Objective style, and criticism.
F	Fluency.
J	Focus, doing the writing, and stating conclusions.
P	Breadth and revision.

Table 7.8: Writing: adding the strengths of the opposite preferences to your own

Consider whether your writing would be improved by any of the following, or by more attention to them.

E	More structure and depth.
I	Writing earlier.
S	Themes and less detail.
N	Examples. Fewer ideas.
T	More 'signposts', flow, and considering impact on others.
F	More analysis and evidence.
J	Revise a bit more and add some details.
P	Add conclusions.

counselling, see Provost (1993), to careers, see Martin (1995), and to intimate relationships, see Jones and Sherman (1997).

Observing type accurately

Most applications of MBTI theory benefit from accurate observation of temperament and/or type (one's own and other people's). Generally, most people observe other people's personalities quite accurately in these respects (Bayne, 1995) but with scope for improvement. Useful strategies for being more accurate are:

1. Look for patterns, over time and across situations.
2. Therefore, treat first impressions as hypotheses.
3. Look for evidence against your first impression, as well as for it.
4. Take situations into account (some situations, e.g. selection interviews, first dates, tend to constrain behaviour much more than others).

There are also several reasons for being careful. First, most of us, most of the time, behave as our preferences suggest, but we can and do behave very differently, too. Behaviour is influenced by many factors, e.g. roles, situations (including who else is there), motives, other personality characteristics, anxiety, stress, mood. Second, it seems likely that accurate judgments are based on several low validity cues (but still valid) rather than a few highly valid ones. Therefore, the cues listed next are valid, but are tendencies only. Highly valid cues have not been found yet, and may never be found.

For E: more talkative, expansive, expressive, louder voice, more colourful clothes, compliment more.

For I: more inward, more serious, tend to 'interview' in conversations and to use qualifying phrases like 'quite' more.

For S: more detailed and practical, less speculative and general.

For N: tend to leap from topic to topic, work in bursts, think in unusual ways, gesture more.

For T: more sceptical and logical, tend to enjoy debates, criticise more.

For F: more cheerful, gentle and sympathetic, smile more, agreeable.

For J: more organized, task-focused, systematic and tidy.

For P: more easy-going, relaxed, likely to switch back and forth between various activities, less tidy.

Personality change

Whether personality changes and if so how much depends on which aspects and levels of personality are being considered (McAdams, 1995, Winter and Stewart, 1995). We know that some behaviour can change fairly easily, e.g. panic attacks can generally be treated effectively and quickly (Seligman, 1995), as can problems with being assertive (Rakos, 1991) and sexual problems (Seligman, 1995). But, at least with current techniques, we know that some characteristics change much less readily, e.g. sexual orientation (Seligman, 1995), and basic personality characteristics (Miller, 1991). For example, according to type theory, people do develop and change but without changing in 'type'. What changes is how developed all the preferences are (including those opposite to a person's own type), and how clear a person is about his or her type. Indeed, the two processes are thought to happen in an almost paradoxical way : as people become more flexible and versatile in their *behaviour* they become clearer about their *psychological type*.

This stability could be seen as gloomy, but an alternative view is that (a) it goes with having a sense of identity: life would be very different if people did not have stable personalities, and (b) it leads to realistic expectations of the effects of counselling. Thus, people who are anxious as part of their personalities (trait anxiety) do not usually change into people who are calm (Miller, 1991), but they can change their attitude towards this aspect of themselves and develop effective ways of coping: 'embrace anxiety, refuse to apologise for it, anticipate discomfort under certain circumstances and adjust your life accordingly' (Miller, personal communication). Similarly, according to type and temperament theory, it is futile for someone who prefers, say, perceiving, to try to become a judging type, or vice versa, but she or he can try to develop their 'other side'.

Conclusion

Myers' theory of psychological type is a constructive and positive approach to people's remarkable diversity. It can contribute to such central aspects of counselling and communication as understanding oneself and others, empathizing more quickly and deeply, helping to establish effective working relationships, managing stress, giving information more effectively, and having realistic expectations about personality change.

Note: Five levels of type theory

Five levels of type theory can be distinguished:

- four pairs of preferences. The preferences are the most widely used level of type theory, and the most investigated (Bayne, 1995; Hammer, 1996).
- the extended analysis, which is concerned with more specific behaviours and suggests five sub-scales (so far) for each preference (Kummerow and Quenk, 1992).
- combinations of preferences, in particular the four 'temperaments' (Keirsey and Bates, 1978) and the 16 types.
- type dynamics (Myers, K. and Kirby, 1994; Quenk, 1996).

- type development (Myers, K. and Kirby, 1994).

Some of the subscales, plus 'mingling' (which is an element of one subscale for EI), the four preferences and the four temperaments were discussed in this chapter.

References

Bayne, R. (1995) *The Myers-Briggs Indicator. A Critical Review and Practical Guide*. London: Chapman & Hall.
Review of ideas, empirical research and applications in counselling, education and organizations.

Carr, S. (1997) *Type Clarification. Finding the Fit*. Oxford: Oxford Psychologists Press.
Very clear and useful booklet on questions to ask and strategies to try, to find your type. 'Type clarification is detective work'.

Hammer, A.L. (1996) (Ed.) *MBTI Applications: A Decade of Research on the Myers-Briggs Type Indicator* Palo Alto, Calif: Consulting Psychologists Press.
Reviews in detail the reliability and validity of the MBTI, and applications in careers, management, teams, counselling education, multiculturalism and health.

Hirsh, S.K. and Kummerow, J.M. (1990) *Introduction to Type in Organisations*, 2nd Ed. Palo Alto Calif: Consulting Psychologists Press.
Booklet containing concise 'bullet' descriptions of the 16 types, with sections on 'potential pitfalls' and 'suggestions for development'.

Jones, J.K. and Sherman, R.G. (1997) *Intimacy and Type: A Practical Guide for Improving Relationships for Couples and Counselors*. Gainesville, Flo: Center for Applications of Psychological Type.

Keirsey, D. and Bates, M. (1978) *Please Understand Me*, Del Mar, Calif: Prometheus Nemesis.
Classic on temperament theory. Lots of ideas and examples. No concern with empirical evidence but many of the ideas are consistent with research findings on the MBTI and the closely related 'Big Five' trait theory of personality.

Kroeger, O. and Thuesen, J.M. (1988) *Type Talk* New York: Delacorte Press.
Exuberant, lots of sweeping, stimulating generalizations from very wide experience as consultants and trainers.

Kummerow, J.M. and Quenk, N.L. (1992) *Interpretive Guide for the MBTI Extended Analysis Report* Palo Alto, Calif : Consulting Psychologists Press.
In depth interpretation of the 20 subscales of what from 1997 is called the MBTI Step II. Step I is the basic MBTI which measures the preferences, and therefore the temperaments and types.

Lawrence, G. (1997) *Looking at Type and Learning Styles* Gainesville, Flo: Center for Applications of Psychological Type.
Includes the best descriptions of the learning styles of each type (56 pp).

McAdams, D.P. (1995) What do we know when we know a person? *Journal of Personality 63* (3) 365–96.

Martin, C.R. (1995) *Looking at Type and Careers*. Gainesville, Flo: Center for Applications of Psychological Type.

Miller, T.R. (1991) The psychotherapeutic utility of the five-factor model of personality : a clinician's experience. *Journal of Personality Assessment 57* (3) 415–33.

Myers, I.B. (with Myers, P.B.) (1980) *Gifts Differing* Palo Alto, Calif: Consulting Psychologists Press.

A careful, thoughtful and original classic.

Myers, K.D. and Kirby, L.K. (1994) *Introduction to Type Dynamics and Type Development*, Palo Alto, Calif: Consulting Psychologists Press.

A clear booklet on complex material.

Provost, J.A. (1993) *Applications of the Myers-Briggs Type Indicator in Counseling: A Casebook*. 2nd edn. Palo Alto, Calif: Center for Applications of Psychological Type.

The only book so far on type and counselling. Clear and practical examples of integrative counselling with clients of all 16 types.

Quenk, N.L. (1996) *In the Grip. Our Hidden Personality*. Palo Alto, Calif: Consulting Psychologists Press.

This booklet (28 pp) is about the 'other in us': behaving dramatically 'out of character'. Here type theory is closer to its Jungian roots.

Rakos, R.F. (1991) *Assertive Behaviour: Theory, Research and Training* London: Routledge.

Seligman, M.E.P. (1995) *What You Can Change ... And What You Can't*. New York: Fawcett Columbine.

Thorne, A. (1987) The press of personality: a study of conversations between introverts and extraverts *Journal of Personality 53* (3) 718–26.

Winter, D.G. and Stewart, A.J. (1995) Commentary: tending the garden of personality. *Journal of Personality 63* (3) 711–27.

Chapter 8

Group membership

Richard Kwiatkowski and David Hogan

We are all members of overt and covert groups; membership of such groups can and does have a profound effect on our functioning at work. In this chapter we wish to explore certain aspects of groups, and to suggest that an understanding of some of the processes present may enhance personal satisfaction, professional performance and indeed, effectiveness. We explore how people are both members of a number of groups and also perceive other people quite easily as members of groups.

We contend that it is helpful to become more aware that in every interaction that takes place in a health care setting we 'represent' other groups. While it may seem obvious to say so, a nurse on a ward round is in a defined role, and in certain ways represents *all* nurses to the other people on the team. The team may know that nurse as an individual, but will nevertheless take all sorts of things for granted, many of them unexamined and pre-judged. (The same is equally true, of course, for any other team member). This can have all sorts of regrettable consequences.

However, through recognizing such perhaps more symbolic aspects of interaction within teams we can begin to sort out the false perceptions from the reality. In this chapter we shall examine various models of how individuals and groups can become aware of their functioning, and therefore enhance their effectiveness. We shall also ask you to consider some aspects of your own functioning in groups, and participate in certain activities that will link the various models to your everyday reality. Finally we shall begin to consider aspects of groups in organizations, though not specifically from an Organizational Development perspective (see French and Bell, 1995).

What defines a group?

Later in the chapter we will ask you to reflect on your membership of various groups, and consider how your membership of them affects you. Although we are all familiar with the concept of groups, the notion itself can sometimes be hard to pin down. Therefore, we will first discuss what characteristics define a number of people as a 'group' rather than simply a collection of individuals.

The following characteristics have been considered to define the existence of a group:

Sustained interaction. Members of a group act and react towards each other over time so that their behaviour becomes interdependent. They are both influenced by and influence the psychological life of the group as a whole.

Perception of belonging to a group. Members of a group will see themselves as belonging to that group and not to others. They will understand who is within the group and who is outside the group; 'in-group' and 'out-group' are terms that are sometimes used here.

Shared group goals. A group will share certain goals or outcomes, whether they are articulated or not; there will be some 'pay-off' to belonging to a group.

Norms will arise. Within a group a set of implicit rules regarding acceptable or accepted behaviour will arise. Group members will know, within certain limits, what to expect from other group members.

Roles may arise. Certain members of a group will adopt certain roles; this may happen formally and officially, or informally and sometimes without overt negotiation.

Personal needs may be satisfied through membership. These personal needs may well be rather different from the group's goals, particularly in an organizational context, where part of the benefit of belonging to a group (or perhaps a team) will be social and personal outcomes.

Affective relationships will develop. Relationships, often containing emotionally charged feelings of a positive (or negative) nature, may well arise as a result of being in a group.

Various theorists (e.g. Goodman, Ravlin and Schminke (1987) or Johnson and Johnson (1994)) have suggested that the above characteristics can be considered when thinking about what it is that defines a group. The list is by no means exhaustive.

Which groups are you a member of?

The above description has deliberately been left largely content free so that we do not bias your thinking concerning the groups to which you belong. The following exercises and questions are designed to make the rest of the chapter more meaningful and useful. We believe that a valuable way for people to make sense of the effects of group membership is to reflect systematically upon their experience of their own group membership.

Activities 1–5

The purpose of these activities is to explore and clarify how you construe your membership of groups. You may wish to make some notes or keep a record; we would certainly suggest that you do so.

1. Consider and reflect on all the people you can remember being in contact with in the last 48 hours. Decide if they can be grouped in any way, for instance if they are mostly nurses, you might simply use that term, or you might make other distinctions such as 'psychiatric nurses', 'practice nurses', 'general nurses', 'sisters', 'ward managers', 'trainees', 'student nurses', 'midwives', and so forth. The title or description or name that you use to describe each group needs to be one that makes sense to you. For instance, it could be 'part of my team' and 'not part of my team', or as broad as 'patients' and 'staff'.

2. Think of all the training courses you have been on, all the professional bodies you are a member of, unions, medical defence organizations, formal and informal networks.

3. Consider the people you regard as members of your 'team(s)'.
Who are colleagues, peers, subordinates, supervisors?
What lines of accountability are present?
What lines of responsibility and reporting relationships are there?

4. List characteristics of yourself which you or others might consider to be important; for example, age, gender, race, class, appearance, sexual orientation, family, marital status, and so forth.

5. Finally, consider ways in which other people might describe you, for instance, district nurse, doctor, social worker, physiotherapist.

For some people a graphical representation (e.g. a drawing, a mind map, or a diagram) is helpful, but in any case it can be salutary to consider just how many 'groups' we come into contact with every day of our lives, and also to consider the groups that we consider ourselves belonging to, or indeed the groups that others may think we belong to.

Our contention is that people represent their groups whenever they interact with others. On some occasions this is less obvious than on others. What is essentially an intergroup encounter may not be recognized as such, and is thought to be a more simple encounter between two separate and distinct individuals. For instance, in talking to a patient in a hospital, social workers, doctors and nurses are all recognized as representing the hospital (to varying degrees) by the patient. However, the professional team members may feel that they are simply chatting informally, or else giving a personal or perhaps a professional view. They may identify themselves, for instance, more strongly with their profession than with the specific hospital they happen to be working at. Similarly, other aspects of identity, such as social class, gender or sexuality may not be recognized as significant to that encounter by either party – although these factors may, in fact, be very important.

One way of conceptualizing these notions is as though you are a nodal point in an immense multi-dimensional array; or if you prefer, a knot in a huge three dimensional net, with numerous links and lines connected to you. These links can be thought of as representing the various groups to which you belong. A tug on a line, depending on the pattern of interconnection and tension present, can pull the knot very gently, or at the other extreme, yank it suddenly out of place.

Models of group process

In thinking about groups it is important to make a distinction between content and process. The content of what actually goes on in groups or teams is often very obvious and visible; however, the way in which items are discussed, tasks achieved, power negotiated, and so forth, is often harder to discern. An old analogy is that gum is the content and chewing is the process. To take this further we might ask how often people are aware of where their tongue is during chewing, or if they prefer one side of the mouth to the other for chewing, or even if chewing dissimilar foods is done in the same or a different way.

Similarly, members of groups – and in particular work teams – are often very aware of the tasks that need to be accomplished, but they may be somewhat less aware of the processes that take place in order to accomplish these tasks; for instance, interaction patterns, how

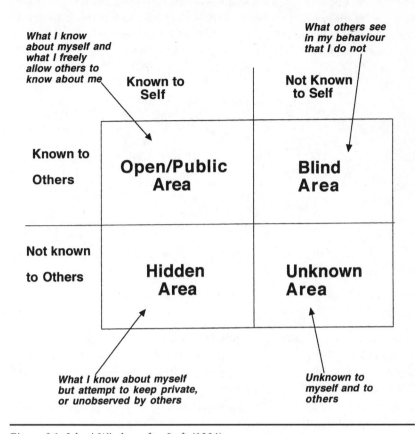

What I know about myself and what I freely allow others to know about me

Known to Self

What others see in my behaviour that I do not

Not Known to Self

Known to Others

Open/Public Area

Blind Area

Not known to Others

Hidden Area

Unknown Area

What I know about myself but attempt to keep private, or unobserved by others

Unknown to myself and to others

Figure 8.1: Johari Window after Luft (1984).

problem-solving takes place, how status and hierarchy influence decision-making, typical patterns of communication, or how the group deals with anxiety.

We shall briefly discuss two models that may clarify process issues in groups. The first will examine individual functioning, or how you are in a group; and the second will look at how you can make sense of what is happening in the group itself.

The Johari Window

A way of thinking about individual processes in groups, and a way of thinking about one's own behaviour in a group is the 'Johari Window'. ('Johari' is derived from the names of the two authors of the concept – Joseph Luft and Harry Ingham.)

As can be seen, for individuals within groups (and perhaps for groups interacting with each other) this formulation presents an interesting form of enquiry. For example, for some people the 'blind area' is comparatively large, thus they may well find themselves puzzled or surprised by others' reactions to them. Similarly, it may be the case that an individual tries to keep his or her 'hidden area' as large as possible, and expends a lot of energy by trying to keep things hidden from others, carefully censoring comments and information.

It can be an interesting exercise to enquire into how your profile changes in different teams or groups and to consider why this might be the case. For instance, you may not wish the hospital administrators (out group) to know what your department is planning, or else you might wish to share fully and frankly some professional problem with your professional peers (in group) – in both these cases the 'Window' would look rather different. Notice here that we are not advocating that you reveal all – in many circumstances it is quite appropriate that the 'public area' is not vast. On the other hand if the blind and unknown areas dominate people's interactions then team-work might become problematic.

Activity 6

You might like to complete a Johari Window for three groups, teams or settings where you would guess that it would look rather different; that is, by moving the vertical and horizontal lines the relative sizes of the areas will be different.

- What might happen if you behaved in one setting in the way you usually behave in another?
- What are you most comfortable with?
- Is there anything you would like to change?
- What might be the consequences of such a change?
- What do you think other people's windows are like?
- Are they dependent on the situation?
- What might happen if next time one of their windows was different?

Schein's observational framework

Before group functioning can be improved on a process level, an understanding of what is going on needs to be gained: a problem for those involved with groups is that they have to learn to distinguish accurately the origin of the information that they choose to gather or use. It is easy to fall prey to all sorts of traps while trying to do this 'objectively'. Under conditions of stress, for example, we can revert to relying on internal data in the form of feelings and suppositions, and not really attend to what is going on in the group in front of us. Many

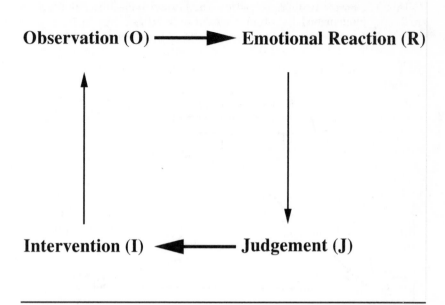

Figure 8.2: The basic ORJI cycle.
From: Schein, E. H. (1988: 64).

of us are not very aware of aspects of ourselves that distort our perception. One model that can help us to become more aware of such distortions is that proposed by Schein (1988).

Schein's framework shows, in a simplified way, the processes that go on within ourselves that affect our overt behaviour. We observe an event (O), we react emotionally to what we have observed (R), we analyse, process and make judgements based on our observations and feelings (J) and we act or behave overtly in order to make something happen, that is, we intervene in some way (I). Both emotional reaction and judgement can be influenced by a number of factors, such as our expectations, any stereotypes we may hold, ways we have of dealing with anxiety, defences, biases and so forth. It is thus important to become aware of the effects of these internal processes in distorting or influencing our perceptions.

A further problem linked to judgements made or action taken on the basis of internal data is that they may well be rational and defensible, that is, they will make sense to us and we may well be able to provide a rational account for our reasons for them if questioned. However, because the data are being distorted, action (I) more often than not will be inaccurate and inappropriate.

The following model (Figure 8.3) expands some of these ideas.

Thus the various traps members of groups can fall into are:

123

GOAL: 1. Learn to distinguish *inside yourself* observations, reactions, judgements, and impulses to act (intervene)

2. Identify biases in how you handle each of these processes

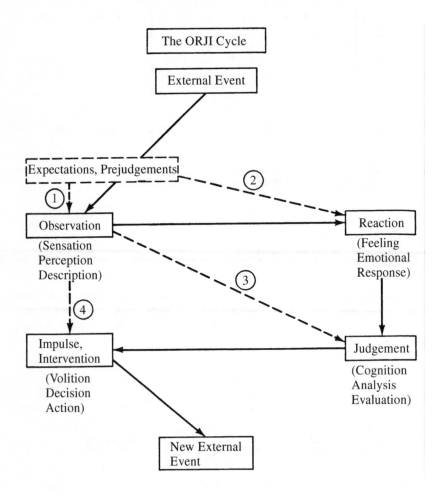

Traps: 1. Misperception

2. Inappropriate emotional response

3. Rational analysis based on incorrect data

4. Intervention based on incorrect data

Figure 8.3: A more realistic depiction of the ORJI cycle.
From: Schein, E. H. (1988: 70).

Misperception. We do not perceive accurately what happens or why it happens because of our pre-judgement, our expectations, our personal defences, stereotypes, and so on.

Inappropriate emotional response. Having misperceived the events in the first place, we allow ourselves to respond emotionally to our initial interpretations without being aware that this response is based on incorrect and inappropriate data or information.

Rational analysis and judgement – based on incorrect data/information. Once we accept our observational and emotional response as 'correct' we are able to reason and explain the event and our reaction to it appropriately and rationally. However, we still arrive at the wrong conclusion and understanding, because our input to our decisions is faulty.

Intervention – made on the basis of incorrect judgement. If our subsequent intervention is based on our apparently rational and 'internally correct' judgement it will invariably be incorrect. If we allow ourselves to intervene without rechecking the whole cycle of elements – that is, checking whether our observation, emotional reaction and the subsequent judgement were correct and appropriate – we may end up acting rationally but inappropriately. Thus, for example we might make worse a situation we intended to improve. A way to facilitate this 'checking' is through open communication with the other people involved, so a shared understanding of what is taking place is reached.

Activity 7

- Think through, and perhaps code – using Schein's framework – a successful group or team event, task, process or goal, and an unsuccessful one.
- What were the differences between the events?
- Does this way of thinking help you to understand what was happening?

For example, if we consider the Johari Window we can begin to think about which hidden parts of ourselves might assist other members of a team if they are disclosed. It is sometimes very difficult to reveal aspects of one's self, particularly in a professional context, and even more so if it implies some lessening of one's professional standing; for instance, asking an 'obvious' question. This desire to save face can

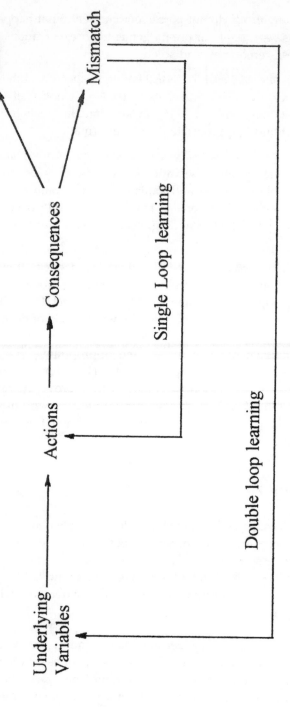

Figure 8.4: Single and Double loop learning – after Argyris (1997) Lecture to the Annual Conference of The British Psychological Society.

have long-term negative effects on team and organizational functioning (Argyris, 1982).

Organizational defensive routines

Chris Argyris (1982) showed that organizations can indulge in single
or double loop learning. By single loop learning he means that an
organization reacts to its environment; by double loop learning he
means that the organization questions assumptions about its own
reactions. The analogy often used is that of a thermostat; it may switch
on the heat at 10 degrees and off at 28 degrees, but it never questions
why this takes place; Argyris suggests most organizations are like this.

The diagram suggests that if faulty information as to the 'goodness'
of outcomes is fed back into the system ('mismatch') then error will
escalate. It is Argyris's contention that through a number of mechanisms, such as unilaterally seeking to save face, we distort this
information on an organizational scale.

This is where the concept of 'organizational defensive routines'
comes in. For example, inconsistencies arise, and people are aware
that, for instance, they are not making their real feelings apparent, say
because of not wishing to 'hurt' another person publicly even though
that person's behaviour is causing difficulties. They act as if this is not
the case, and further make undiscussable the fact that their lack of
reaction is inconsistent with the true situation; and even further, they
make the fact of its undiscussability also undiscussable. Thus organizations tend to increase the errors inherent in any system by 'pretending' that the situation is different from what it really is. See also de
Board (1978).

Activity 8

You may like to consider:

- What are the major sources of 'error' in your group and
  organization?
- Are the underlying causes of this discussable?
- What are the undiscussable topics in your group or organization?
- What might happen if they were discussed?
- Who do you fear might be 'damaged' if they were discussed?
- What steps could your team or organization take to become more
  appropriately 'open' to acknowledging error?

Conclusion

In trying to make sense for ourselves of what is happening in our
teams we need to consider that perception within groups is by no

means a simple process: the cost of poor communication to our clients and patients, our teams and organizations and to ourselves is considerable. Through an awareness of some of the aspects of group functioning we can begin to improve communication and effectiveness. Groups are also, of course, a source of information, reasoned decision-making, enjoyable comradeship, instillation of hope, sources of support, identity, social activity and fun. Awareness of some of the processes present in groups can mean that we can enhance and address these aspects as well.

References

Argyris, C. (1982) *Reasoning, Learning and Action*, San Francisco, Calif, Jossey Bass.

In this work and in subsequent books and articles Argyris elaborates his views of single and double loop learning and organizational defensive routines, where error builds on error, and particularly if it is kept hidden (although often widely known).

De Board, R. (1978) *The Psychoanalysis of Organisations*, London, Tavistock.

A good summary of a range of work, including that of Lewin and Bion as well as Menzies. Clearly and concisely written.

French, W.L. and Bell, C.H. (1995) *Organization Development: Behavioral science interventions for organization improvement* 5th edn. New Jersey, Prentice Hall.

A key text for the last 20 years in organizational development. We prefer their formulations to that of Egan and others, who have transposed individual models to the group or organizational contexts.

Goodman, P.S., Ravlin, E. and Schminke, M. (1987) Understanding groups in organizations. *Research in Organisational Behaviour*, 9 121–73.

This article considers the fact that groups within organizations are often called upon to 'produce'. This factor tends to be neglected in other psychological writing.

Johnson, D.W. and Johnson, F.P (1994) *Joining Together: Group Theory and Group Skills* 5th edn. Boston, Mass, Allyn and Bacon.

An excellent book for people who are interested in making groups work; it covers much of the relevant literature as well as including a large number of structured exercises that can assist in understanding aspects of group functioning.

Luft, J. (1984) *Group Processes: an Introduction to Group Dynamics*, 3rd edn. Calif: Mayfield.

Schein, E.H. (1988) *Process Consultation: Volume 1 – Its Role in Organisational Development and Volume 2 Lessons for Managers and Consultants*, 2nd edn. Reading, Mass., Addison Wesley OD Series.

One of the key authors in this area. The two volumes are slim and easy to read (although expensive on a pennies-per-page basis); however, we judge the insights provided to be extremely worthwhile.

PART 3

SPECIALIZED SKILLS AND SETTINGS

Chapter 9

Talking to children and adolescents about life, death and sex

Paula Nicolson

Children and adolescents are a neglected group in counselling and communication textbooks aimed at medical and health practitioners, as they are not assumed to be typical of those seeking help. However, young people comprise a high proportion of health care consumers in their own right, as well as being involved, to varying degrees, with health problems in family life such as caring for the mental or physical well-being of their parents, or guardians or another family member.

A working knowledge of psychological theories of child development facilitates health professionals' awareness of children's capacity for understanding their own and other people's health-related experiences. Theories of psychological development focus upon the way that psychological processes (thinking, memory, emotions, social capacities and behaviour) evolve through a combination of social and biological influences from infancy to adulthood. Understanding psychological development is important in professional-patient communication, when the patient is a young person, when parents are being advised on relevant procedures in their child's health care or when the young person is involved with a member of their family who is ill.

These are complex processes and need to be understood not as prescriptions but as the context from which interaction may be understood. Health care professionals need to take account of both verbal and non-verbal signals that the child, parents and other staff use – and the effects of these on the consultation.

The extent to which information about psychological theory may be used in day-to-day encounters is limited, but without some under-standing of developmental psychology it is likely that communication will be curtailed and information will lack value. Effective communi-cation with children and young people, however, ultimately comes about through a combination of psychological knowledge and practi-cal experience.

In this chapter I identify stages that children and young people go through in the developmental processes and their importance for handling information on difficult subjects such as death and sex. I also begin to demonstrate how health professionals might use this knowl-edge to develop their effectiveness in working with this group.

Children's understanding of the body

Jean Piaget's approach to children's cognitive development is particu-larly useful as a starting point for an awareness of how they make sense of the human body. Piaget, concerned with the development of human thinking and reasoning, was the first to demonstrate that children see the world and reason about events in a very different way from adults. It is important to bear this difference in mind in all communication with children.

Piaget constructed a developmental model of children's intellectual maturation in which he suggested that children *interact* with their environment from infancy, modifying their understanding of them-selves in the world based upon their assimilation of new knowledge that emerges from these interactions. Piaget was not, however, advo-cating the centrality of the environment in the developmental process. He argued that *biological* maturation was fundamental to cognitive development. Until a child reached a particular cognitive developmen-tal stage (which was age related) he or she did not have the capacity to understand certain features of the world. An overview of his theory is in Appendix 1.

Conservation

Psychologists have subsequently developed and fine-tuned Piaget's initial concepts and research findings, but the underlying ideas and approach remain important for communicating with children. A key feature of Piaget's approach was his exposition of the notion of 'conservation'. He considered that grasping the concept that some things remain the same in quantity and form, even if they appear superficially different, to be pivotal in his model of cognitive develop-ment. This realization tends to happen when the child reaches the age of 6 or 7. Then the child is able to discern that, for example, a grouping of five buttons remains constant in number even if the configuration is altered. Until the child had grasped that concept they were likely to insist that when buttons are moved from, say, being tightly grouped to being spread out, that the second formation was 'bigger' than the first (see Bee, 1981).

This has implications in a number of ways for how children understand illness in the family. Thus they themselves may believe that a parent is ill on one day, but not on the next because they have got out of bed or are behaving differently. Similarly, they may not see that they themselves need to maintain certain health-related behaviours on more than one occasion. For instance, a young child may obey the advice about not running around a school playground because of their condition on one day, but this does not mean they will be consistent or understand that they need to continue to be so. For older children, who have grasped the concept of conservation, failure to meet adult demands may be more to do with boredom, or acting out and intentionally transgressing rules rather than not grasping the importance of the health-related advice.

Context

One of the key findings that illustrates the difference between children at different stages of cognitive development is the way that information is understood. So for young children it has been shown that contextualization of information is vital. Therefore, when giving instructions about medication (or supporting parents doing this) it is necessary to modify information for different age groups.

To tell a child: 'don't drink milk or you will be sick', will not mean much to a child under about the age of 7. To make those instructions meaningful, it would help to tell the child a story about the way milk may affect them, how they might feel, and how biscuits and water would be better alongside the medicine so that they won't get pains in their stomach.

The younger the child the more 'contextualization' is needed. It may be helpful, for example, with under-7s to use drawings to show the 'tummy ache'. It might be effective to get the child to embellish the tale, to show they have understood, but don't lose the message! Sometimes children can repeat instructions, appearing to show that they have understood, but this may not be the case. They may have perceived the exercise to be a comprehension game, or they may not have realized the urgency of the instruction.

This means that a health professional talking to a child needs to be aware of

- how far to make information sensible to a child at various stages of his or her development, and

• how to make sense of what children mean when they explain themselves to adults.

In all cases, asking the child for feedback to check they have understood is essential.

Children and disease

Psychologists who have used Piaget's approach to human reasoning and understanding have demonstrated on a practical level that there are indeed clear distinctions between what children at various ages are able to grasp in relation to the human body. The younger the child is, the more *contextualized* an explanation needs to be, as indicated above. However, even if an elaborate story is woven around explanations, children under about the age of 5 still cannot grasp certain concepts with ease, particularly the idea of bodily damage as irreversible or death as permanent. For example, if children between the ages of 5 and 10 are asked to describe what human bodies contain, some studies showed that overall:

1. 5 to 6-year-olds know that bodies contain blood and bones, because they can see and feel them, but this group of children can only list up to three things inside the human body;
2. by the age of 7, children understand that a heart is in the body because, even though they can't see it, they can feel it beating;
3. by the age of 9 or 10, children are able to list up to eight internal organs, such as muscles, liver, brain and lungs, which they can't see.

The younger ones also think in terms of what is put into the body, and what comes out, as being the *extent* of the issue. When these children are asked to name the most important part of their bodies, younger ones focus on the external parts, such as the nose, the feet and the hair, and see the nose as being particularly important for breathing. However, by the age of 10 they understand that lungs are as important as noses for breathing, and they have some idea of the biological function of other organs.

What then is the most effective way to explain to a 5-year-old how to cope with an asthma attack? Restricted breathing is likely to make anyone panic and be unable to cope with their medication and regain stability. While older children and adults will have a basic understanding of what is happening to them and how to cope, even if they do panic sometimes, a 5-year-old is unlikely to respond in the way that is most likely to alleviate their symptoms. This is in part, at least, because they cannot relate their shortening breath to the fact that they have lungs which are internal. They connect their problem to their noses and mouths, which seem to be the source of the breathing difficulties. Further, younger children may fail to relate any particular attack to a previous one, or may be too troubled in their breathing to grasp the underlying logic of *how* to breathe and get themselves into an appropriate state to administer medication or find their inhaler. Thus they need practical help, with the focus on action rather than comprehension.

Similar age differences have been found in relation to understanding digestion and food intake. Special diets, for example, need to be explained in terms of making the child 'big and strong', particularly when talking to under-9s, rather than in terms of the negative effects of the wrong food.

To understand children's limitations in relation to this is potentially useful for explaining health care, illness and medical or surgical procedures, as well as for finding out from children about pain, discomfort and other symptoms. Children under 10 do not appear to understand the disease process or the finality of organ damage or death; instead they see damage and death as resulting from *external* agents and observable phenomena, such as bullet wounds or being run over. They also appear to believe that someone can avoid death, which indicates that perhaps they believe that death and disease is the fault of the victim. There is also a clear and important danger that young children may see the illness or death of a parent or sibling as being 'my fault'. This may cause many years of trauma and stress if not handled sensitively, honestly and directly.

Children, emotion and death

The death of children

For health professionals, death or impending death of the patient represents a degree of failure, and this is sometimes difficult to deal with in oneself or colleagues, patients and relatives. This is likely to hamper effective communication.

Cognitive developmental psychologists' work made it clear that death is a difficult concept for young children to understand intellectually – particularly because of its permanency. However, children *do* die and children lose close relatives through death. So how do you tell children about their own impending death or the death of others? It is important to be clear and ask for feedback to ensure that the child has understood. However understanding and emotional reactions to death need to be held together by the health professional trying to assist the child, which is a hard task for both parties. The principles and findings from studies of cognitive development are useful but do not explain the *emotional* aspects of development, which are important when communicating about death. John Bowlby, who worked from a psychoanalytic perspective, studied loss, separation and death in childhood, adolescence and adulthood. His work has made a major contribution towards understanding how children cope with separation, loss, dying and the death of others.

Psychoanalysis, on which Bowlby's work is based, is underpinned by the theories of Sigmund Freud. A key aspect of this work is the idea of the human *unconscious*, which houses both primitive instincts and drives, and emotions and thoughts which are too painful to face.

The human mind operates a series of defence mechanisms in order to protect itself from intense psychological pain, such as that generated by the prospect of one's own death or that of a loved one. One of these defences is 'denial'. Research studies and psychoanalytic therapists have continuously shown that we all operate a system of denial about death (both our own and that of others). This is not to say that adult human beings fail to understand the rational basis of death, but it is the emotional process with which we appear unable to cope. This is particularly true of doctors and other health care professionals, especially if they are working in an area where death is common. Doctors on cancer wards typically *claim* to treat each patient as an individual, while observations of what they actually do suggest their focus is on something other than the person – such as pain alleviation – thereby avoiding discussions (which patients often initiate) about the process of dying.

This denial by avoidance is even more clear when health professionals are working with children who are dying. There have been examples of special funds set up to send very sick children on a 'once in a lifetime' trip. Sometimes the publicity that surrounds dying or terminally ill children makes them into 'superstars', a process that enables the child, the parents and even the health professionals to avoid facing the painful and ugly reality of illness, physical deterioration and death. In a recent case in the UK, public hostility was directed against a health service team that refused a child an operation for a bone-marrow transplant on the grounds that it would be painful and unlikely to be successful. These doctors were publicly denounced for being concerned about finance (which was one element in their argument for not doing the operation) rather than children. A public appeal ensured the operation was carried out privately, and although the child gained some extra time, she did in fact die. What is the rationale of these kinds of public efforts to prolong children's lives in this way? There is no doubt that any death, but particularly that of a young person, is a tragedy. But it also seems there is an element of social denial and the operation of a social defence against the guilt which such public cases engender.

The aim is overtly to make the child's last days active and happy, when this may not be in the child's best interests. Denying that a child is dying, seriously lets the child down – both clinically and emotionally. It is important that health professionals help children and their parents understand that they are reaching the end of their life, so they can tackle the grief process and, as far as possible, reach a state of peace of mind.

Kübler-Ross, working with terminally ill adults, developed a psychological profile of the emotional experience of dying – suggesting that this is a normal and emotionally useful pattern, which should be facilitated rather than blocked. The process that Kubler-Ross described goes from denial through to anger, to attempts to postpone death, to depression and finally to acceptance of its inevitability. To enable this is to enable the child or young person to understand what is happening to them and to achieve peace of mind as far as possible. If the denial is prolonged, by publicity, fund raising and so on, the child and the parents may be unprepared for the end and thus have less chance of achieving peace.

The death of others

Death in the family is difficult for all young people, even for those who have reached adolescence and thus have a clearer understanding of what death means. For instance, it is now generally accepted that a diagnosis of cancer in an adult has an emotional impact on the whole family. It is also the case that effective and honest communication between multi-disciplinary health care teams, patients and their families, reduces anxiety and increases well-being, while the converse exacerbates stress. Failure to reveal bad news does not protect the recipient. They are likely to intuit that something is not making sense and this may be very worrying.

The potentially traumatic effects for adolescents following a cancer diagnosis on a parent, and the deleterious implications for their behaviour, mental and physical health, may be expected from studies of the literature on adolescence as a pivotal and potentially vulnerable stage of psychological development (Erikson, 1959). Further, literature on young people's reactions to family problems such as parental separation and divorce (Wallerstein and Kelly, 1974), and the implications of parental death on young people's mental state and behaviour (e.g. Dyregrov, 1994) reinforce the impact of the cancer diagnosis and the fear of, as well as the reality of, parental death. Reactions to parental cancer are likely to lead to trauma resulting not only in behavioural problems, but confusion and distress for a young person trying to understand his or her own reactions. It is also the case that unacknowledged emotional distress at this sensitive developmental stage may lead to life-long emotional and psychiatric disorders in a significant proportion of adults (Bowlby, 1988). It is therefore vital that health professionals allow time and opportunity for these young people to express their fears and emotions in a supportive environment. In that, they are no different from adults, but their specific understanding of death according to their developmental stage and experience needs to be taken seriously.

Talking with children about sex and reproduction

Another complex and difficult area for health professionals is to talk to young people and children about sexual behaviour because this frequently occurs in the context of sexual abuse. Cognitive developmental psychology indicates that very young children's understanding of sexual intercourse is limited, so that use of anatomically correct dolls with very young children has been useful for enabling communication both for giving information and seeing what children understand about their experiences (see Glaser and Frosh, 1988). However, it is important to use this information with caution. Psychological studies suggest that 9-year-olds are capable of understanding sexual intercourse in relation to reproduction, but do not necessarily understand that somebody might have sexual intercourse either for pleasure or in an abusive way. This makes understanding what they report potentially difficult. Therefore, once again the child needs to be allowed to describe what happened, step by step rather than to put a meaning or intention on actions of either themselves or the others involved. It is also important at this stage not to allow the discussion between the professional and child to focus on physical or emotional pain, because that again influences how they describe events.

Moreover, psychoanalytic theory, based on Freud's psycho-sexual developmental stages, indicates that from infancy there is an unconscious understanding of sexualized pleasure and that from birth to adulthood children experience sexual development via particular focuses on erogenous zones, for example, the mouth, the anus, genitals, at different stages and ages. These perspectives are potentially conflicting and therefore may have implications for diagnoses of sexual abuse and communication between the professional, the child and the perpetrators, in that some adults argue that children collude and in some cases even encourage sexual relations. Collecting and understanding this kind of evidence takes time and collaboration between different professional groups and between those professionals and the children and adults involved.

It is also important to note that under the age of about 5 children's memory of events is poor. They do not spontaneously rehearse or commit incidents to memory in the way that adults do. However, if rehearsal of an event is suggested, then they can do this. It is necessary, though, to treat memories with caution, because constant interviewing and describing particular events may exaggerate a memory or distort it. A child, for example, may be convinced that an event took place because they have talked about it several times. It is only when a child reaches the age of 9 or 10 that the spontaneous rehearsal of memories becomes more common and evidence therefore more reliable.

Talking to adolescents about sexual health

Adolescence is often seen as a difficult stage of life and one when sexuality is biologically and emotionally important. The work of the psychoanalyst Erik Erikson has made one of the most influential contributions to understanding the conflicts that young people experience when trying to establish a separate identity – they are at odds with their families, with their developing bodies, with the emotions that accompany these rapid changes as well as the mixture of fear and excitement that the future promises them (see Appendix 2).

One clear area in which adolescents come to the attention of health professionals is in relation to their sexual behaviour – they have moved through puberty, are seeking to establish an identity and gain intimacy with others (see Erikson, 1959) and their social lives often revolve around sexualized activities such as going to parties, dances, clubs and so on. A high proportion of young people are routinely sexually active by the time they reach 18 (Lees, 1993).

Adolescents talk to each other about sexuality and sexual behaviour some of the time, but they are very unlikely to discuss such things with their parents or other adults. Sexual behaviours may lead young people into being at risk of pregnancy, sexually transmitted diseases and HIV/AIDS which occur not only because of ignorance, but because of various value systems held by young people that are not understood by the adult health professionals.

Significant examples of these mismatches emerged in a study of health-related youth work in Sheffield (Thomas and Nicolson, 1997). Some health and youth worker professionals considered that a key element of their job is to prevent very young (especially legally under-aged) people having sexual intercourse. However, most young people *are* sexually active. They do not always want to admit it because they are still bound up in the culture that believes that casual sex is not virtuous and believe that they themselves will be judged accordingly. This makes communication difficult because health professionals may not want to be seen to condone sexual relationships but on the other hand they want to enable the young people to engage in positive and healthy relationships.

One point of conflict between health and youth workers and the young people we studied was the notion of 'risk'. The workers were concerned that the young people, who were clearly engaged in sexual activities, used condoms for protection from pregnancy and infection. However, it seemed that, particularly with young people from lower socio-economic group backgrounds, risk-taking was an integral part of their lives. For example, to use a condom with a partner meant that they were then suspected of being unfaithful, and some young people would rather take a risk with their own health than contemplate the breakdown of their relationship on that basis.

A second point of conflict was that the young women did not perceive that pregnancy was a risk in the way the health workers did. They knew they would have a baby sooner or later, and if they were out of work, with few attractive long-term prospects, pregnancy and motherhood was potentially a positive experience for them.

Health professionals, in this context, had to redirect their focus towards enabling the young women to make an informed and self-concerned choice about when and with whom they would become pregnant rather than 'leaving it up to chance'. However, this is very different from the notion that young women have to be helped to avoid pregnancy.

Another key issue in health work with young people is sexism and sexually aggressive behaviour. Exploitation and verbal and physical abuse were routine for several young women who, while not seeing such behaviours on the part of their boyfriends as desirable, did not have other possibilities from which to choose. They assumed that this was what it meant to be a woman. The decision of how to combat this was difficult for the workers, but they chose to work separately with the young women and men, building up the self-esteem in both groups, and particularly focusing on masculinity with the boys. The intention was to show them alternative ways of being 'men' rather than 'putting them down' for being men in the way they had been.

Underlying almost all matters of communication and sexual health with adolescents is the need to ensure that young people increase their self-esteem and hold a positive image of their own worth. It is often difficult for health professionals to do that because of the semi-visible gap – most young people look like young adults, and health professionals expect them to respond to the same 'logic' that they themselves hold in their middle-class value system. Adolescents may have the cognitive capacity to make sense of the adult value system, but they have their own cultural values, and personal insecurities are obstacles to effective communication.

Conclusions

This chapter suggests that health professionals who understand aspects of psychological development will be better able to communicate with children and young people on sensitive issues such as death and sexuality. They not only need to be sensitive to the *emotional* side, but also to the extent of children's and young people's *intellectual capacities*.

Appendix 1: Overview of Piaget's Theory

Piaget believed that children actively construct their understanding of the world by interacting with it. At different periods of their development they have the capacities for different kinds of interactions and arrive at different kinds of understandings.

He gave these developmental periods names:

1. The sensory motor-period:

From birth until two years. Here the child begins to develop a sense of object constancy and understands that s/he can act intentionally in relation to the world.

2. The pre-operational periods:

From two until seven. The child is egocentric – unable to believe anything happens in the world unless they are the centre of the action.

3. The operational period:

divided into the period of *concrete operations* from seven until eleven when the child begins to understand more than one aspect of a situation, understands notions of conservation and reversibility, and moves beyond complete egocentricity; and the period of *formal operations* from eleven until adulthood. At this stage the child begins to deal with abstractions.

At around the age of six or seven the child begins to grasp the concept of 'conservation' when the child understands that for example when liquid poured from a tall to a short, but wider beaker, the amount remains the same.

(see Helen Bee: *The Developing Child* for a more detailed reviewof this theory)

Appendix 2: Erikson's approach to understanding adolescence

Erik Erikson believed that over the life course an individual goes through a series of distinct developmental stages with a specific task at each stage.

The stages are partly defined by cultural expectations, partly by biological stage and partly by the psychological context in which the child is growing.

Between the ages of 13–18 and the adolescent passes through the 'Identity versus role confusion stage'. The tasks here are to adapt a sense of self to the physical changes of puberty, make occupational choices, achieve adult-like sexual identity and search for new values. (Erikson, 1959)

References

Bee, H. (1981) *The Developing Child*, New York: Harper & Row.
  A clear and useful text which outlines all major psychological theories of development and some research findings relating to them.
Bowlby, J. (1988) *Loss, Sadness and Depression, Vol 3, Attachment and Loss*, London: Hogarth Press.
  A classic text using clinical case studies to inform theory.
Dyregrov, A. (1994) Childhood Bereavement: Consequences and Therapeutic Approaches, *ACPP Review, Vol 16*, 4.
Erikson, E. (1959) *Identity, Youth and Crisis*, London: Faber and Faber.
  Classic developmental theory particularly important for the study of adolescence and the growth of identity.
Glaser, D. and Frosh, S. (1988) *Child Sexual Abuse*, Basingstoke: Macmillan.
  Using case studies and theory to provide an excellent introduction to working with sexual abuse of children.
Lees, S. (1993) *Sugar and Spice: Sexuality and Adolescent Girls*, Harmondsworth: Penguin.
  Feminist study of adolescent girls which differs from the traditional understanding of girls as seen in Erikson's model.

Thomas, K. and Nicolson, P. (1997) *Wybourn Way Forward in Health: An Evaluation of a Health-Related Youth Work Project*, Sheffield: Trent Health.
Original research which explores the role of health and youth workers with deprived adolescents.

Wallerstein, J.L. and Kelly, J. (1974) The effects of parental divorce: the adolescent's experience. *In A. and C. Koupernik (Eds) The Child and His Family*, New York: Wiley.
Details of children's experiences during and after divorce.

Chapter 10

Talking about sexuality and sexual problems

Paula Nicolson

There are three ways in which sexual behaviour and sexuality are important in effective communication between health practitioners and their clients and patients.

1. Sexuality influences every social encounter – between patients and professionals and between everyone who works in the organization. Thus all need both to be aware of this and also to be able to undertake discussion of sexual issues when they arise, clearly, ethically and without embarrassment.
2. Doctors, midwives, nurses and physiotherapists have intimate physical contact with patients in their care. This means that they potentially disturb their patients' sense of their own private space, even when they carry out the examination or treatment impeccably.
3. Most health professionals are also likely to help patients directly with reproductive or sexual problems at some time in their careers – even if they are not specialists. These problems can range from questions about relationships to anxiety about infertility or abuse.

Being aware of sexuality in our self and in others is a taboo in Western industrial society. However, because sexuality is so fundamental to human contact the taboo needs to be addressed. In this chapter I explore assumptions about sexuality and the norms of sexual behaviour in the context of health care, suggesting that awareness of these issues enables effective communication about all levels of sexual problems. I begin by exploring beliefs about what is normal and then outline the main sexual problems and their treatment.

Understanding sexuality and sexual behaviour

Underlying all forms of sexual therapy and most client–professional interactions are a set of beliefs about what is *normal* sexual behaviour. But what does 'normal' mean in this context? Most people take for granted that 'normal' sex is what they have been brought up to accept, emerging from a mixture of exposure to the mass media, the education system, gossip, rumours about others' transgressions and what parents or caretakers have permitted them to know and do. Unless an individual falls foul of the law, the majority of the population believes their desires and behaviours to be normal. By this knowledge they judge others. Health professionals are rarely challenged about their assumptions concerning sexual behaviours, either during their training or in their everyday practice, so that their opinions on what constitutes normal sex is taken for granted and this influences their professional judgment. However, there are wide variations in how patients and professionals behave, which suggests possibilities for misunderstandings and a clash of values.

Much of popular and professional knowledge is derived from the work of sexologists, a multi-disciplinary group of scientists and clinicians who study and conduct clinical work on sexuality and sexual behaviour. They include biologists, sociologists, counsellors, psychotherapists, psychoanalytic, biological and evolutionary psychologists, psychiatrists, genito-urinary medicine specialists and gynaecologists. There appears to be little active communication between researchers and practitioners from these different perspectives and between the sexologists and critical commentators such as feminist and critical sociologists or psychologists.

Sexual myths and cultural values

There are clear links between mainstream sexological viewpoints and popular beliefs, however, particularly concerning the differences between female and male sexuality. The ways in which researchers perceive men and women's normal sexual needs do not seem to have changed a great deal in the last 100 years and often contemporary clinical decisions and assumptions reflect this, i.e. that perceptions have not changed.

Ideas about sexuality which underpin contemporary sexology and popular ideas can be seen in the work of Havelock-Ellis and Freud in the early 20th century. Their assertions are basically that men are *active*, responsible for heterosexual behaviour, that men *need* sexual intercourse, that they *naturally* pursue women and they do not take 'no' for an answer. Conversely women are seen to be sexually *passive*, resisting male advances because they do not *need* sex for its own sake. Current forms of treatments, particularly for primary sexual dysfunctions (see later in this chapter), reflect those myths.

Ellis created a scientific 'stir' when his work was published. He was subsequently applauded for assigning sexual desire to women (a radical idea in Victorian culture), but as the following quotation shows, his description of female sexuality is highly flawed.

> A special and detailed study of the normal characters of the sexual impulse in men seems unnecessary if only because it is predominantly open and aggressive. The sexual instinct in women is much more elusive ... manifesting itself in the phenomena of modesty and courting.
>
> (Ellis, 1905: 189)

> Some of the most marked characteristics of the sexual impulse in women, moreover, – its association with modesty, its comparatively late development, its seeming passivity, its need of stimulation, – all combine to render difficult the final pronouncement that a woman is sexually frigid.
>
> (Ellis, 1905: 295)

Ellis' radical view that women are not sexually frigid but only *seem* passive, that they want to be courted and need stimulation, has been seen by some as a 'rapists charter'. This view persisted in modified form, however, from the early part of the 20th century to beyond the apparently liberated 1960s. The following two quotations illustrate this:

> ... the accomplishment of the aim of biology has been entrusted to the aggressiveness of men and has been, to some extent, independent of women's consent.
>
> (Freud, 1933: 131–2)

> ... the main determinants of adult rates of heterosexual activity in our society is the level of male commitment.
>
> (Gagnon and Simon, 1973: 198)

It seems it is difficult for lay people and health professionals to take on board an image in which men may not actively pursue sex or that women actively do so. Texts on sexual problems and popular magazines demonstrate this clearly. Female 'promiscuity' is deemed a problem, as is low sexual desire in men. What is important in this context is that both men and women appear to adopt this view of gendered sexual behaviour as being normal. It has slipped into cultural myth with little dispute. Women traditionally, were not only assumed to be asexual socially, but also biologically and psychologically, in that they neither desired nor experienced pleasurable sensations through sexual behaviours. Sex and the pursuit of sex was for the man's pleasure and for reproduction. Many people, both scientists and non-scientists, have therefore argued that the acknowledgment of any sexuality on women's behalf was 'better' than in the asexual Victorian and pre-Victorian times, and it is widely assumed that since the 1960s women have been liberated and this double standard abolished. This is clearly not the case. Contemporary sexual etiquette and beliefs demonstrate unequivocally that little has changed since sexological science emerged at the turn of the 20th century.

Science and myth

The mid-20th century saw application of more rigorous methods of investigation, The Kinsey Institute's social surveys and the laboratory studies of Masters and Johnson being among the most ground-breaking.

The Kinsey research published in the early 1950s about the sexual attitudes of men and women (see Gebhard and Johnson, 1979) shocked the population of the USA, who were confronted with evidence that was contrary to their expectations. The realization emerging from the data that for both men and women, for instance, homosexuality and homosexual behaviour was widespread, and that everyone had the potential to engage in homosexual activities or have those desires, shocked the nation. The previous assumption had been that homosexuals were a discrete, psychologically disturbed and deviant group of the population. Some commentators still take that view, although nowadays the contemporary liberal climate of 'acceptance' is more visible.

Kinsey's work further indicated that women had sexual desire, masturbated and wanted to achieve orgasm during intercourse (although this frequently did not happen). Although there is now a prevalent comfort with these facts about female sexuality, they were controversial and counter-intuitive when published. They are, however, still treated as 'problem areas' in that, as indicated above, women may be socially condemned if they are seen as *too* sexual.

Masters and Johnson produced two important volumes, *Human Sexual Response* (1966) and *Human Sexual Inadequacy* (1970). These were based on a series of experiments in which they measured physiological and psychological responses to various sexual activities, including heterosexual and homosexual intercourse and masturbation. They identified a *response cycle* in both male and female subjects which had similarities (see Figure 10.1).

The Kinsey and the Masters and Johnson research disposed of

Phase 1 –Excitation; 2 – Plateau; 3 – Orgasm and 4 – Resolution

In men;
1 – was characterized by erection, 2 – by sexual flush and tension, 3 – by contraction of the involved organs and ejaculation, and 4 – in decreasing congestion

For women;
1 – was characterized by lubrication, blood congestion in labia and nipple erection, 2 – by sexual flush and tension, 3 – muscle contraction (uterus, vagina and labia and erectile sphincter, which may be repeated many times and 4 – again, characterized by decreasing congestion

Figure 10.1: The response cycle.

myths about female asexuality and homosexuality as an independent category. They also tackled the myth of the vaginal orgasm by showing that women had clitoral orgasms and were potentially multi-orgasmic. Also, female satisfaction in heterosexual intercourse is not influenced by their partner's penis size.

During the 1970s and 1980s there was a widespread belief that regular, satisfying sex was a basic human right and for that reason sexual therapies developed in Western industrial societies. However, although some of the detail has changed, and women are now perceived in some contexts and sub-cultural groups as actively sexual, this female image contravenes the persistent double-standard that exists. Studies of young people's sexual development (e.g. Holland *et al*, 1990) all draw attention to the double-standard which means that women still have to 'pretend' to leave the sexual overtures to their male counterparts or fear being labelled a 'slag'.

What, then, is normal sexual behaviour? What standards do health professionals and patients use to assess whether, and to what extent, they have a sexual problem? How is 'good and satisfying' sex to be identified? Health professionals and clients are immersed in these gendered images to some extent, and their problems are identified in that context.

The psychology of sexual problems

Health professionals are increasingly consulted by patients with sexual problems, partly because of public awareness of sexual issues and partly because of a widespread popular desire to make the most of any sexual experience. Common issues brought by clients are:

- Why do I no longer enjoy sexual intercourse with my partner?
- How can I make time for sex in my life?
- What are the consequences of confronting my partner with my lack of desire?
- Might I be gay?
- How do I prevent pregnancy/become pregnant?

Consultations with people who have sexual problems require the health professional to discuss intimate aspects of the patient's life in a straightforward way. It is important to understand that the language that patients use may be different from the professionals' own language: both professionally and privately. For example there are class, cultural and gender differences in words used to describe sexual behaviours and parts of the body. There are educational and class issues that surround the ability to recognize and seek help in certain areas, particularly with issues of sexual orientation. However, the fact that members of certain social groups might find it easier to explore the possibility of homosexuality, does not necessarily mean that they find it easier to accept it in themselves or their partners. Recognition by a hitherto self-identified heterosexual person that they may prefer a potential sexual partner of their own sex, is likely to be traumatic – not because it is not what they want for themselves, but because of the social stigma, which in some cases is internalised as self-disgust.

Presenting with anxiety about sexual problems

If someone comes for help with a sexual matter they may not find it easy to make themselves or their needs clear. Some people find it difficult to articulate their own needs even to themselves. They may find it difficult to express their fears and what they might want from the professional. It may be helpful for professionals to check out what a patient means when they use particular words and similarly to check that patients understand the words used by the health professional. Thus, paying careful attention and checking that interactions have been understood, is an important part of the process that is both a means of establishing a common meaning and ensuring that the professional and client have engaged sufficiently.

Sex is an embarrassing topic, especially for the person who has the problem, but sometimes for the health professional as well. Thus, not everyone presents their symptoms clearly and sometimes clients fail to acknowledge, even to themselves, the sexual element of their distress. Some people will find devious ways to draw attention to their sexual worries under another guise. For example, they may ask whether something is normal. One female GP reported to me that women come to see her for 'permission' to avoid sexual intercourse. She arrived at this conclusion after several years of working in a busy inner city practice. She realized that she was frequently asked whether it would be healthier to avoid intercourse at various times during the menstrual cycle, during pregnancy or during and after the menopause. Closer questioning on most occasions revealed that sex between that woman and her partner had been unsatisfactory for some time prior to the interview. The woman may have suffered pain on penetration, or be unfamiliar with what is effective contraception, worried about more pregnancy or is running out of excuses to refuse sex because it seems to be just one more demand upon her.

In such a case it is often difficult for the health professional to know where to start – is it a sexual or a relationship problem? If any physical symptoms can be removed from the equation then it is important to treat the relationship. This kind of presentation often accompanies secondary dysfunction (see below), and clients are too anxious to face the fact that their sexual behaviours or their relationships may be in difficulty and prefer the possibility of a hormonal 'excuse'.

There are also clear connections between the way people evaluate themselves sexually and the cultural stereotypes discussed above. Some men, for instance, believe they should be wanting to have sex almost all the time and with most potential partners, and they will see themselves as having a problem when this is not the case. This difficulty may be most acute after the breakdown of a long-term relationship while the man is still suffering a grief reaction. Instead of actively going out to find a new partner, or seeking sexual encounters following 'nights out on the town', a man may simply want to stay at home or have quiet evenings talking to his friends. Distress about this may lead him to be referred to a doctor, counsellor or therapist for excessive drinking or drug abuse, violence or depression instead of presenting himself directly with a sexual problem.

Some women exhibit anxiety about initiating sex and seek professional help, even within a long-term, stable relationship, for fear of being labelled 'promiscuous' or unfeminine, or because they themselves believe this desire and behaviour is *in fact* an indication that they are 'unnatural'. It is therefore important to establish the difference between a person's beliefs and the reality of their sexual functioning.

A student came to see me for career advice. She was halfway through her PhD and wanted to do voluntary work in a developing country as she felt she needed to put something back into the world. She came two or three times to discuss her application for this work and how she might leave her doctoral studies while she was abroad. However, she made it clear during these meetings that she was religious, believing that sex should take place only within marriage. Not only was she feeling that her boyfriend was pressuring her into having intercourse, but she was not experiencing any sense of physical desire. After several consultations she decided to finish her PhD and tell her boyfriend that she was not ready for sex. She further decided that she needed the opportunity to consider whether or not she was gay.

Clinical researchers in the area of sexual behaviour and problems have clarified two broad categories of problem that patients present: *sexual dysfunctions* and *sexually transmitted infections*. In the following sections I outline some of these.

Problems associated with sexual dysfunction

Sexual dysfunction refers to sexual activities which the client, their partner or a professional, considers to be outside the norm. Individuals who seek help with sexual dysfunction are usually unhappy about their sexuality and sexual behaviour, believing that their problem is influencing their life in a negative way.

It is difficult to determine the extent to which sexual dysfunction of any kind is present in the population as a whole. How do health professionals gain knowledge about the extent and types of sexual dysfunctions that exist in society? Sexual surveys provide some information, but they tend to be unreliable, partly because people do not always tell the truth about their sexual behaviours for a variety of reasons. (They might exaggerate their capacities and desires or they might do the opposite – depending on their beliefs about what is normal and healthy). Also, the majority of returned responses from general population surveys are from the younger age groups – thus there is relatively little information on middle aged and older people. This is at least in part because it is assumed that only young people are interested in sex. Also, the generation currently over 60 was not socialized into being able to talk freely about sex, which would inhibit their participation.

Clinical studies that provide data on people who have presented with sexual problems are useful in providing material on patterns of referral. However, they describe the behaviours only of those who are aware or enthusiastic enough to seek treatment. Thus, knowledge of the overall distribution and types of sexual behaviours in the general population is unreliable.

However, there are some data available on how many people refer themselves or are referred for specialist counselling and medical help, and that number is increasing. Sexual problems are more visible now in the 1990s as there is less taboo or stigma associated with asking for help. There is also an increased belief that clinical help is available and effective, and a greater acknowledgment that sexual problems can disrupt or be caused by other areas of life (for example, relationships and work) and that these problems may have roots in childhood emotional and/or physical problems.

Sexual dysfunctions have always been and continue to be defined narrowly in relation to (usually) heterosexual intercourse. Thus, for men the concerns tend to be associated with whether they can achieve and sustain erections and ejaculate. With women, concern is often with whether they can become sufficiently aroused to receive a penis into their vagina and whether they are able to achieve orgasm during intercourse.

Classifying sexual dysfunctions

Sexual dysfunctions are characterized as to whether they are primary, in that the individual has always had a particular difficulty, or secondary where the problem develops at some stage in the course of an otherwise problem-free sexual life (Hawton, 1991).

Contemporary classifications of sexual dysfunction are as follows:

Disorders of sexual arousal, which in women includes lack of desire and excitement, and in men erectile dysfunction and impotence (erectile failures).

In these cases it may be that clients want to have sex with their partner, indeed may feel sexually excited, but they are prevented by either the inability to achieve an erection or lack of lubrication. Worry about their partner's reactions, fears about their physiological functioning and memories of sexual failure all serve to exacerbate this kind of problem.

These difficulties, particularly if they are secondary dysfunctions, have a number of potential causes, although in the majority of cases they are brought about by problems at work or pressures in relationships. For example, fears of being made redundant, anger about being passed over for promotion or that a partner has been unfaithful are all common causes of sexual dysfunction for both men and women. However, as with all sexual dysfunctions, it is quick and simple to have a medical check to eliminate the possibility of any physiological reasons before the emotional or psychological difficulties are addressed.

Talking about lack of sexual desire is often very difficult when the people involved are in permanent and loving relationships. Not to want to have sex with someone is frequently perceived as a major betrayal and so it is not unusual to try to hide this problem. On the whole men find this more difficult to do, particularly if they have no way of either achieving or sustaining an erection.

The vital ingredient for the counselling relationship is to enable the client or patient to talk, freely and without the fear of judgment, with the health professional enabling them to explore the extent of the difficulties and the best means of changing the current situation.

Disorders of orgasm, which include premature and retarded ejaculation in men; and for women, the inability to achieve orgasm, particularly during sexual intercourse. More men report premature orgasm and more women report problems with achieving a climax.

The increase in reported incidents of impotence or erection failure has been attributed to the increased sexual awareness, activity and demands of heterosexual women, and the problem may be alleviated only by enabling the man to increase confidence in his own sexual abilities. When women were more generally considered asexual, those women who found themselves not gaining pleasure (in any sense) from intercourse saw it as their own problem, rather than a problem for the couple, which is the preferred view nowadays.

Some people do have difficulties achieving orgasm at a primary level which may be the result of childhood trauma, possibly sexual abuse or rape. However sometimes this may simply be because an individual as a young child had seen a couple having sexual intercourse and been disturbed by it. Very often a series of counselling or therapeutic interviews enables the client to come to some degree of resolution and begin the healing process.

Disorders of sexual satisfaction, which includes both non-sexual and sexual aspects of relationships. There may be a problem in terms of satisfaction even if a person has regular orgasms.

Since the 1960s 'sexual liberation', and the ideas and research that accompanied these political changes, it has also become incumbent upon women as well as men to 'enjoy' sex, particularly sexual intercourse. There are many reasons that people do not enjoy sex, which include the presence of pain or discomfort (painful erections for example), a poor physical self-image, and anxieties about the relationship. Some people, despite overt signs of pleasure and physical involvement, maintain deeply held guilts about their sexuality which prevent that sense of pleasure.

How might the health professional work with clients in such cases? This assessment can be achieved only through enabling the client to talk and express themselves about the issues that concern them. The ability to listen, ask non-directive questions and be empathic (see chapters 3 and 4) are basic but powerful skills for enabling this process.

Physical sources of sexual problems

There are sometimes physical sources of sexual problems that can be easily assessed. Prolonged use of illegal drugs (such as heroine and cocaine) and alcohol diminish sexual appetite as well as ability. The side effects of some prescribed drugs can influence sexual physiology, but these influences are easily diagnosed and possible to treat, provided the client is willing. Drugs and alcohol can also bring about very short-term sexual difficulties which normally disappear once the substance has passed through the person's system (Hawton, 1991).

Problems associated with infection

Infection caused directly as a result of sexual activity varies in the extent to which it has serious long-term health implications. Such infections range from mild disorders dealt with by a course of antibiotics, to those that are life threatening such as HIV/AIDS. Health professionals will have to face patients with all of these conditions, either as a direct part of their work, or when the client comes to see them for other reasons, but who has such a disease. The most problematic of course is HIV/AIDS, where professionals as well as clients still experience fear and misunderstanding about its transmission and treatment. HIV/AIDS remains a threat despite the fact that knowledge has increased dramatically over the past 10 years and that cases may have receded (but the prolonged incubation makes this difficult to know).

In 1991 in England 1,259 new cases of AIDS were reported. Since 1982 the cumulative total reported had been 5,059 of whom 3,113 had died. In 1991, 2,120 reports of HIV antibody positive occurred in England. Between 1984 and 1991 14,537 cases were reported in all. Between 1990 and 1991 there was a 1 per cent increase in other sexually transmitted diseases, which ran counter to the previous downward trend since the 1980s.

The presence of such an infection as HIV/AIDS has implications for emotional reactions and sexual behaviour. It is therefore important to discover the person's version of how they were infected, and also to gain from them a sense of their sexual patterns of behaviour at the moment, in order to make appropriate decisions.

Breaking bad news

The following should be considered when breaking bad news:
- that the person will be shocked and may be angry
- they will experience a sense of loss
- they will feel grief and a sense of bereavement.

It is crucial that they are referred to a specialist service or counsellor who can enable them to cope with these feelings, because anxiety and stress reduce chances of recovery or health maintenance. It is also important for the health professional to enable the patient to change their behaviour, to protect both the patient and others with whom they might have contact. It cannot be assumed that the patient will make rational decisions. Thus the counselling strategies required are:

• to help the sufferers come to terms with the condition. This involves helping the client to talk about their feelings, their beliefs about how they contracted the virus, their anger and possible need to attribute blame as well as express their fears of what is going to happen to them. They may have fears of dying alone, painfully and in fear. On a practical level it is helpful to explore the resources for helping people with AIDS die in a more peaceful context.

• to protect the health of those with HIV and prevent them from spreading the infection. This involves dealing with the feelings and fears that cause anxiety in the patient. The anxiety in itself is likely to reduce their physical capacity to withstand illnesses to which they are vulnerable. They may be encouraged to have counselling perhaps with a combination of yoga, art therapy or some form of relaxation technique that they can practise when they feel panic or anxiety emerging.

• to deal with rational fears and misinformation. This may be done through providing written information alone in some cases. However, it is more likely that a combination of literature, support groups and practical advice is the most effective intervention.

• to support carers. This is vital, and sometimes very difficult because of the fear engendered by the virus and its consequences, often because of ignorance. Information is important but carers themselves also need to be helped to come to terms with the emotional difficulties of the person who has the virus and the social stigma and the issues which that raises.

• to support other professionals. Other professionals are likely to suffer from the same kinds of ignorance and prejudice as the general population. Those who specialize with these kinds of patients therefore have much to offer by way of information, advice and support. It is very important to recognize that not all colleagues have a tolerant and informed view of AIDS patients.

Key aspects of these skills are discussed in other chapters of this book.

References

Ellis, H. (1905) *Studies in the Psychology of Sex*. Vol 1, New York: Random House.

Freud, S. (1933) *New Introductory Lectures in Psychoanalysis*, trans. J. Strachey. New York: Norton (1965).

Gagnon, J.M. and Simon, W. (1973) *Human Sexual Conduct: The Sources of Sexuality*. Chicago: Aldine, excerpted in M. Brake (Ed.) (1982) *Human Sexual Relations: A Reader*, Harmondsworth: Pelican.

Gebhard, P.M. and Johnson, A.B. (1979) *The Kinsey Data: Marginal Tabulation of the 1938–1963 interviews Conducted by the Institute for Sex Research*. Philadelphia: Saunders.

This provides a detailed breakdown of the questions, findings and statistics which informed the Kinsey Institute's reports on sexual behaviour of men and women in the late 1940s and early 1950s.

Hawton, K. (1991) *Sex Therapy: A Practical Guide*. Oxford: Oxford University Press

A good basic overview of sexual dysfunction and available treatments.

Holland, J., Ramazanoglu,C. Scott, S., Sharpe, S. and Thompson, R. (1990) Don't die of ignorance – I nearly died of embarrassment, *WRAP Paper 2*. London: The Tufnell Press.

This paper outlines some aspects of recent research into the sexual experiences of young people, demonstrating that double standards of behaviour for young women and men still exist and that these resonate with early 20th century beliefs which disadvantage young women in particular.

Masters,W.H. and Johnson,V.E. (1966) *Human Sexual Response*. London: Churchill. A source text based on the original and innovative work of these researchers. Interesting and informative.

Masters, W.H. and Johnson, V.E. (1970) *Human Sexual Inadequacy*. London: Churchill.

Chapter 11

Working with infertility

Christa Drennan and Sallie Rumbold

Infertility can devastate lives. It is often a hidden problem, and affects couples and individuals in many different ways. It can cause an emotional pain that is hard to quantify or explain. It is a commonly held view that one in seven couples have problems conceiving. Templeton (1992) suggests that 14 per cent of couples in Western society will be troubled by infertility and that 3–4 per cent of couples will eventually remain childless involuntarily. Health professionals are therefore likely to come into contact quite frequently with clients for whom infertility is a problem.

We work together as part of a multidisciplinary team within an NHS assisted conception unit (ACU). One of us is a counsellor and the other a nurse/co-ordinator. In this chapter we first describe the emotional process through which clients who are affected by infertility may pass, regardless of whether treatment is pursued or not. We then look at fertility treatment in the UK and its psychological impact upon the client. The final section discusses the specialized role of the fertility counsellor in a dedicated ACU. We use the term 'client' throughout the chapter to mean any person or persons troubled about their fertility.

The emotional impact of infertility

Most people assume that they will have a choice about whether or not to have children. Therefore the loss or potential loss of one's ability to conceive requires a reappraisal of the future, and time to grieve over what may never be. The process can be complicated and long and broadly resembles other bereavement processes. However, there are important differences. For example, Diane and Peter Houghton(1987) suggest 'three negations' as consequences of childlessness. The first is 'thwarted love' – being unable to fulfil the desire to give parental love. The second is 'peripherality' – the feeling of being peripheral to the family-based society that so many people with children take for granted. The third negation experienced by the childless is called 'genetic death' – the painful loss of the ability to reproduce biologically.

Moreover, each menstrual period or course of fertility treatment can induce its own grief process, with the raising of hopes and the potential for great disappointment and despair. It is a complicated grief in that there is no body to mourn, and no recognized ritual for saying goodbye. The loss is often not acknowledged by others and it becomes difficult to seek and accept support.

A process model for working with infertility

There are several models for the emotional impact of infertility, e.g. Jennings (1995), Read (1995), Lee (1996). The model described below is broadly based on the grieving process proposed by Kübler-Ross (1973). We use it to provide a structure within which we describe the feelings most commonly experienced by clients with infertility issues.

Shock
Disbelief/Denial
Bargaining
Isolation
Anger and Guilt
Depression and Anxiety
Acceptance

Figure 11.1: A process model for infertility.

As with other types of bereavement, this process is not linear. Each client has a unique response, moving in and out of different stages of the process at different times in their lives. We find it useful to keep this model in mind when working with these clients. It helps us to keep a sense of perspective when dealing with such a wide range of emotions. Clients often feel as if they are going nowhere, just marking time, and we use the model to provide a sense of process. An awareness of the bereavement process, and linking it to infertility can help clients to understand and manage their feelings. In our experience loss of a sense of control is a major factor for almost all individuals experiencing problems conceiving, and this is intensified if treatment is sought and people become 'patients'. For some clients the trauma comes as much from being denied the decision of whether or not to have children as from living with childlessness. Hope seems to run like a thread throughout, keeping clients 'on hold' and stopping them from coming to terms with life without children.

Shock

Being told by a health professional that you have a fertility problem can come as a great shock, even though the client may have been aware for some time that there may be something wrong. It is difficult to respond well to a client's distress in a busy clinic where privacy is hard to come by and time is limited. This can be compounded by the fact that the client and the health professional may be new to each other.

Clients respond to bad news in a variety of ways. Some are visibly distressed and cry and plead for help. Others react angrily and focus their anger on the health professional. Others seem cold and detached. Almost all feel a need to understand why this has happened to them. Many feel guilty and ashamed as though a dark secret has been uncovered or as if they are being punished for past misdeeds.

The client's reaction can leave the health professional feeling useless, frustrated and upset, and the temptation can be to offer treatment or investigations that are not really appropriate. The shock and distress can mean that information is either not heard or is misunderstood and may well need clarifying later. Sometimes clients need time and space to appreciate fully the information they have been given before they can consider their options.

Denial/disbelief

Infertility is a difficult loss to accept because the loss is not tangible. Because there are often no definites and no certainties it is difficult to deal with and denial is commonplace. Indeed, clients often put off seeking advice or medical help for a long time for fear of discovering that they have a fertility problem. For many, approaching a doctor for help and advice also means saying, 'I want a child', and therefore means believing it too. There may be a fear that to long for a child will mean risking great hurt and disappointment if it never happens.

While there is hope of having a child, clients cannot fully come to terms with the possibility of being childless. There is also no treatment without hope, and however hard clients try to prepare themselves, disappointment is inevitable if treatment is unsuccessful. Clients tend

University of Nottingham
School of Nursing & Midwifery
Derbyshire Royal Infirmary
London Road
DERBY DE1 2QY

to focus on the present and on their current stage of treatment, avoiding anticipating the future and what it may hold.

Bargaining

Bargaining behaviour is often difficult for health professionals to cope with. Some clients may plead and beg as if somehow the health professional can perform a miracle. Some want assurances that if they change an aspect of their lifestyle, such as reducing stress or stopping smoking, then the reward will be a pregnancy. This reassurance is impossible to give and can leave the health professional feeling helpless.

Some clients strike bargains with themselves. They promise themselves peace of mind in return for having at least tried every avenue open to them to become pregnant. They tell themselves that the only way that they can live with their infertility in the future is with the knowledge that they have tried everything. And some clients employ rituals, which Naish (1994) calls 'magical thinking'. For example, they take a particular route to the clinic, or wear the same clothes to each visit, in the hope that the pay-off will be a baby.

Isolation

Infertility, like grief, is a difficult issue to discuss. Feelings of shame and guilt can add to a sense of isolation. For some clients, confiding in their family creates more stress than it alleviates. Infertility may mean that other members of the family have potential losses to deal with too, such as never having grandchildren. Some clients find therefore, that they are giving support rather than receiving it. Two other factors can also increase isolation. First, our society is pronatalist in that it encourages the view that having children is a natural and fulfilling progression in adulthood. Childless couples are therefore seen as unnatural (Monach, 1993). Second, many clients have difficulty being around people who are pregnant or who have children, and their feelings of envy limit even further their ability to receive support (Cranshaw, 1995).

Some couples are pulled together and their relationships are strengthened and deepened by the process, but some find that they are pulled further apart. Sex can become a means to an end rather than a meaningful and pleasurable experience. In cases where there are underlying problems that are not being addressed, for whatever reason, these problems can be brought to a head, sometimes leading to the breakdown of the relationship.

Men and women tend to be affected emotionally in different ways by infertility. For many women, becoming a mother is part of their identity, and being pregnant and being able to give birth and to nurture is a significant issue. For men, being able to reproduce is often linked to feelings about their virility and masculinity. Men and women seem to cope differently with infertility. For example, women appear to face the issues more readily and will seek help alone (Lee, 1996). Men may take longer to come to terms with the issues, particularly if the problem is one of male infertility. In these cases women will often have to deal with their own distress as well as comforting and encouraging their male partners. This can cause difficulties in relationships in that both parties may have different agendas or may be moving along the grieving process at different stages at any one time.

Anger

Clients with infertility problems are often angry. This can be due partly to frustration at the slow and lengthy investigations they may be undergoing. Clients often complain of being ignored or 'lost in the system'; of conflicting information and having 'wasted time'. They may be mistrustful of health professionals due to previous bad experiences.

Anger may also be caused by feelings of guilt or blame. Previous terminations of pregnancy or pelvic infections, or not seeking help earlier for example, can result in clients feeling guilty and responsible for their infertility. This guilt can result in anger that can be projected on to others such as the doctors, nurses and counsellors with whom they are in contact. Clients can also be angry at the unfairness and injustice of their situation and anger at others who seem to be able to have children easily and whom the client feels do not 'deserve' to be parents.

Guilt

Anger and guilt are two different ways of dealing with pain. The angry may blame others and the guilty may blame themselves. Feelings such as envy, jealousy and anger can be uncomfortable for the client. They may feel guilty about these feelings and as a result not wish to express them. It can be helpful to acknowledge that such feelings are understandable and very common. Many clients feel guilt about past experiences such as termination of pregnancy and feel as if they are somehow being punished. There is often a need to 'overwrite' their experience of themselves as unsuccessful in producing a baby, needing a positive experience to make up for what they have done, or failed to do.

Depression and anxiety

For many clients, depression is never very far away, but is kept in the background while there is hope, however small. The next cycle of treatment, or another test, or another appointment can give the client something to focus on. When there is no focus many clients are overwhelmed by despair and depression. Anxiety often accompanies depression, with symptoms such as sleeping and eating disturbance, low libido and low self-esteem. Panic attacks are a common reaction. Such feelings, and the debilitating pain that accompanies them, can push people back on to the treatment path again in an effort to keep them at bay, repeating an exhausting cycle of hope and despair.

Acceptance

For many clients, accepting that there is a fertility problem is difficult enough, but the reality that they may never have children is much harder to accept. People are rarely told categorically that they will never have children. Technological advances can mean the reawakening of hope long after a client accepts their childlessness. The decision to end treatment does not always mean that the client has abandoned hope. For many, each menstrual cycle carries some hope, however small, but each menstrual period can further chip away at a woman's self worth (Pfeffer and Woollett, 1983), making acceptance and resolution hard to come by.

For those who accept that they cannot have children, the freedoms of childlessness are valued, although they may not compensate for not having children. Reinvestment is possible, in relationships with family, partners, friends, and other people's children, in work and in careers, and in the creation of a meaningful and fulfilling life (Bryan and Higgins, 1995; Powell and Stagoll, 1992).

Fertility treatment in the UK and its impact on the client

Fertility investigations, support, advice and medical or surgical intervention are available in the UK for people who are having problems conceiving. In many cases subfertility, and sometimes infertility, can be resolved by surgery or by drug treatment. Other kinds of infertility are essentially incurable, and in such cases treatments circumvent the infertility rather than cure it, allowing people who are technically infertile to have children. The best known method of achieving this is via *in vitro* fertilization (IVF) – the 'test tube' method. There are new developments occurring all the time, and patients in the UK are now routinely offered procedures that were not available five years ago. Success rates are relatively low. For example only 14.5 per cent of couples will achieve a live baby following IVF treatment (HFEA, 1996).

The Human Fertilisation Act 1990 followed the Warnock Committee Report of 1984, which looked at the legal, social and ethical implications of the new reproductive technologies. The Human Fertilisation and Embryology Authority (HFEA) was set up as an independent body, funded partly by licensed treatment centres and partly by the tax payer. As well as licensing and regulating treatment and research centres the HFEA also publishes a code of practice giving guidance to centres on how they should carry out licensed activities. A centre must be licensed by the HFEA to carry out any fertilization treatment that involves the use of donated eggs or sperm, the creation of embryos outside the body, the storage of eggs, sperm or embryos, or any research on human embryos. Currently in the UK, licensed centres are inspected annually by the HFEA.

In the UK, there is at present (1997) no national policy for providing and funding fertility treatment and no national criteria regarding suitability for treatment. Each health authority makes its own decision regarding funding. Some health authorities do not fund any fertility treatment and others have strict criteria for funding, such as age limits and types of infertility. Waiting lists for funded treatment can be long. Many clients are therefore faced with a choice of either self-funding or forgoing treatment altogether.

Investigations, treatments and monitoring procedures are personal and physically intrusive. Clients often feel that their privacy has been invaded, and may find routine visits to the clinic upsetting. The client tends to take on the traditional role of patient, with all the powerlessness that tends to accompany it. Even when the fertility problem is the male partner's, treatment is focused on the female. During treatment the male is marginalized, and has only a supporting role, which some men find difficult. In cases where donor sperm is used the male partner may feel completely redundant.

Fertility treatment is a controversial subject and is often reported in the media. New treatments create new moral dilemmas, and many people express concern about the techniques used, and interference with the natural 'miracle' of creating life. Clients have not only to deal with their own feelings and thoughts about these controversial issues, but also the opinions of those around them, and those expressed by the media.

Advances in reproductive technology have raised our expectations for a successful outcome, yet more often than not these expectations are not met in reality. The client, the counsellor, and the whole multi-disciplinary team sit uncomfortably somewhere between being realistic and having hope.

Working with a high failure rate, even though it is the norm in this field, affects all members of staff, and sometimes the client is allowed to carry the hopes and needs of the staff, and can be left feeling that they have let everybody down if the treatment does not work. Some clients feel like failures themselves when they do not conceive after fertility treatment. It can seem as if the process has an inbuilt bias towards failure, that fertility treatment creates an emotional environment detrimental to conception. Some people find the whole process so stressful, and so intrusive, that they often wonder how they will ever conceive while under such strain.

The role of the fertility counsellor

The HFEA stipulates that people seeking licensed fertility treatment *must* be given a suitable opportunity to receive counselling about the implications of taking the proposed steps before they give their consent (HFEA, 1995). No one is under an obligation to accept counselling, although the HFEA believes it should be encouraged and presented as a positive part of the treatment process. In response to this clause, and to the needs of this particular client group, many fertility units now employ the services of a specialized counsellor.

The British Infertility Counselling Association (BICA) has published a leaflet providing guidelines for practice and training recommendations for fertility counsellors. They suggest that training should include the skills of working with grief and bereavement, working with couples as well as with individuals, and an appreciation of the dynamics of psychosexual dysfunction. BICA also recommend that the counsellor should have knowledge of the medical and scientific procedures used in reproductive medicine, and the ability to work, if necessary, within a multi-disciplinary team. We add to this list the knowledge and skills required to work effectively with clients from different cultures (see Chapter 6).

The role of the fertility counsellor is delicately balanced between being an active part of a multi-disciplinary team and being a separate and independent service. The counsellor/client relationship should not be confused with other role relationships, and it is not an information or advice-giving service (see Chapter 1). Yet a practical knowledge of fertility treatment helps the counsellor understand what the client is either considering, experiencing, or has gone through. Clients tend to assume that the counsellor has some knowledge of the treatment options and what they entail, and often wish to discuss their thoughts and feelings about the treatment. Concerns over waiting lists, the cost of treatment, or the effects of the drugs, for example, are all issues discussed regularly in counselling. Some knowledge of the treatment process also assists the counsellor when facilitating the decision-making that arises at each stage of treatment. The fertility counsellor explores with the client the impact of the treatment, both physically and mentally, and helps them identify how best to support themselves. Fertility counsellors are able to draw from the experiences of previous clients, which may help others to prepare for the treatment and its impact. Counselling can help clients to feel more in control.

Fertility counsellors work with couples as well as with individuals. Discovering that they have fertility problems, and that the choice of whether or not to have children may not be theirs, has a fundamental impact both on individuals and on their relationships. People often employ very different coping mechanisms. This can mean that although both partners are going through the same process, they deal with their pain and their stress differently, and the relationship between them can become strained.

Counselling can facilitate communication between partners by focusing on the relationship as well as on the individuals. Some couples use counselling to voice doubt and ambivalence; others declare support and commitment, or ask for commitment to be confirmed, or for their differences to be accepted. Clients may find it beneficial and perhaps easier to communicate such things in the presence of a counsellor than alone with a partner.

The HFEA suggests that the length and content of counselling, and the pace at which it is conducted, should be determined by the needs of the individual concerned (HFEA, 1995). The need for flexibility is great. Clients can undergo fertility investigations and treatment for a number of years, with varying needs at different stages of the process. Some clients have one-off sessions, some negotiate long- or short-term contracts, and others see the counsellor when a problem arises, or a decision needs to be made. For some, discovering that they have problems in conceiving uncovers other problems that need addressing, and which they bring to counselling. Counselling contracts often do not 'end' in the usual way, leaving the door open for returning at some time in the future. Sometimes during counselling it becomes clear that a better understanding about a particular part of the process may alleviate some of the stress or help the decision-making process, and in our workplace the counsellor may suggest or even facilitate a meeting with the appropriate member of the team, enabling the client to make informed decisions about his or her own treatment.

There are some aspects of the HFEA code of practice that fertility centres interpret individually. Staff, including counsellors, are obliged to consider the ' welfare of the unborn child' (HFEA, 1995) as well as that of the infertile couple. In practice this means that some sort of assessment of suitability may take place. Different centres do this in different ways. For example, some treat only married couples, some only heterosexual clients, others may routinely request information regarding suitability from the clients' GP. Some may voice concerns over individual clients, and find them unsuitable for treatment under this clause. The fact that some sort of selection process goes on affects the client/counsellor relationship. A counselling session needs to be a safe place to express thoughts and feelings without the client thinking that this may somehow affect their fertility treatment. As part of establishing a safe and trusting relationship, the fertility counsellor clearly separates counselling from any kind of assessment, and defines the boundaries of confidentiality by being explicit about any way in which the 'welfare of the unborn child' clause may affect the client/counsellor relationship.

Sometimes a treatment centre asks the counsellor to be part of an assessment process. People who wish to donate eggs, sperm or embryos, or who wish to become surrogates, are generally screened for suitability. If the counsellor is participating in this process, the fact that an assessment is taking place is made explicit by the counsellor. The client's motives, expectations, and understanding of the physical and emotional impact on themselves and their family, are all issues that may be discussed and evaluated.

Infertility is experienced within all cultures, and the clients' cultural context is an important factor for counsellors to be aware of. Whatever their value systems, clients with different cultural beliefs and practices need the counsellor's respect and not to have the counsellor's own values imposed upon them. Different cultures and religions create different pressures. Many religions place great emphasis on fertility and on producing children, and in some societies infertility means failure and loss of status, and can lead quite directly to divorce. Some clients, who have grown up and been educated in the UK, and have adopted Western values, may be coping with pressure from their extended family with more traditional views. Issues such as infertility, fertility treatment, openness, using donor sperm or eggs, single parenting, same sex couples and monogamy are all influenced by culture and religion, and clients will make their decisions within this context.

Although fertility counselling is supported and encouraged, and we try to present it as a positive thing for clients to do, anecdotal evidence suggests that only about 10 per cent of those seeking fertility treatment have counselling. We think there are contributing factors particular to this client group that keep this figure low. Fertility treatment is time consuming, with frequent and regular clinic appointments, and adding counselling to these visits increases time away from work. Perhaps some clients fear that they may be judged as not coping if they request counselling, and that this may affect their treatment. Perhaps there is a fear of the power of 'negative thought' – that if too much emphasis is placed on the negative, this somehow influences the outcome of treatment. Some clients are in a state of denial, and do not want to be reminded of the reality of their chances of achieving a pregnancy, and of facing the prospect of a future without a baby. The majority of assisted conception units (ACUs) are private, and counselling may not be included in the cost of treatment.

Many clients have said, in retrospect, that they wished that they had had more counselling in the early stages, either before they began treatment, or after initial investigations (Pengelly, 1995). Offers of fertility treatment can set up unrealistic expectations of success, and often without allowing the client much time to come to terms with the diagnosis and its implications.

Feelings of ambivalence when treatment does result in a pregnancy, particularly if it is a multiple pregnancy, are not uncommon, and clients experiencing these can also benefit from the support of the counsellor. If the fertility counsellor sees clients only in the ACU, they may not always meet the needs of these clients. Those who wish to talk to someone before they seek treatment, and those who find it hard to return to an ACU when they are no longer undergoing treatment, or are ambivalent about pregnancy, may find it easier to talk to a counsellor outside the ACU.

The HFEA and fertility counselling

The HFEA identifies three different 'types' of counselling to be offered by the fertility counsellor: implications, support, and therapeutic. Their code of practice states that each fertility centre *must* make implications counselling available, and *should* provide support and therapeutic counselling.

Implications counselling

Implications counselling is defined as aiming to 'enable the person concerned to understand the implications of the proposed course of action for themselves, for their family, and for any children born as a result' (HFEA, 1995 : 31). It combines the general issues relevant to infertility with the exploration of potential social and emotional issues. This is particularly important when a couple is considering treatment using donated eggs, sperm, or embryos, and many treatment centres strongly advise couples to have counselling before deciding on this course of action. Proceeding with this treatment when either partner has not fully come to terms with not only their own or their partner's infertility, but with being the parent of a child they are probably not genetically related to, may have a detrimental effect both on the couple and the child. A difficulty for both client and counsellor is trying to anticipate how one might feel – somehow to predict the future and ask themselves, 'how will I feel if . . . ?', 'how will I feel when . . . ?', 'what if . . . ?, It is important to consider these questions before they arise because of the life-long implications for all concerned.

Whether or not to tell the child about its genetic origin is one of the main issues raised during implications counselling. This issue needs to be focused upon before any course of action is taken, because if the potential parents are considering keeping its origin a secret from the child, then as few people as possible should know and carry the secret. The responsibility of carrying a life-long secret, and the potential damage if the child finds out by accident, need to be considered to protect the child. If the inclination is to tell the child of its origins, many people want to explore when and how this should be done.

There are additional issues if the client wishes to use a known donor as opposed to an anonymous one. In these situations the donors themselves are also encouraged to have implications counselling. Fertility counsellors tend to have certain key questions that they ask clients to consider during implications counselling. When we are counselling we make explicit such an agenda. Implications counselling can feel like some sort of assessment procedure because of the agenda, and clients may feel that there is a right or wrong answer to the questions raised. This is an important issue, as the counsellor may have very strong feelings which need to be put aside, particularly about whether the child has a right to know of its origins.

Support counselling

At various stages throughout the whole process, from diagnosis to resolution, the client may benefit from support. This can be provided by friends, family, or partner, but the process is long and many people lose their support as time goes on and people get on with their own lives. Clients often feel as though their lives are 'on hold' while they are undergoing treatment, and it may be only the counsellor who can stay with them as they go through yet another cycle of treatment. Some clients choose not to keep telling people when they are 'having another try', to avoid having to share their pain if it doesn't work, thereby isolating themselves even further. If treatment fails or is withdrawn or denied, or if a pregnancy is found to be ectopic, or ends in miscarriage, or if investigations uncover previously unknown problems, support counselling can help clients to come to terms with their situation. Support groups, both national and local, can also help to reduce isolation and provide a much needed peer group.

Therapeutic counselling

Infertility may have the effect of unmasking other, older, pain. Any number of issues can be brought to the fore by the experience of infertility. In answer to the 'Why me?' question that plagues so many,

past sexual behaviour, old losses, and frequently previous terminations of pregnancy and miscarriages are linked by the client to their
infertility. Depression, anxiety, low self-esteem, cultural issues, relationships, sexuality and many other issues may be brought to the
counselling session (Naish, 1994), and the counsellor may decide to
refer the client to other services outside the centre.

Appendix 1: Useful organizations

British Infertility Counselling Association (BICA)
   69 Division St., Sheffield S1 4GE
   Information Officer: 0171-354-3930
   The major professional association in the UK for fertility counsellors.

CHILD
   43 St Leonards Road, Bexhill-on-Sea, East Sussex, TN40 1JA
   Ph: 01424-732361
   A self-help organization for those experiencing fertility difficulties.

DI Network
   PO Box 265, Sheffield S3 7YX
   Contact Line: 0181-245-4369
   A network of people who have used or are considering using donor
   gametes.

Human Fertilisation and Embryology Authority (HFEA)
   Paxton House, 30 Artillery Lane, London E1 7LS
   Ph: 0171-377-5077
   The UK statutory body responsible for licensing and regulating
   certain forms of infertility treatment and research

ISSUE
   114 Lichfield Street, Walsall, WS1 1SZ
   Ph: 01922-722-888
   The largest self-help group for people with fertility difficulties.

References

Bryan, E. and Higgins, R. (1995) *Infertility: New Choices, New Dilemmas*.
   London: Penguin.
Cranshaw, M. (1995) Offering woman-centred counselling in reproductive
   medicine. In S. Jennings (Ed.) *Infertility Counselling*. London: Blackwell.
   Some useful chapters for fertility counsellors, and counsellors in general.

Houghton, D. and Houghton, P. (1987) *Coping With Childlessness*. London: Unwin Hyman.

Slightly outdated in terms of fertility treatment, but none the less a comprehensive discussion of the whole process, by a couple who have been through it themselves.

Human Fertilisation and Embryology Authority (1995) *Code of Practice*. Paxton House, 30 Artillery Lane, London E1 7LS.

Essential reading for those working with clients undergoing licensed fertility treatment.

Human Fertilisation and Embryology Authority (1996) *The Patients Guide To DI and IVF Clinics*. Paxton House, 30 Artillery Lane, London E1 7LS.

Contains annually updated statistics and success rates for all licensed ACUs in the UK.

Jennings, S. (1995) Birthmasks: ritualization and metaphor in fertility counselling. In S. Jennings (Ed.) *Infertility Counselling*. London: Blackwell.

Kübler-Ross, E. (1973) *On Death and Dying*. London: Routledge.

Lee, S. (1996) *Counselling In Male Infertility*. London: Blackwell.

A useful and interesting book about male infertility, with the focus more on infertility in men than on counselling.

Monach, J.H. (1993) *Childless: No Choice. The Experience of Involuntary Childlessness*. London: Routledge.

Naish, S. (1994) *Counselling People with Infertility Problems*. Rugby: British Association for Counselling.

Slim, concise, easy-to-read volume aimed at counsellors generally, but also useful for all health professionals interested in this field.

Pengelly, P. (1995) Working with partners: counselling the couple and collaborating in the team. In S. Jennings (Ed.) *Infertility Counselling*. London: Blackwell.

Pfeffer, N. and Woollett, A. (1983) *The Experience of Infertility*. London: Virago.

Powell, S. and Stagoll, H. (1992) *When You Can't Have a Child*. Sydney: Allen and Unwin.

A series of interviews with people who are involuntarily childless, focusing on their emotions and coping strategies.

Read, J. (1995) *Counselling for Fertility Problems*. London: Sage.

Templeton, A. (1992) The epidemiology of infertility. In A.A.Templeton and J.O. Drife (Eds) *Infertility*. London: Springer-Verlag.

Chapter 12

Solution-focused brief therapy: from hierarchy to collaboration

Harvey Ratner

Solution-focused brief therapy is a recently developed approach, first receiving attention in the USA in the mid-1980s. The pioneers of the approach are Steve de Shazer (1988, 1994) and Insoo Kim Berg (1991), who are directors of the Brief Family Therapy Center in Milwaukee, and Bill O'Hanlon *et al.* (1988, 1996). A number of other writers have helped to establish the approach as a significant contribution to the field of counselling by demonstrating its applicability to the widest possible range of client problems, such as work with survivors of sexual abuse (Dolan, 1991), clients with eating disorders (McFarland, 1995) and alcohol problems (Berg and Miller, 1992). In the UK the Brief Therapy Practice, which consists of therapists with backgrounds in the health service and social services, was established in 1989 in London to provide training in the approach and to offer a counselling service, and has published articles and books (e.g. George, Iveson and Ratner (1990), and Lethem (1994)).

'Patients are willing to share responsibilities for their health. They are educated and interested in co-operation. The physician–patient relationship is beginning to shift from a strict hierarchical relationship to a collaborative one' (Honsig, 1989: 445). This is an era of partnership with patients and clients, where the patient's own views are sought so as to maximize the effects of treatment in this increasingly cost-conscious age. Solution-focused brief therapy offers the counsellor or therapist a range of useful techniques and questions, but most importantly it enables clients to generate their own solutions, by focusing on the ways that patients have found to deal with the problem, what works for them, and their ideas about the future without the problem. Thomas Honsig's article begins with a hospital consultation between two nurses and a doctor around the bed of a patient suffering from acute pancreatitis caused by his drinking, and is an example of how solution-focused thinking can be adapted to the complex situations to be found in health care settings, where the convenience of quiet interview rooms and hour-long sessions are a far-off luxury.

> Patients' goals are appreciated and clarified. Physicians reduce their efforts to convince patients of the 'one and only right way', and patients will start changing on their own. Physicians can leave most of the work to them. It is necessary for physicians (and medicine as a science) to learn there are several ways 'to get to Rome' and that there is more than one Rome. Barriers between physicians and patients, as well as between patients and their goals, decrease.
>
> (Honsig, 1989: 447)

Background and theory of the approach

The pioneers of solution-focused brief therapy have acknowledged an indebtedness to Milton Erickson and to the systemic field of family therapy. Observers will see that there are similarities to other approaches, including cognitive-behavioural and reality therapy, but they will readily recognize that there is a very marked difference from psychodynamic approaches.

From the hypnotherapist Erickson was taken the concept of 'utilization', i.e. harnessing the client's own strengths and unique ways of doing things, and of utilizing a fantasy about a future in which the client's problem is solved (de Shazer, 1988). From John Weakland and the Brief Therapy Center at the Mental Research Institute in Palo Alto (Watzlawick, Weakland and Fisch, 1974) was taken an approach that saw problems arising not from underlying pathology but from a client's restricted sense of how to deal with life's difficulties – particularly the common but often misguided view that 'one must try, try and try again'.

Perhaps the single most distinctive idea that the Milwaukee team brought to the tradition was the concept of the 'exception' to the rule of the problem. To Erickson's idea of utilizing whatever clients bring they added that, despite what many clients will say initially, namely that the problem is 'always' happening, it is possible to demonstrate that there are nearly always exceptions, i.e. times when the problem is happening less or not at all. These times contain within them the seeds of the solution: if the client can be enabled to discover for themselves what they did to bring about these exceptions, then they are on the way to undermining the apparent domination of the problem in their lives. They discovered, for example, that in two-thirds of cases clients report positive changes in the time between making the first appointment and attending the session (Weiner-Davis, de Shazer and Gingerich, 1987). Thus, if the counsellor remembers to ask about pre-treatment change in the first session, clients will start to become aware of how they themselves can solve their own problems, and the change process can be seen to have started even before the client came into therapy. The counsellor doesn't need to tell clients what to do; the client has only to 'see' that they have got what it takes to solve their own problems.

Perhaps the most famous of all solution-focused questions is the 'miracle' question:

> Suppose that tonight after you go to sleep a miracle happens and the problems that brought you to therapy are solved immediately. But since you were sleeping at the time you cannot know that this miracle has happened. Once you wake up tomorrow morning, how will you discover that a miracle has happened? Without your telling them, how will other people know that a miracle has happened?
>
> (de Shazer, 1994: 95)

This question helps clients to construct imaginatively their preferred future for when the problem is solved. Once this has been done, then any exceptions to the problem that are discovered can be seen as evidence that the client is already able to achieve aspects of their solution picture.

Thus, the radical feature of solution-focused therapy is the split it proposes between *problem* and *solution*. It proposes that there is no intrinsic value in exploring the history of a problem or trying to understand how it came about. The therapist is interested only in maximizing the non-problem or solution talk in the session. *Whatever* problem the client presents with, the solution-focused therapist will approach it in the same way: what is the client's preferred future, and what evidence (the exceptions) is there that it is achievable?

Assessment

Brief therapy offers no framework for the assessment, diagnosis and classification of problems. The approach is about *change* and can offer no particular insights as to why people have the problems that they have. This does not mean that a brief therapist is somehow duty-bound by the solution-focused model to ignore problems. For a start, most clients want their therapist to understand something of the pain and trouble they have been having. A sympathetic counsellor will enable the client to feel rapport. At the appropriate moment the counsellor will acknowledge something of what the client has been experiencing, and then ask a specifically solution-focused question to help the client move on. For example, 'I think that what you have been saying is that you've been worried about this for a long time; so what would tell you that today's meeting had been useful to you?' Furthermore, if a person is at risk of harming him or herself or others, the brief therapist will of course want to assess the degree of harm, but will be clear that this activity is essentially separate from the therapeutic one, as protection will always come before therapy. A goal that is illegal, dangerous or unethical will be challenged as such, and if a convincingly safer goal cannot be generated then the therapist would take whatever steps they can to protect the client or others, such as speaking to the GP about hospitalization or to social services when children are deemed to be at risk.

Where the therapist has a medical responsibility, 'a profound knowledge of basic traditional medical diagnosis and treatment is a foundation for being accepted and heard by patients and the hospital system' (Honsig, 1989: 449). Honsig gives several case examples of how expert knowledge can be used to win a client's co-operation and to promote health; in one example an older man with chronic asthma, who had spent more time in inpatient treatment than at home over the previous four years, was helped to return home permanently by being told after a long examination of his heart that further treatment could be tried 'because your heart is very strong and healthy'. The attention to his wishes (to spend time with his grandchildren) coupled to focusing on his healthy organs and treating him as basically a healthy 84-year-old man were the key features of the 'treatment'. A further example of how medical expertise is built into the process of the therapy is to be found in Barbara McFarland's work on brief therapy with eating disorders, where she describes the use of weight charts for patients with anorexia, and where it is made a condition of the therapy that if their weight falls below a certain level then hospitalization will result (McFarland, 1995).

Elements of a session

One of the features of this approach that new practitioners report as appreciating the most, is the structure it offers for a session, with a 'toolbag' of techniques to be used at different times. As in most therapies, it is in the first session that the distinctiveness of the approach can be most clearly discerned. Given that research has shown that a large number of clients attend for one session only, and a majority of them report a satisfactory outcome to their single session therapy (Talmon, 1990), it makes sense to make as much as possible of the first encounter. The ideal first session will include:

- preferred future (goal) questions. The therapist will probably start by establishing the client's hopes for the session and then move on to an exploration of a future in which the problem is non-existent.

- exception questions, where the therapist engages the client in a search for signs of the preferred future happening now and in the past, and of other resources, including coping abilities.

- measuring change. Solution-focused therapy makes considerable use of 'scale' questions (to be discussed later) to assess the extent of changes already made in relation to the client's goals, and to clarify what the next step might be.

- the session ending with the therapist offering the client compliments on their strengths and asking if they want a further session.

In second and subsequent sessions the emphasis will be on exception and scale questions, presuming that the goals for the therapy have already been established in the earlier part of the work. If goals remain unclear, or if they change, then there will be a return to preferred future questions.

Preferred future questions

A client who was seen after his doctor had prescribed anti-depressants for him said he was in a quandary about a relationship he was in, and his goal for the session was 'to get my head clearer about what I want to do'. (In this case he was later asked *two* miracle questions, about what might happen if the relationship ended or if it continued, and this gave him the incentive to focus on the positive aspects of the relationship in future.) In other situations a client might describe his or her goal in terms of the absence of something, e.g. 'I don't want to drink so heavily', 'I don't want to go on bingeing and vomiting'.

Faced with these sorts of vague responses, the brief therapist seeks descriptions in which behaviours are described in as concrete, small and specific detail as is possible, e.g. in what situations and with whom the client will show confidence; the therapist also looks for what will indicate the presence, not the absence, of something e.g. when the client is no longer so anxious, what will they be doing instead?

Of course, there is also a small group of clients who may be unable to describe a goal at all. This is usually because the client's attendance for therapy has been required, or at least been felt to be so, by someone else. A woman in her 20s, with a psychiatric history, was unable to say what she wanted from the therapy, and so she was asked how other people who were concerned about her, such as family members, would know that the sessions were useful to her. Although she was unable to think of anything, she remarked that 'I never seem to know my own mind'. She agreed that she would like to start to 'have a mind of my own' and so the search was on to elucidate what would be different for her when she *would* know her own mind, and to find examples of times when she already *did* know her own mind. In other cases, clients, especially those in statutory situations, will accept someone else's goal for them as long as it will make their life easier for them in some way, even if this means only that they will no longer need to attend further sessions!

A single mother, Anna, who had come to the UK from Italy ten years earlier, had been investigated by social services following reports that she was over-chastising her 2-year-old daughter Sophie, and had left her unattended at home. She was unhappy about being referred for counselling but acknowledged that unless she made some changes then social services would be likely to intervene more rather than less in her life. With a goal of reducing the involvement of professionals in her life she was able to consider what changes in her relationship with her daughter she would need to make. Such a situation would be familiar to health visitors who are sometimes accepted by parents more easily than social workers (who have overt statutory authority) and are therefore in a special position to help clients work out the changes they need to make.

In this case the following sequence – with both Anna and Sophie present – ensued (note that in this case, as in others referred to in this chapter, names and certain details have been changed to protect the clients' identities):

Therapist: Let me ask you a question. It may sound a very strange question. I want you to imagine tonight, when you're asleep, a miracle happened. A miracle happens when you're asleep, and takes away the reasons why you are here today. But you're asleep.

Anna: Right.

Therapist: You don't know the miracle has happened but when you get up in the morning you start doing things differently. Sophie starts doing things. People tell you things are different, a miracle has happened. What would you see different?

Anna: The miracle has happened? Well, the morning, when I get up, I don't attend to myself, so it's difficult . . . (shakes head).

Therapist: This is after the miracle (leans forward).

Anna: You know ...

Therapist: You attend to yourself, yeah?

Anna: No, not just myself. I don't mind attending to her.

Therapist: Right.

Anna: (thinking) Well, I think it's me who has to change not her. 'Cause when I'm good then she ... (Sophie shows Anna her drawing).

Therapist: She responds to you being different?

Anna: Yeah, she responds, the communication will be better between us.

Therapist: Right, so what would be different for you after the miracle? What would you be doing differently?

Anna: I would just be more relaxed, more in control of everything. This is it isn't it, control?

Therapist: Great. O.K, so you being more relaxed, more in control, what would you be doing when you're more relaxed?

Anna: Nothing much more, maybe I could read ... (Sophie tries to get her mother's attention again and Anna shows her a book). What exactly do you mean what do I do? I don't want to do nothing special you know.

Therapist: Well, people do different things when they relax, some people it's just to read the paper or watch TV. Other people ...

Anna: Oh, I love reading, yeah.

Therapist: You love reading?

Anna: Yeah. I wondered whether you wanted me to say something like that or something different.

Therapist: Yes, anything.

Anna: Reading and knitting (Sophie puts her head in her mother's lap).

Therapist: She wants you to read to her now!

Later on the miracle picture was developed further:

Therapist: So, you notice that she responds to you when you're relaxed, when you're relaxed it's good for her. So what other things do you do when you're relaxed? What will you do when the miracle happens? How will you know it's happened?

Anna: I can read, I can clean. You know, sometimes you can't even clean. Powder everywhere, lipstick, everything. I could go for a walk. Oh, I love going for walks with her and she looks in the windows and things. Sometimes, I walk for ages and ages.

Therapist: Good.

Anna: And that's not her fault, sometimes I'm in a rush, like in the morning, 'cause I'm going out. That rushing kills me. But that's my fault again (smiles) . . . just doing things . . .

It is worth considering the words of a worker in the field of HIV and AIDS who was asked whether the use of the miracle question might not engender a sense of false hope in the client:

How, ethically, can you ask the miracle question? The outcome of this disease is well known. My response after some considerable thought was, 'how can you *not* ask the miracle question?' I have asked the miracle question to every HIV + client that I have seen and have recorded and tracked the answers. I have yet to ask it at some point during a client's therapy when it failed to highlight difference – hope? It has always seemed to clarify for the client some part of their life in which there already exists some forward control, some scintilla of agency in the course of this mercurial disease'.

(Chilton, 1995: 11)

The therapist needs to pay attention to the wording of the question. 'Imagine a miracle happened and solved the problem that brought you here' is more 'realistic' than 'imagine a miracle happened and your *life* became as you wanted it to' – who, being asked that, could avoid referring to lottery wins and so forth! Someone with a chronic disease, who would naturally be tempted to say that if a miracle had happened they wouldn't have become ill in the first place, could be told that 'the miracle would not be a big one but a small one that helped you cope better'. For example, 'we both know that a full recovery from this disease is unlikely, yet if a miracle were to happen while you were asleep and you found that you were living your life in a way that did yourself justice, what would you be doing differently? How would others know?' And where a client still surprises one with a seemingly unrealistic scenario, the aim should still be to maximize the client's own potential within the situation. One client, for example, answered that she would 'wake up in the morning and my husband would be there in the bed with me'. On further exploration it transpired that the client had been divorced for ten years and her ex-husband had started a new family elsewhere and was currently in prison! In such situations it is useful to remember to make a distinction between 'means' and 'ends': the client might think, as here, that the means to a goal are the presence of someone else, but the actual end that is aimed at is something different about the client herself. Therefore, the therapist focused on how the client would be different *in herself* rather than focusing on the magical relationship with her husband, and very soon the client acknowledged the unlikeliness of the scenario but stayed focused on what she wanted specifically for herself.

Exception questions

Exceptions are signs that the miracle picture is already starting to happen. They act as a kind of bridge to the attainment of goals. A client suffering pain will, with patience and perseverance, be able to talk about moments when he or she copes better with the pain and is able to live a more 'normal' life.

It is obviously important for clients to be able to attach some significance to the exceptions that have been unearthed. Counsellors are familiar with the 'yes, but . . . ' response, such as clients saying that better days happened because the 'sun was shining', or a client with an alcohol problem saying that they he or she drank less on a particular day because 'I ran out of money'. It is essential to help the client to identify their part in the process of change and to find a way to 'blame' the client constructively for any better outcome, thereby increasing their sense of responsibility and agency. Asking how the client is different *in him or herself* on a sunny day and then perhaps locating times when they have felt that way even when it wasn't sunny would be a way forward. Similarly, reminding the client that even when they have been short of money they have at times made sure that somehow they got the alcohol they wanted, will help to emphasize that on the occasion under discussion something different happened: 'so how were you able to resist the urge this time?'

Paul was a 26-year-old homeless man who was referred by his GP because of alcohol problems and depression. His miracle picture included being happier, having friends and keeping off the drink. When exceptions were pursued, he was able to recall that the week before, when he had got a new pair of glasses, he had been happy to be able to read a newspaper; a casual reference to keeping some of his belongings at a friend's house elicited the evidence that he had more than the one friend he had stated he had at the start of the session; and he had managed to go for three weeks without drinking until the day before the session. To Paul, each of these exceptions seen separately was not significant – he was, for example, demoralized by the drinking he had done the day before – but as the exceptions accumulated he began to acknowledge that he had made more progress than he had originally thought.

Scale questions

Scale questions are among the most versatile of all brief therapy 'tools'. The aim is to ascertain where the client feels he or she is *today* and then to focus on what the next *small step* would look like. Almost anything can be rated on a scale, from progress towards the miracle being attained, to how well the client is coping; from their confidence that change is possible to an evaluation of their actual commitment to doing something about it.

Examples of scale questions are:

- With zero representing you when you were at your worst (e.g. when you were hospitalized) and 10 representing the day after the miracle has happened, where would you say you are today?' 'At what level would your partner say you were?' 'Let's say you had moved up one step on the scale, what would you be doing differently then?'

- With zero representing you being so overwhelmed by your pain that you felt unable to do anything except sit down all day, and 10 representing you managing to do all the things you want to do ... '

- With zero representing you being totally unable to cope with your partner's sickness, and 10 representing you coping as well as you might, so that you can still get on with your life ... '

- With zero representing your having no confidence whatsoever that things can improve, and 10 representing your total confidence that things will improve, where would you say your confidence is right now?'

A scale can be used to assess risk, along the lines of: 'with zero representing that you will definitely kill yourself before our next appointment, and 10 representing there is no chance you will do this ... '

A 27-year-old woman, suffering with bulimia, rated herself at only 1 on a scale where zero represented being totally dominated by the bulimia and 10 represented no longer having to struggle with it. The scale therefore graphically revealed the extent of her despair but enabled her to concentrate, not on the gulf that appeared to separate her from her miracle picture, but on just the next small step towards it, which involved considering how she might manage to go for a few hours at work in the morning without bingeing and vomiting.

Subsequent sessions

Typically, the second and any subsequent session will open with the question, 'what has been better since we last met?' The 'what' of the question presupposes change and urges the client to focus on positive changes rather than on negative events. Life has its ups and downs and so of course there will have been some set-backs. The key is to acknowledge such things, but to direct the client's attention to change in order to enhance their sense of possibilities for the future. An exceptions search is thus initiated from the very beginning, and every possible difference is scrutinized to see what the client has done, and may be able to continue to do.

In the second session, two weeks later, the therapist asked Anna:

Therapist: So what's been happening that's been good for you?

Anna: (smiles) Well not too much really but my friend says Sophie's been seriously reformed now so . . .

Therapist: Reformed . . . (nods head) . . . really?

Anna: You know Paula, my friend who used to think Sophie was spiteful and . . . that's what she said . . . (shrugs).

Therapist: Fantastic! What has Paula seen that's different?

Anna: I don't know but she keeps saying she's very . . . she's a reformed girl now. She doesn't push other children. She's very . . . more well behaved. Yeah that's it.

Therapist: Great, great. Do you feel good about that?

Anna: Of course, of course (smiles).

Therapist: Yeah. That's good, that's good. What do you reckon it's due to? What have you done?

Anna: Oh. I haven't done nothing. But, er . . . em . . .

Therapist: So how do you explain it?

Anna: Maybe I am more aware of her needs 'cause I come here.

Therapist: Good, good. What sort of things have you noticed when you've become more aware?

Anna: I try to make her know that I'm in control. I keep using this word, it's not nice. A control thing. But I think she likes it, rather

181

than ... She doesn't like it when it seems I don't know what I want of her.

(Sophie gets up and walks to the blackboard)

> *Anna:* She likes it when I'm fair with her I think.
>
> *Therapist:* Right. How do you know she likes that?

Scale questions can be employed to measure the progress made. They offer a simple method of confirming that a client has moved on and therapy can end. Many clients will drop out of therapy when they have reached only 5 or 6 on the scale, because they now appreciate that they have the resources to take themselves on without the need for further therapy; other clients might wish to arrange follow-up sessions to review progress. Anna, for example, had three sessions (there was a four-week gap between the second and third sessions) by which point she was at 7 on the scale; a follow-up meeting was scheduled for two months later and she had then reached 8. In theory all sessions after the first can be seen as follow-ups, evaluating the progress the client has made towards the goals that were established in the first session. In reality, if the goals were still unclear then further clarification will be needed in later sessions, and of course some clients may need to change their goals or introduce new ones for new problems that might arise.

Chronic pain, support and the relief of stress

John Weakland was well known for advising his trainees to 'go slowly!' This is not a contradiction of the idea of *brief* therapy. It is a reminder that the therapy must fit the client and not the other way round, and if the client were to feel that their counsellor was pushing them too hard in the direction of change then they would be likely to feel that the counsellor has not understood the extent of their pain, or their feelings of hopelessness.

In relation to clients with chronic pain, it has been found helpful to look closely with clients at what they hope to be able to do when the pain will bother them less, and then to look for exceptions, i.e. times when they already cope with the pain sufficiently to be able to do some of the things they want to do. It is essential to look for the *smallest* of exceptions: when clients are invited to observe the detail of their daily lives it becomes apparent that the pain varies in intensity. In short, the solution-focused therapist would not be focusing on trying to get rid of the pain, but on what the client will be able to do, and is already doing, in spite of the pain.

Similarly, it is sometimes necessary to help the client to accept that what they are experiencing is normal given their circumstances, and that a realistic goal may be to cope with the situation better rather than to think it can be transformed entirely. Many clients, for example, benefit from having their symptoms of post-traumatic stress identified as such, so that they might move beyond feelings of self-blame and begin to recognize that they are reacting 'normally' to terrible events. From a therapist's point of view, what matters is what the *client* believes about themselves and what *they* feel they can achieve. One client, who described herself as having 'chronic low self-esteem', was being seen for her agoraphobia. Despite having suffered with the complaint for 20 years, she was still susceptible to taunts from her family that 'you don't have a real problem: it's all in your mind'. She asked the therapist if *he* thought she had a 'real' problem. The therapist replied that as her life was considerably disrupted by her symptoms then it seemed undeniable to him that she had a real problem, but what mattered was what *she* felt she could do about it. She was asked to imagine herself in 10 years time as a 'wiser, older self' (Dolan, 1991) and to think what the wiser self would think had been the best way to deal with her situation. After some thought she said that the older self would advise her 'just to accept that I have this problem'. She was then asked what the older self would advise her to *do*, and she said, 'to take small steps, a day at a time'.

It is perfectly natural for clients to fear a relapse, but solution-focused thinking suggests that if the client focuses on *preventing* a relapse occurring, such as trying to stop themselves drinking or getting depressed, then a relapse will be *more likely* to occur. The guard against relapse is the same as in all solution-focused work: to keep focused on what the client needs to do *instead* of drinking, etc. If the client believes that they have a condition, e.g. that they 'are' depressive, then, as before, the brief therapist will seek to co-operate with such a view and try to learn what the client would feel is the best way they can cope with the situation. If the client feels that medication, for example, is useful to them, then the therapist would want to support them in that while seeking from time to time to help them evaluate that the medication is still being helpful. Clients might suggest that positive changes are due only to the medication, and the counsellor, while accepting that the drug has been helpful will, for example, ask what the client is doing to enable the medication to be as helpful as it has been.

With clients who appear to need, and indeed request, ongoing support, it is obviously important to assess regularly with the client what 'support' means to them, and how the counsellor is continuing to be helpful. Sometimes this support is for the relatives and carers of the patient and it enables them to cope better in difficult circumstances, which may of course have a beneficial spin-off for the patient as well. As EunSook Park has written of solution-focused brief therapy in relation to family medicine, 'this model has relevance not only to psychosomatic or stress-related medical problems but also as a tool to help support behaviour change and to gain family co-operation for the management of medical illness' (Park, 1997: 84), and in a case example describes how 'I told him that it was clear from our talk that doing something is more helpful than trying not to get nervous, and that I agreed with him that the harder one tries to avoid stress the more difficulties one gets caught in. Therefore, I agreed with him that concentrating on something to forget the stress was a good idea' (Park, 1997: 85). The author concludes that 'it seems to me that no other treatment model would have brought about more beneficial information from the patient in a brief, 18-minute session and in the process have given the patient more hope and confidence', and that 'since the model requires the patient's self-discipline and responsibility, both the physician and the patient share less burden and there is no danger of over-intervention' (Park, 1997: 86). It could be added that, as EunSook Park is writing from Seoul, this also represents a demonstration of the cross-cultural sensitivity of the approach; for a further discussion of this point see Berg and Jaya (1993), and also, for particular reference to gender issues, Lethem (1994).

Does it work? Of course!

A group of brief therapists have recently been puncturing the growing pride of their colleagues as to the effectiveness of solution-focused brief therapy, by stating that research shows that *all* therapies are equally effective – and are brief as well! Scott Miller, a former associate of the Milwaukee team, and his colleagues have studied psychotherapy outcome studies going back many years and have concluded that:

- 'Virtually all of the available data indicate that the different therapy models, from psychodynamic and client centred approaches to marriage and family therapies, work about equally well' (Miller, Duncan and Hubble, 1997: 2).

- Data collected over the last 50 years consistently show that the average client attends only a handful of sessions *regardless of the treatment model employed* (ibid., p.5).

- The influence of a particular model in terms of outcomes amounts to only 15 per cent (ibid., p.29); other factors, such as events outside of therapy and features of the relationship itself between client and therapist, are far more significant (ibid., p.36). It should be noted that one of the features of events outside of therapy to which the authors refer are client resources and strengths, and it is precisely these factors that are central to solution-focused thinking anyway!

Important – and sobering – as it is to be reminded about these findings, it is clearly still important to demonstrate that solution-focused brief therapy is effective. It is also the only conclusive way to answer the charge this writer has frequently encountered, namely that by not addressing possible underlying causes or function of a problem, then the changes that come about in brief therapy are likely to be only superficial and short-lived.

As a relative newcomer to the scene, solution-focused brief therapy is still in the early stages of being formally evaluated, yet the studies that have been done are certainly very encouraging. A recent study of the Milwaukee team's work found a 77 per cent success rate in 3.7 sessions (De Jong and Hopwood, 1996). The study examined rates of success for different problem presentations and found evidence that the approach is applicable across the board of client problems. The study also examined the possible influence of typical client – therapist variables such as gender and race, and found nothing of significance, thereby offering an endorsement of the client-centred nature of this approach. In Britain the most significant study to date has been that of Alasdair Macdonald, a consultant psychiatrist, and his team. They followed up a sample of clients with mental health difficulties and also contacted their GPs for their views on outcome. The success rate has been 64 per cent, with an average of 3.35 sessions per client; as in the Milwaukee study, variables such as social class have not been found to be of significance (Macdonald, 1997). In Sweden, an interesting study of work in prisons was carried out and is a rare example of research that has included a control group. The study found impressive evidence for the success of solution-focused brief therapy in reducing the rate of recidivism after leaving prison and, notably, a reduction in drug use and mortality among those who were recipients of the therapy (Lindforss & Magnusson, 1997). The implication therefore is that changes wrought through brief therapy are long lasting, and not superficial.

Criticisms of solution-focused brief therapy

The most common criticism this author has encountered is the fear that to do solution-focused brief therapy the therapist has to pressure the client into discussing only the positive, thereby 'whitewashing anything negative' (Efran and Schenker, 1993). It is feared that the approach disqualifies a client's experience, by preventing them from talking about their suffering. Such comments appear to misunderstand a fundamental aspect of the approach, which is to attend, first and foremost, to the client's wishes and experiences, and to be respectful and curious – features, surely, of all good counselling methods. 'No amount of technique will disguise the therapist's lack of listening skills, lack of faith in the client's ability to know what is good for him (sic), and miscomprehension of the philosophical thinking that generates questions ... the questions articulated by solution-focused therapists are expressions of an attitude, a posture and a philosophy' (Berg, 1994: 14). Sometimes a therapist who is new to this approach, and is eager to use the questions and be as brief as possible, ends up being not so much solution-focused as 'solution-forced' (Nylund and Corsiglia, 1994). They seem to forget the essential need, as in all counselling, to acknowledge and validate (O'Hanlon and Beadle, 1996) a client's experience, and to hear the client talk about painful experiences for as long as it takes for the client to feel that they *have* been acknowledged. If clients feel disqualified, they will either terminate the therapy or argue even more strongly for the seriousness of their problems. Like everybody else, they need to feel heard.

Finally, the fear has been voiced that because the approach relies on a few essential question areas then the therapist (or perhaps the client) will get bored or irritated with 'strings of stock questions' (Efran and Schenker, 1993). Someone new to the field may well be tempted to use the questions mechanically, acting as if a miracle question will indeed produce miracles! Again, it is necessary to reiterate that, as with all good therapy, the crucial ingredient is the therapist's curiosity and respect.

References

Note: There has been little written specifically about solution-focused brief therapy in relation to health care, although there are authors who write about related issues, as mentioned in the text. As an introduction to the approach, the BT Press publications are recommended, as is almost anything by de Shazer, Berg and O'Hanlon.

Berg, I.K. (1991) *Family Preservation: A Brief Therapy Workbook*. London: BT Press.

A very handy how-to-do-it text with numerous practical examples of the various questions.

Berg, I.K. and Miller, S.D. (1992) *Working with the Problem Drinker: A Solution Focused Approach*. New York: Norton.

Berg I.K. and Jaya, A. (1993) Different and same: Family Therapy with Asian-American Families *Journal of Marital and Family Therapy 19(1)*, 31–38.

Berg, I.K. (1994) A wolf in disguise is not a grandmother *Journal of Systemic Therapies*, 13(1), 13–14.

Chilton, S. (1995, Dec.) Immanence, miracles and HIV+ clients *News of the Difference* (a Brief Therapy Newsletter) 4(3), 11–12 New York.

De Jong, P. and Hopwood, L. (1996) Outcome research on treatment conducted at the Brief Family Therapy Center, 1992–1993. In S.D. Miller, M. Hubble & B. Duncan (Eds) *Handbook of Solution Focused Brief Therapy.* San Francisco: Jossey-Bass.

de Shazer, S. (1988) *Clues: Investigating Solutions in Brief Therapy.* New York: Norton.

de Shazer, S. (1994) *Words Were Originally Magic.* New York: Norton.
The first section is a complex exploration of philosophical and linguistic themes, but the rest of the book contains some of the best published case examples of the approach.

Dolan, Y. (1991) *Resolving Sexual Abuse.* New York: Norton.
An extremely important contribution, devoted to a particularly challenging area of work, with numerous helpful ideas and techniques.

Efran, J. and Schenker, M. (1993) A potpourri of solutions: how new and different is solution-focused therapy? *Family therapy Networker 17(3),* May/June, 71–74.

George, E., Iveson, C. and Ratner, H. (1990) *Problem to Solution: Brief Therapy with Individuals and Families.* London: BT Press.
The first British text on the approach, with lengthy case examples.

Honsig, T. (1989) Stories, reflections and miracles: new approaches to introducing Family Therapy to inpatient settings *Family Systems Medicine* 7(4), 443–53.

Lethem, J. (1994) *Moved to Tears, Moved to Action: Brief Therapy with Women and Children.* London: BT Press.
An important British contribution to thinking about how gender and power issues are accounted for in this approach.

Lindforss, L. and Magnusson, D. (1997) Solution-focused therapy in prison. *Contemporary Family Therapy* 19 (1), 89–103.

Macdonald, A. (1997) Brief therapy in adult psychiatry – further outcomes *Journal of Family Therapy* 19(2), 213–20.

McFarland, B. (1995) *Brief Therapy and Eating Disorders.* San Francisco: Jossey-Bass.

Miller, S.D., Hubble, M. and Duncan, B. (Eds) (1996) *Handbook of Solution Focused Brief Therapy.* San Francisco: Jossey-Bass.
An extremely useful book as it contains many examples of applying the approach in different contexts, including psychiatry and grief work.

Miller, S.D., Duncan, B and Hubble, M. (1997) *Escape from Babel: Toward a Unifying Language for Psychotherapy Practice.* New York: Norton.

Nylund, D. and Corsiglia, V. (1994) Becoming solution-forced in brief therapy: Remembering something important we already knew *Journal of Systemic Therapy* 13(1), 5–12.

O'Hanlon, B. and Weiner-Davis, M. (1988) *In Search of Solutions: A New Direction in Psychotherapy*. New York: Norton.
A very clear and simple introduction to the ideas and techniques.

O'Hanlon, B. and Beadle, S. (1996) *A Field Guide to Possibility Land: Possibility Therapy Methods*. London: BT Press.

Park, E. (1997) An application of brief therapy to family medicine *Contemporary Family Therapy 19(1)*, 81–88.

Talmon, M. (1990) *Single Session Therapy*. San Francisco: Jossey-Bass.

Watzlawick, P., Weakland, J. and Fisch, R. (1974) *Change: Principles of Problem Formation and Problem Resolution*. New York: Norton.

Weiner-Davis, M., de Shazer, S. and Gingerich, W. (1987) Constructing the therapeutic solution by building on pretreatment change: an exploratory study *Journal of Family and Marital Therapy 13(4)*, 359–63.

Chapter 13

Communicating about ethical dilemmas: a medical humanities approach

Rowena Murray

Medical humanities is a practical strategy for health professionals. It has worked in the Glasgow group, a mixed group of health professionals and others, over the past eight years to produce conversations about ethical dilemmas – conversations that would probably not have taken place otherwise.

Ethical dilemmas are often seen as the 'big issues', like genetic engineering or abortion, issues which regularly attract the attention of the media, are the focus of philosophical debate and require rigorous monitoring by committees or professional bodies. Dilemmas can also be discussed, or revealed, when decisions are to be made about resource allocations. Communicating about such issues can be fraught; we each have our own views, and there is rarely any forum in which we can air them. It sometimes seems easier to skirt around these difficult areas and get on with the work.

Ethical issues are also 'daily dilemmas', decisions about, for example, how best to give information, how much time to spend with people, how best to offer support, how to find some support for yourself or how to give your attention to someone you do not particularly like or respect. Over time, this type of dilemma can be just as demanding, perhaps more so, as the 'big issues':

> Ethical choices seldom appear in the abstract or otherwise undisguised; more often, they are embedded in the mundane and parochial, linked inescapably to our daily affairs.
>
> (Garvin, 1991: 287)

There may be pressure not to talk about them. Daily dilemmas may simply become a fact of life: we accept that we do not have enough time to talk to patients, or students or relatives. However, left unaddressed, these dilemmas can have powerful effects both on the well-being of the individual and on professional practice.

Questions of conscience, of roles, responsibilities and values, all of which can shape professional identity, are generally excluded from professional discussions and professional development after undergraduate years. Taboos, role conflicts and ambiguities may therefore become a very personal burden for the individual health professional. These issues may be subsumed under professional conventions. Moreover, as the health professions strengthen their conventions and rhetorics, with degrees and evidence-based research, for example, there may be increasing territorialism. As waves of change hit the health professions there are philosophical and strategic arguments to be conducted at all levels and these changes may present dilemmas for health professionals.

Where do health professionals engage with such issues? When can they air their views freely? How can they address these ethical dilemmas constructively? How will they find the time? And why should they? Is there any guarantee that it will help them in their work; will they be more effective, more efficient, with patients or students?

This chapter outlines one method for stimulating and structuring discussion of ethical dilemmas: medical humanities is a sounding board for difficult issues. A short definition of this approach is provided, along with a worked example to show how it functions in practice. This example can be used as a starting point for exploring in groups such issues as bereavement, mental illness, health promotion, and patient-centred care. A rationale for this approach is provided in a selective summary of the literature, along with doubts and reservations that have been raised. Evaluation of the impact of medical humanities on practice is at an early stage; initial reports from participants in the Glasgow medical humanities group are provided here. It is a forum for exploring ethical – and daily – dilemmas that is not too rarified, nor too abstract, nor too intimidating, which costs almost nothing and takes up hardly any time.

Medical humanities: effects and critiques

Medical humanities involves using literary texts on medical subjects to prompt discussion. Because a literary text is open to many interpretations it often has the effect of opening up a surprising range of readings. This variety of responses can reveal underlying assumptions and attitudes. Unlike case study discussions, where there is an imperative to arrive at a decision, in medical humanities discussions there is no drive to find right and wrong answers. The structure, while flexible, provides a loose framework for reflection, and the literary text provides a focal point.

Two major journals are devoted to scholarship on medical humanities: *Literature and Medicine* (Johns Hopkins University) and *Medical Humanities Review* (University of Texas). They illustrate the variety of interesting approaches that use literature and narrative in healthcare settings. For example, Chambers (1994) looks at narratives written by ethicists. Chambers argues that the case study reflects the writer's view of a moral issue or dilemma, rather than the objective view that is often claimed. Chambers concludes that such writing skills are therefore part of, not apart from, medicine and healthcare:

> I shall examine five examples of case presentations from bioethicists who have distinct approaches to ethical issues in medicine and show that in all instances the ethicists' stylistic choices in their case presentations are reflections of their particular approaches to moral decision making . . . Case presentation thus must be seen as a part of – not apart from – the rhetoric of the bioethicist; in short, ethicists persuade through narrative style.
>
> (pp. 60–1)

Best (1994) uses extracts from case discussions to show how healthcare professionals use narrative not only to report but also to create shared understanding and meaning; health care professionals in this study not only reported what was happening with a patient, but included judgement and opinion in what purported to be factual reports. Healthcare teams, patients and families are shown going through the same process of generating their own narratives and meanings, causing Best to reflect on how agreement can be reached, among all these 'stories', about what '*the* story' is (p. 104):

> Collectively generated narratives make the process of story construction highly visible, much more so than narratives generated by individuals.
>
> (p. 105)

Particular training effects are also claimed for narrative in medical settings. For example, Shafer and Fish (1994) argue that patient and physician narratives can be 'a powerful tool to accentuate the individuality of the patient for all physicians' (p. 124).

Positive effects on trainees and professionals have been claimed for medical humanities, specifically in nursing, medicine and physiotherapy. For example, Darbyshire (1994) describes a course, including literature and other arts which, he argues, helped students to think and learn in new ways, while learning about caring:

> Hearing these participants speak of how they formed meanings around reading, seeing, thinking, learning and practising interpretively, highlights the new thinking and learning which seemed to occur in the new home that these students found within this course.
>
> (p. 862)

Young-Mason (1988) argues that literature can help students to develop an understanding of moral and ethical dilemmas, with literary texts offering role models for the 'purposeful, humane behavior of the professional nurse' (p. 299). Young-Mason also addressed the difficulty of sustaining this behaviour: 'This article . . . specifically discusses the ways in which deceitful behavior injures the nurse as well as the patient, and it demonstrates factors that, at times, cause nurses to deceive' (p. 299).

Radwany and Adelson (1987) argue that 'literary classics' can help in teaching medical ethics. Hackler (1994) proposes that medical humanities could help to create the 'well-rounded doctor' by ensuring that medical students received a 'balanced education' (p. 266). Self (1993) provides an empirical assessment of three different approaches to humanistic medical education.

Having established a medical humanities group in the UK, Thow and Murray (1991) observe that there is potential for medical humanities to develop group skills, communications and an increased awareness of the patient's point of view. In one-off medical humanities sessions, participants said that they enjoyed the discussions, and so enjoying reading and talking about literature are other important and immediate effects (Murray and Thow, 1995).

Although little evaluative work has been done to substantiate such claims for the potential of medical humanities, a study of the Glasgow group shows that participants find that medical humanities has had an effect on them. Initial analysis of interviews shows up several recurring effects for this group:

- They feel they have developed empathy.
- They have improved their communication and group skills.
- They have a deeper understanding of other professional groups and of the patient's point of view.
- They have 'tuned' their listening skills.

Others, however, have expressed 'doubts.' For example, Rogers (1994) questions what can be seen as the promotional writing about medical humanities for promoting its potential but not developing the discipline:

> First of all, I take it for granted that any discipline worthy of the name should produce its own critics, but there is very little internal

critique in medical humanities ... Second, in contrast to its self-satisfied exponents, I do not believe that the medical humanities, as it currently stands, are a properly integrated part of the educative process. Third, there is a major problem about power. Patriarchy is alive and well in the hospital setting. There is relentless evidence that those who teach and work in the medical humanities both accept and maintain existing power hierarchies.

(p. 347)

Wear (1992) supports this view, questioning the usefulness of medical humanities, if it has been 'colonized' by the medical curriculum, even to the extent of the 'medicalization of ethics enquiry' (p. 202). Wear sees a flaw in medical humanities, where it mimics the perceived methods of science, using the 'master's tools':

And even though I doubt that anyone could arrive at a unified theory that guides the practice of all physicians ... I find myself and my colleagues covertly, perhaps unconsciously, appraising our practice in the medical humanities with that of scientists and clinicians, with the latter installed as the regime of truth ... This is odd: our domains are different; our protocols are different; our cognitive styles are different from our basic science and clinical colleagues.

(p. 202)

There are arguments here for integrating medical humanities in the curriculum; there are also arguments against. There are arguments for making narrative a part of medical discussions; there are arguments for keeping it apart. Overall, however, the literature suggests that there is great potential in medical humanities as a mechanism for reflective practice, and that the version of medical humanities we have developed in the Glasgow group has had positive effects and has proved a safe forum for discussion of ethical dilemmas among healthcare professionals and others. It is this type of informal group that is proposed and illustrated in the rest of this chapter.

Medical humanities in practice: 'Not Wordsworth'

The version of medical humanities developed both in Murray (1997) and in this chapter is not about 'the classics', nor about literary aesthetics or developing a high level of literary analysis. It is about using literary texts to stimulate discussion of both personal and professional issues, with individuals free to choose how much or how little they reveal of their views to partners in a 'pair-share' or a plenary discussion.

'Not Plato'

To philosophers and ethicists this form of medical humanities may seem lacking in rigour and consistency. We have no fixed agenda, no conceptual framework and no collective 'accounting' of our journey or lessons learned in these discussions. We have had, until recently, no measures of the outcomes of our experience of being in these discussions. The flow of our discussions has been unpredictable. This is part of the enjoyment and stimulation: there is always an element of the unexpected in other people's responses. The openness of the structure preserves the spontaneity.

This version of medical humanities is for a wide spectrum of people, including health professionals. We even had the publisher, who sponsored our medical humanities roadshow, as an active participant in his first medical humanities discussion. No literary training is needed.

In the Glasgow group we have used a variety of literary texts, including contemporary and local writers, journals and journalism. We have read first-hand, first-person accounts, commentaries on specific conditions and analyses of such commentaries. The aim is to include different points of view in our readings. We have also tried to avoid intimidating participants with 'Literature', with a capital 'L'.

Worked example

A one-hour session is outlined, with guidelines on getting discussion started and keeping it going. Reflective writing, which we have found an essential and enjoyable aspect of our group's work, is explained. Finally, reactions of different groups who used this text in discussion are provided. Their reactions show the range of responses, and this diversity may itself be a topic for discussion.

The text for this illustration is an extract from Janice Galloway's novel *The Trick is to Keep Breathing* (1989, reprinted 1991: 19–23). This extract was used with a group who were hoping to start a new medical humanities group; the extract has proved an effective starting point. It also has the potential to raise a number of different ethical dilemmas.

The subject of this extract is one of a series of home visits by a health visitor to a woman who is experiencing a breakdown or depression, has stopped eating, has had difficulty accepting the validity of the treatment offered by a number of health professionals, lives alone and is spending more and more time alone.

Extract: *Janice Galloway's* The Trick is to Keep Breathing

By twenty past I'm running along the twisty road between the houses to the shop for biscuits. She likes biscuits. I get different ones each time hoping they are something else she will enjoy. I can't choose in a hurry. I can't be trusted with custard creams so deliberately don't get them. Chocolate digestives are too expensive ... I get flustered at these times, but I know I'll manage if I try harder. These visits are good for me. Dr Stead sends this woman out of love. He insisted.

I said, I'm no use with strangers.

He said, But this is different. Health visitors are trained to cope with that. He said she would know what to do; she would find me out and let me talk. *Make me* talk.

HAH

I'm putting on the kettle, still catching my breath when she comes in without knocking and frightens me. What if I had been saying things about her out loud? I tell her to sit in the living room so I can have time to think.

Tray
    jug
        sweeteners
          plates
            cups and saucers
              another spoon
                christ

the biscuits
the biscuits

I burst the wrap soundlessly and make a tasteful arrangement. I polish her teaspoon on my cardigan band. No teapot. I make it in the cup, using the same bag twice, and take it through as though I've really made it in a pot and just poured it out. Some people are sniffy about tea-bags. It sloshes when I reach to push my hair back from falling in my eyes and I suddenly notice I am still wearing my slippers dammit.

Never mind. She smiles and says

Well!

This is to make out the tea is a surprise though it isn't. She does it every time. We sit opposite each other because that's the way the chairs are. The chairs cough dust from under their sheets as she crosses her legs, thinking her way into the part. By the time she's ready to start I'm grinding my teeth back into the gum.

HEALTH VISITOR   So, how are you/how's life/what's been
                  happening/anything interesting to tell
                  me/what's new?
PATIENT   Oh, fine/nothing to speak of.

I stir the tea repeatedly. She picks a piece of fluff off her skirt.

HEALTH VISITOR   Work. How are things at work? Coping?
PATIENT   Fine. [Pause] I have trouble getting in on time,
                  but getting better.

I throw her a little difficulty every so often so she feels I'm telling her
the truth. I figure this will get rid of her quicker.

HEALTH VISITOR   [Intensifying] But what about the day-to-day?
                  How are you coping?
PATIENT   OK. [Brave smile] I manage.
HEALTH VISITOR   The house is looking fine.
PATIENT   Thank-you. I do my best.

This is overdone. She flicks her eyes up to see and I lower mine. She
reaches for a biscuit.

HEALTH VISITOR   These look nice. I like a biscuit with a cup of
                  tea.

We improvise about the biscuits for a while, her hat sliding back as she
chews. She doesn't like the tea. Maybe she eats so many biscuits just to
get rid of the taste . . .

This is the fourth time we have played this fucking game.

The first time was the worst. I went through the tea ceremony for five
minutes then tried to get the thing opened up.

What are you supposed to come here for? I said.
She just looked.
What's it for? What are we supposed to talk about?
She said, I'm here to help you. To help you try to get better. I'm
here to listen.
But I don't know you from a hole in the wall. I can't do it.
She said, You can tell me anything you like. I assure you it goes
no further and I've heard it all before . . .

She knew how I felt. Did I think doctor hadn't given her case notes?
She knew all about my problems. Did I want her to tell me a true
story? Her niece had an accident on her bike once. And she thought,
what'll happen if Angela dies? what'll happen? But she prayed to God
and the family rallied round and they saw her through to the other
side. That's what I had to remember. She knew how I felt; she knew
exactly how I felt . . .

She smiles and stands up but guilt is spoiling the relief. I get more guilty as she waddles towards the door, tumbling crumbs from the folds of blue coat, fastening up one top button, ready for the outside. My temples thunder as she touches the door and something buzzes in my ear.

You Always Expect Too Much.

Structure

The structure for discussing literary texts that we have developed in the Glasgow group over the past eight years has three phases:

- initial reflection
- discussion of a question
- further reflection

Initial reflection allows participants to realize their own reactions to the text, find their own starting point and voice their own views. Alternatively, discussion of a question provided by the facilitator directs participants' attention to the text and focuses on its ambiguities. In the final stage – further reflection – participants reflect individually on their initial reactions, and on discussions that have taken place, and may reassess their views. The facilitator can take responsibility for ensuring that time is allocated for all three phases or that flexibility allows for discussion to run on. A discussion of the Janice Galloway extract could take an hour:

Initial reflection

Five minutes' private writing, in sentences, rather than notes, to encourage the development of a thought, rather than simply recording it, on the question:
Do you think this health visitor is an effective facilitator?
Plus pair-share, discussing writings and views   15 mins

Discussion

Group's responses to the question
Other points raised by the text
Focused discussion of the text   30 mins

Further reflection

Five minutes' writing, in sentences rather than notes, on the question:
What are the implications for . . . ?
Plenary & conclusions   15 mins

TOTAL   60 mins

Writing

Private writing – i.e. writing not to be read by anyone else – is based on Peter Elbow's (1973) technique of freewriting. Participants write freely for five minutes, without stopping, in sentences rather than notes. This kind of writing seemed a bit strange at first but it has become one of the most enjoyable periods in each session, and one of the most reflective. The prompt for starting to write, for those who need one, can be quite open, encouraging participants to give their first impression of, or gut reaction to the extract. In pairs they then discuss these initial reflections, revealing as much or as little of their freewriting as they choose.

Questions

The question used to prompt discussion of this extract was, 'Do you think this health visitor is an effective facilitator?' The answer may seem obvious. Some will say, 'Obviously, yes!'; others, 'Clearly, no!' This question is not, however, designed to create confrontation, but to allow for a wide range of answers. Participants are encouraged to link their answer to the text, to find some connection between their answer and what in fact the text says.

Discussion

Discussion of answers to this question, and reasons for the answers, can take up most of the session. This discussion is frequently a mixture of narration and reflection: narration, as people draw on their own experiences, their own anecdotes, their own 'texts'; and reflection, as they consider other people's responses and anecdotes.

Participants often use this discussion as an opportunity to think aloud. Some have changed their minds as soon as they put their thoughts into words. Some have taken the opportunity to develop an opinion. While the medical humanities discussion can be used as a sounding board, the text is the focal point.

Facilitator

We have had some discussion about whether or not the facilitator has to be a literary expert, or someone with an Arts background or training. We have decided that it probably helps if they do, if he or she can provide guidance on techniques for analysing texts. Without this skill the discussion can stray quite far from the text, in a stream of personal and professional narratives. The facilitator should have the skills to redirect the discussion back to the text.

A literary specialist may also be more tolerant of ambiguities in texts, and perhaps more skilled in dealing with them. They may be more comfortable with the absence of 'right-or-wrong' answers than those with a scientific training. They may also be adept at helping others to feel comfortable in discussion of amibiguity in texts.

However, the medical humanities discussion of a literary text has, in our group, been quite different from seminars in English literature. For example, readers' personal opinions and personal experiences are included. Discussions about the author's intentions, and identification of authors with texts are included. These might well be excluded from academic literary discussion. The medical humanities facilitator and group participants would have to reach some agreement about whether 'anything goes' in discussions, or whether boundaries to interpretation should be set.

As in any group management situation, the facilitator has to decide whether or not to be the 'filter' for all comments made by the group; should participants address comments to the facilitator or to each other? Medical humanities works best, I feel, when the facilitator is not the filter for the discussion; this requires the person who plays this role to have group management skills:

> Any analysis of the ethics of discussion leadership must eventually wrestle with the question of fairness. . . . Complications arise from the multidimensional character of fairness. In discussion settings, one must consider not only fairness to the individual, but also fairness to the class, the discussion process, the material, and the instructor's own individual morality. Because efforts to respect one type of fairness often lead to conflicts with another, instructors must frequently engage in a delicate balancing act'.
>
> (Garvin 1991: 289)

Running a medical humanities discussion may therefore present ethical dilemmas for the facilitator.

Further reflection

Participants take stock, reconsider, sum up or revise their views. The mechanism for this reflection can again be five minutes' freewriting. Some participants enjoy simply having five minutes to follow their own thoughts. Others welcome a prompt for writing, such as, 'What are the implications of this discussion for ... ?' A number of options can be used to complete this question: implications for your own practice? for your communications with patients? for your view of mental illness? for your definition of mental health? for your facilitation skills? A pair-share, where participants air these reflections with one other person, can regenerate (or replace) the final plenary discussion.

Reactions

This discussion of Janice Galloway's novel threw up a wide range of issues: patient-carer relations, power and resources, communications skills and styles and many others. Several different discussions of this extract, with different groups, have produced recurring questions:

- How do we communicate with patients?
- How does the dynamic alter when we are on their ground?
- How do we know when we have communicated effectively, or not?

The question, 'Is this health visitor an effective facilitator?' threw up a wide range of responses. Some participants assessed the health visitor's performance on criteria they used in their work. Some did this without realizing they were doing so, believing that they were giving a neutral view. Others related it all to their own approach to working with patients.

The responses to this question included both yes's and no's. The 'yes' group gave several reasons for their answer: the health visitor's visits are effective in stimulating the patient, prompting her to prepare for this visit; the health visitor is sensitive to this patient's taste for irony; the patient wants to get better, so the health visitor has not done any harm; the health visitor does just enough to keep the woman talking; even if the conversation is superficial, stilted and scripted like a play, there is some exchange taking place; she leaves pauses, while she thinks, rather than speaking in a constant stream of smalltalk; it is unrealistic to expect them to have genuine communication at this stage; she is performing the function of a 'crash mat', absorbing all the patient throws at her.

The 'no' group gave equally diverse reasons for their answers: the health visitor is simply making the patient feel worse; the patient has become even more anxious before and during her visit; she fails to attend to the patient, picking fluff off her coat, for example; her questions are too routine, too obvious and there are too many, too quickly; the health visitor does not reflect back what the patient has said; she misses the most obvious of cues; she is patronizing.

All the discussions of this text have come back to point of view: we remind ourselves that we are seeing everything from the patient's point of view. We see the health visitor only through her eyes. The scene is therefore coloured by her attitudes, her thinking and her illness. This means that the description of the health visitor is not objective.

However, both positive and negative sides of the health visitor's performance do emerge, and participants' interpretations were not neutral either. They revealed their own definitions of 'effective facilitation'. In the course of further discussion, focusing on the detail of the text, they could work out for themselves the extent to which their interpretations had been coloured by their own beliefs.

A group of students who participated in a discussion of this text, and this question, came to a number of realizations about professional practice. Some points related to their limited clinical experience, others were more reflective: having to wear different hats with different patients, using clinical language carefully, so that patients understand, striking a balance between the professional and the personal touch. They had begun to address two daily dilemmas: 'Where do you draw the line?', 'How do you protect yourself?'

Thus, what were referred to as 'daily dilemmas' early in this chapter have been addressed. Fundamental questions have been raised about how participants communicate with patients, how they define their roles and which established 'approach' they use in these roles. Perhaps more importantly, it has been clearly and relatively comfortably established that there are differences in these approaches, and that some of these differences may be personal as much as professional. As one participant in an evaluation interview put it, having to listen to someone putting a view with which you do not, and cannot, agree can, in a safe forum, release some of the pressure and 'heat' out of difficult issues.

Where there is complete disagreement, as on the question of professional distance, for example, to take a daily dilemma – or on abortion, to take one of the big issues – it is unlikely that people will change their views. However, the value of medical humanities is that people can develop, and maintain, their skills of listening to each other, even when strong differences of view become apparent.

There are occasions when even trying to have your say on a matter becomes a dilemma: when to speak? how to get people to listen? When the pressures to conform or remain silent become too strong, the individual voice can be supressed and perhaps lost. This is where reflective writing can be helpful in enabling people to voice their views in security. Whether or not they choose to share these views in discussion with others, they have at least put them into words. Medical humanities discussions may also enable participants to voice these views aloud to others.

Conclusions

Medical humanities can be used to create a safe forum for the discussion of ethical dilemmas. Open to many interpretations, the literary text can be a sounding board, at once like and unlike a case study. This kind of forum could be a mechanism for reflective practice.

My book on medical humanities (Murray, 1997) provides enough information for others to try the approach for themselves, and examples of literary texts, so that everyone can have a copy of the same texts without breaking copyright law. Guidelines for structuring discussions are included, along with basic vocabulary and concepts for talking about literary texts. Themes for discussion are suggested, such as death and dying, ageing, sexuality and power. The role of the facilitator is described. Writing activities, for private reflection, are explained and illustrated with examples. The argument that literary texts can complement medical and scientific texts in the education and development of health professionals is made more fully there.

Finally, reading literary texts about medical subjects has been for medical and health practitioners in our group, and for others, a semi-professional 'excuse' to read, and enjoy, literature again.

References

Best, P.C. (1994) Making hospice work: collaborative storytelling in family-care conferences. *Literature and Medicine*, 13, 93–123.

Chambers, T.S. (1994) The Bioethicist as author: The medical ethics case as rhetorical device. *Literature and Medicine*, 13, 60–78.

Darbyshire, P. (1994) Understanding caring through arts and humanities: a medical/nursing humanities approach to promoting alternative experiences of thinking and learning. *Journal of Advanced Nursing*, 19, 856–63.

Elbow, P. (1973) *Writing Without Teachers*. Oxford: Oxford University Press.
   Explains practical strategies for developing writing skills. His technique of freewriting is effective in stimulating ideas, developing fluency in writing and 'unblocking'.

Galloway, J. (1992) *The Trick is to Keep Breathing*. London: Minerva.

Garvin, D.A. (1991) A delicate balance: ethical dilemmas and the discussion process, in Christensen, C.R., Garvin, D.A. and Sweet, A. Eds. *Education for Judgement: The Artistry of Discussion Leadership*. Boston: Harvard Business School.
   A collection of essays on orchestrating questioning, listening and responding in groups.

Hackler, C. (1994) Medical humanities: creating the well-rounded doctor. *Health Care Analysis*, 2, 266–69.

Murray, R. and Thow, M. (1995) A medical humanities roadshow: 'spreading the word'. *Physiotherapy*, 81, 95–106.

Murray, R. (1997) *Ethical Dilemmas in Healthcare: A Practical Approach Through Medical Humanities*. Cheltenham: Stanley Thornes.
   This book was written with healthcare professionals in mind. It provides texts and topics for medical humanities discussions. There are guidelines on managing a medical humanities discussion and vocabulary for talking about literary texts. The approach is practical, with outlines for discussions and examples of discussions in the Glasgow medical humanities group.

Radwany, S.M. and Adelson, B.H. (1987) The use of literary classics in teaching medical ethics to physicians. *Journal of the American Medical Association*, 257, 1629–31.

Rogers, J. (1994) Doubts about medical humanities. *Health Care Analysis, 2,* 347–350.

Self, D.J. (1993) The educational philosophies behind the medical humanities programs in the United States: an empirical assessment of three different approaches to humanistic medical education. *Theoretical Medicine, 14,* 221–229.

Shafer, A. and Fish, M.P. (1994) A call for narrative: The patient's story and anesthesia training. *Literature and Medicine, 13,* 124–142.

Thow, M. and Murray, R. (1991) Medical humanities in physiotherapy: education and practice. *Physiotherapy, 77,* 733–736.

Wear, D. (1992) The colonization of the medical humanities: a confessional critique. *The Journal of Medical Humanities, 13,* 199–209.

Young-Mason, J. (1988) Literature as a mirror to compassion. *Journal of Professional Nursing, 4,* 299–301.

Chapter 14

Rehabilitation counselling

Pamela Griffiths

Rehabilitation counsellors usually work as part of a multidisciplinary team in rehabilitation centres (government and private, e.g. amputee units, spinal cord injury units), hospices, hospitals, residential homes, pain clinics, alcohol and drug abuse centres, sheltered workshops, mental health centres and GP clinics. Key components of courses in rehabilitation counselling are education in psychosocial aspects of disability, concepts of rehabilitation, major counselling and personality theories, ethical practice and research methods. North American and Australian programmes include an additional emphasis on vocational testing and vocational development. In the UK, rehabilitation counselling is taught at post-graduate level and is usually a development for a professional already working in the rehabilitation field. Following graduation they may negotiate to use their counselling skills as an aspect of their current role, or negotiate a new role as a rehabilitation counsellor on the team. Their counselling remit may cover people with disability and chronic illness, their carers and members of the multidisciplinary rehabilitation team. Some rehabilitation counsellors develop a specialism, e.g. working with people who are deaf or visually impaired.

Over the last 20 years there has been a gradual shift in the perception and understanding of disability in Western culture. Models such as the ICIDH (International Classification of Impairment, Disability and Handicap) published by WHO in 1980 began to recognize that impairment, disability and handicap were different aspects of the disabled person's experience (Wood, 1981). It showed that the impairment leads to a lack of ability to function (disability) and that the resulting handicap depends on society's attitudes and ability to construct an accessible environment. The debate continued as the literature increased, notably in the autobiographical accounts of people with disabilities, e.g. Ashley (1973), Sutherland (1981), Campling (1981), Morris (1989), which show the limitations of a medical model. Many people with disabilities were offended by a 'professional construction of disability as adjustment' (Lenny, 1993: 237) which implied that it is disabled people who have the problem. Researchers such as Oliver (1993) argue that what is needed is 'an epistemology and methodology which takes as its starting point the central idea that disability is socially created' and that definitions of disability should not be based on 'able-bodied assumptions about disability' (p.65). Counsellors in this field may then need to consider their role as encompassing being an advocate and activist in removing the environmental constraints and prejudices that sometimes exist in the local community, rehabilitation centres and hospitals.

Rehabilitation: a process of transition

Rehabilitation often begins with a period of crisis. The initial crisis may be precipitated by acute injury or illness, the diagnosis of chronic illness or the discovery of congenital impairment in a young baby. In a systems view of society the crisis will touch family, friends, carers and health-care professionals. In recent years there has been considerable discussion concerning models of adaptation to disability which postulate stages or phases of psychological process. However, writers such as Trieschmann (1988) contend that there is insufficient empirical support for such models, and Lenny (1993) warns that disabled people 'can feel deeply oppressed by the application of grief and stage theories that do not accord with their experience.' In fact, in many autobiographical accounts people with disabilities do not experience their disability in terms of loss. It remains useful for counsellors in this field to consider models of adaptation as an indicator of process, while remembering that it is good practice to check the quality of the research on which the model is based.

Robertson (1992) reminds us that 'similar to the need for physiological homeostasis, individuals have a need for social and psychological equilibrium' (p.133). This equilibrium is disturbed at times of crisis, and new coping responses may be required in order to negotiate the transition towards integration. Early models of adaptation to disability were based on Kübler-Ross's (1969) model of reactions to death and dying, e.g. Matson and Brooks (1977) who explored the process of people adjusting to multiple sclerosis. More recently, Schlossberg (1984) described the process of assimilation as a person moving from total preoccupation with the transition to integration of the transition with his or her life. Livneh (1986a) reviewed more than 40 stage

Table 14.1: *Model of Psychosocial Adaptation to Physical Disability (Adapted from Livneh 1986a)*

Theme	Marked By
Initial impact	Shock and anxiety
Defence mobilization	Bargaining and denial involved
Initial realization	Mourning and/or depression, Internalized anger
Retaliation/rebellion	Externalizing anger and aggressiveness
Reintegration/Reorganization	Acknowledgement (cognitive) Acceptance (affective) Reconstruction (behavioural)

models of psychosocial adaptation to physical disability and incorporated them into a single model comprising five broad stages (Table 14.1).

In 1991 Livneh and Antonak developed a multidimensional inventory to explore the multiple aspects of adapting to disability called the RIDI scale (Reactions to Impairment and Disability Inventory). Their study using this inventory found a different ordering to the broad categories in Table 14.1: first a 'non-adaptive phase' with depression and internalized anger followed by shock, anxiety and externalized hostility, then an adaptive phase where there was acknowledgement and adjustment; denial appeared independently between the two phases. Their findings showed that individuals can regress to earlier stages and skip a stage, and they emphasize that stages overlap.

Livneh and Antonak (1991) also showed that the stage of denial particularly warranted further attention. French (1993a) describes the complexity of denial for people growing up with a disability. She shows the stress of living up to 'other people's ideas of "normality"' and explains how children may try to deny their disability to avoid the anxiety and distress of family and friends. The implication is that some children may spend years in a form of denial that considerably affects their sense of self and development of identity.

Another model of how individuals experience the transition of rehabilitation also evolved from models of grief and loss. This is the concept of chronic sorrow that is 'not constant yet is chronic and recurs periodically' (Teel, 1991: 1317). It occurs when an emotionally close relationship is permanently disrupted, such as when a spouse is brain-injured or when the hoped-for child is born with a physical or mental impairment. Chronic sorrow may be the experience of carers of a person with a disability and part of their transition may be for them, and those who support them, to gradually understand that it is a normal process in this situation. It is suggested that individuals may resolve the chronic sorrow by withdrawing from the relationship (e.g. divorce), or eventually no longer perceiving it as a loss.

Finally, it is important to consider that if the disabled person experiences trauma at the onset of the disability he or she may have post-traumatic stress disorder (PTSD), as may any friends or relatives who were present at the time of the trauma. It is important that the possibility of PTSD, which may include intrusive imagery and avoidance of situations, is recognized by health-care professionals and an appropriate referral made.

Strategies for counselling intervention

It is clear that there is no universal order of stages and time-scale for a person to adapt to a disability, although there are indications of the nature of the stages that a person may experience. Livneh and Antonak (1991) remind us that factors influencing the process of adaptation may include 'human variability (and uniqueness), differential levels of severity and chronicity of disability, mode of disability acquisition, sociocultural and environmental conditions' (pp. 311-2). Robertson (1992) summarizes the main variables affecting outcome as: characteristics of the transition, the environment and the individual. The implication for the rehabilitation counsellor is to stay close to the client's unique experience and to validate that experience. The counsellor's knowledge of stages of adaptation, chronic sorrow and PTSD may help the counsellor to understand the experience and to normalize it for the client. However, it is the freedom the client has to experience his or her understanding of this feeling that will enable the client to take the risks involved in being himself (Rogers, 1967).

For example, following a head injury a young man had reduced function on one side of his body and used a stick to walk. He was no longer able to work as a builder. He felt that it was 'shameful' that he could no longer provide for his family and that his brother and father no longer respected him. To mask his sense of shame he exerted his authority more strongly at home, fiercely clinging to the only role he knew. His tenacity, which earlier had helped him to cope with painful exercise programmes, now distorted into a stubborness that disrupted his relationships with those people who were close to him. In counselling he gradually became more able to explore his conflict between acknowledging his pain and remaining the responsible head of the household. He explored his view of himself as a man and the

Table 14.2: A Framework for Counselling Adults in Transition
(Adapted from Schlossberg, 1984)

Theme	Corresponding Stage from Egan (1975)
Individual pervaded by the transition	Exploration
Disruption: relationships are changing	Understanding
Transition is integrated	Action

role models he had had as he grew up. He learnt to evaluate his assumptions by ascertaining the views and experiences of his family and discovered an improved level of communication at home that he had not experienced before. The specific characteristics of this individual and his environment were crucial factors in the counsellor understanding how to facilitate his rehabilitaion.

Schlossberg (1984) has constructed a framework for counselling adults in transition which is based on Egan's (1975) model of exploration, understanding and action, and she has used the stages to parallel her concept of the transition process (Table 14.2). The correspondence between Egan's model and Schlossberg's stages of the transition process will now be examined as a means to evaluate counselling interventions in rehabilitation.

Exploration

At the start of counselling there may be a dilemma for the counsellor as to how much of the client's medical records to review. Sometimes the referrer will note issues for the counsellor to be aware of. These may include sensory deficits, such as the client being deaf and needing to lip-read, the client being dysphasic (unable to find words), or severely visually handicapped so that he or she may rarely, or never make eye contact with the counsellor. There may be a report on the client's cognitive level and/or a perceptual assessment. These assessments are particularly appropriate following a head injury or a stroke. These reports need to be carefully considered, usually with the client, as their findings may affect the structuring of the session. For example, the sessions may need to be shorter if the client has a limited attention span, or the counsellor may need to sit in a particular part of the room if the client is not attending to one half of his or her visual field.

Other considerations may include an awareness of the client's medication regime e.g. it may be more comfortable for a client in physical pain to attend counselling after taking his or her pain tablets.

Similarly, if a client has a blocked catheter or breathlessness during a session, it may be necessary to end a session earlier than planned. Although these details may be found in medical records or referral details they would need to be explored with the client. The advantage of exploring these details with the client prior to reading any notes is that the client's perspective is heard with no 'filter' of another person's view. Bear in mind that clients in the rehabilitation field may have had to explain aspects of their disability many times prior to talking to you.

An elderly woman, following a stroke, wanted to talk about a possible reconciliation with her son. She believed that her son might visit her in the hospital and she was anxious about the visit. After 10 minutes she became too tired to speak but asked the counsellor to stay. They agreed to have 30-minute sessions and at times the woman spoke monosyllabically using much non-verbal communication which the counsellor would often verbalize to confirm her understanding. The woman said she felt supported in the talking and the silences and that 'this helped her to think'.

An aspect of opening negotiations that may take time to establish may be deciding the venue. Some clients may be house-bound or bed-bound and boundaries around the venue will need to be considered. Cubicle curtains in a hospital ward may not feel private enough so it may be preferable to see a client in a day-room or other available office, if this is possible. Home visits may necessitate agreements to curtail all interruptions, e.g. unplugging the phone, not answering the doorbell and requesting an hour's privacy from family members. Time spent early in the sessions to construct a mutually agreeable contract on these issues will enable the later sessions to maintain a clearer focus.

The phase of exploration corresponds to the stage where the client is pervaded by the transition and the non-adaptive phase of psychosocial adaptation. Clients may be at varying degrees of comprehending what has occurred, and possibly experiencing shock, anxiety and depression. A man who had a stroke and was taken to hospital said later: 'suddenly one evening, everything sort of collapsed, nothing seemed real, just everything stopped'. A woman who fell on her floor at home with a stroke rolled around the floor all night trying to find a way to get to the door and summon help. Health professionals need to set agendas that are sensitive to the patient's state of shock. People in shock cannot absorb a lot of new information and often wish to stay still and be kept warm until they have begun to digest their new experience.

Clients sometimes claim to have had insufficient information about their condition and prognosis. The counsellor may need to acknowledge the difficulties of absorbing so much new information at once, as well as exploring with the client ways to obtain more information. In some situations it may be the rehabilitation counsellor's role to reinforce certain details about the client's new condition. The experience of the non-adaptive phase can transform a person emotionally, behaviourally and cognitively so that the team may have no sense of the client's personality prior to the illness or disability. A client with extensive burns on her legs screamed abuse at health-care staff for four days. Her relatives later commented with astonishment that they had never before heard her swear or raise her voice. Counselling intervention to demonstrate an empathic, congruent and non-judgemental approach will help to stabilize the client. Boundaries may need to be reinforced to help clients to contain their anxiety. This may occasionally include the use of behaviour modification approaches established with the client and consistently held by all members of the rehabilitation team. These could be negotiated with the client and are in effect 'ground rules' for the management of extreme behaviours such as aggression.

The literature strongly advocates a person-centred humanistic approach in the early counselling phase. Livneh (1986a) advocates more affective and/or insightful counselling approaches in the earlier phase, with cognitive-behavioural and action orientated approaches in the later phase. This view corresponds with that of Prochaska and DiClimente (1982) who present a model of change comprising four stages. They advocate that verbal processes are more important in the first two stages ('contemplation' and 'determination'), and behavioural processes in the last two stages ('action' and 'maintenance'). Their view is that the flexibility of an integrative approach recognizes the needs of the client at each stage and provides a more balanced view.

In contrast, Lenny (1993) advocates a person-centred approach throughout. Lenny emphasizes the importance of the counsellor having a non-judgmental approach and not imposing meaning on the situation or labels on the person which may already have been part of the client's negative experience. For this reason she argues that a psychoanalytical approach is not appropriate. She suggests that the person-centred approach will more fully enable a client to make sense of the relationship between 'individually experienced impairment' and 'socially imposed disability'.

A key finding of Oliver's (1995) research into counselling people with disabilities was that 'the medical model of disability can disempower the disabled client and be the cause of many of their psychological difficulties' (p.275). One of the most frequently repeated items in her findings was that counselling needs to be flexible in approach and not have just one theoretical orientation. This finding concurs with Livneh (1986a) and again suggests the need for an integrative approach.

Understanding

The middle of the transition is described by Schlossberg (1984) as a time of disruptions and changes in relationships. Egan (1975) recognizes the middle phase as a time when there is a deepening in the relationship between counsellor and client and there is a need to understand some of the dynamics around the presenting issues. According to research on the psychosocial stages of adaptation a client may be experiencing a degree of realization marked by depression and anger as he or she begins to assimilate losses relating to role, body image, physical capacities and relationships. In order to facilitate the growing awareness and beginning of assimilation in the client, several counselling strategies may be considered. The choice of method will be guided by listening to the client's experience, and evaluating his or her personality and physical and mental capacities.

Facilitatory methods such as reflection and clarification may need to be supplemented with those of confrontation. Cognitive approaches may be found to be powerful, as 'individuals with disabilities are indoctrinated by the same attitudes, prejudices, and stereotypes as mainstream society' (Vargo, 1992: 79), which inevitably produce barriers in the process of adjustment. Vargo shows that these attitudes are products of cognitions and self-verbalizations and that a cognitive approach could help overcome any resulting dysfunctional behaviours. A cognitive behavioural approach uses a stimulus-response technique and recognizes the importance of thought (cognition) as a psychological filter mediating between stimulus and response. Many people with disabilities may have self-defeating verbalizations that affect their feelings and this process may be evident in research which shows that the degree of adjustment to a disability is independent of the severity of the impairment (e.g. Ben-Sira, 1983).

Other methods that are helpful in exploring the dynamics of a situation and accessing feelings include: gestalt, applications of games and script analysis from transactional analysis, and assertiveness skills explored in role play. Creative approaches may be particularly valuable when the client has little or no verbal abilities. These approaches comprise art, keeping a journal, drama (perhaps with mask painting), visualization and guided imagery and sand trays. When integrating the creative experience with a client who has little speech it is useful to have cards with a range of words on, which the client may point to, or select, in order to express their understanding of the process. Some of these approaches may require creative adaptation of tools, such as thicker brushes, or crayon handles, or a counsellor may need to place the figures in the sand tray with guidance from the client.

Some creative approaches may be used in a group context that involves clients and carers. This approach has been used in hospices in Sweden and England. The creative work may become a mirror for the internal processes of the group or the individual. Counselling may be a part of the group process if this is what the group agrees, or it may be available on request as the project evolves. One project, which was focalized by a rehabilitation counsellor, developed a mural for the day centre allowing those involved to take part at their own rate. The resulting mural was celebrated by those who took part and by the local community. The project was gently facilitated by practising Rogers' (1967) core conditions of empathy, congruence and unconditional positive regard.

A wife with a newly-dependent husband found that she was scolding him in a way that she never had before his illness. Using the techniques of transactional analysis it was found that her transactions often used the words 'should' and 'if I were you'. This is the ego state of the critical parent and it seemed to be accessing introjected scripts relating to her experience of parenting. Her way of coping with the dependence of her husband was to relate to him as parent to child. This dynamic was communicated in her behaviour, speech content and tone of voice. By raising her awareness to the level of the transactions she was using she became able to move into the adult-to-adult ego state transactions more often and also to express some of her feelings about the transition they were both experiencing.

The body may become the focus of the counselling and this could be utilized in the creative work. Some clients will have become more aware of their bodies than ever before. The predominant initial experience can be a sense of limitation. Clients may find freedom in painting with their hands. Indeed, some counsellors have encouraged clients to paint their own bodies as a means of accepting and remembering their body. Counsellors with expertise in bodywork may find it appropriate to facilitate understanding and assimilation of the experiences by the use of massage or gentle touch on areas of the body that have been damaged or neglected. This approach may promote a sense of wholeness. As always, this approach would be introduced only with the consent of the client, and with the client in control. Time must be allowed to explore and integrate feelings that are touched in the session.

Somatization may be an aspect of bodily sensations, and attending to them could help the client to access feelings that have been repressed and discounted. Clients may become aware of conflicts and deep concerns as they remember how they used to express themselves through their body.

A young mother with multiple sclerosis despaired that 'I can no longer hug my children'; a middle-aged woman, following an ileostomy, mourned the loss of her sex life. Grief and anger may be acknowledged and new perspectives and forms of expression may be explored. Concerns about sexuality may be expressed indirectly and may sometimes need referral to a sex therapist. Two adolescent boys with developing muscular dystrophy were chastised for making frequent jokes with sexual innuendo whenever young female staff were near. In a counselling situation their anxiety about their ability to have sexual relationships could have been addressed.

During this phase the client may become most acutely aware of the split between his or her old sense of self – before the illness or trauma – and the emerging new sense of self. The sense of transition creates unease which may manifest in mood swings and varying cognitive presentations. The counsellor needs to provide safe boundaries to hold the client's unease as he or she seeks to find a new sense of wholeness with a different construction. The counsellor using a client-centred or phenomenological approach may find that an attempt to understand the possible meaning or learning from the situation may help to bridge the split and promote integration. This approach may be viewed as more transpersonal. Matson and Brooks (1977), studying the adjustment process of people with multiple sclerosis, found that some people felt that multiple sclerosis had 'afforded them the time to get in touch with the more essential values in life' (p.248). Similar viewpoints have been expressed in studies with individuals who have had cancer (LeShan, 1990; Siegel, 1990) and heart attacks (Dossey, 1991). Lyons *et al.* (1995), reviewing experiences of people with chronic illness and disability, found that people often take stock of priorities, including the value they place on close relationships. Such insights reflect a depth of working and can sometimes enable a client to touch a sense of authenticity in their being that they never knew before. It is important that the counsellor readily admits to not having all the answers (Bennet 1984) so that the client sees the vulnerable 'humaneness' of the counsellor, thereby closing a potential split between 'all-able, all-good professional worker and the all-helpless, all-bad customer' (Shearer 1986: 111).

Action

This phase corresponds to the time when the client may be integrating the transition and the later stages of psychosocial adjustment involving acknowledgement, acceptance and reconstruction. Livneh and Antonak (1991) characterize this phase as the 'adaptive' phase. Both Prochaska and DiClimente (1982) and Livneh (1986a) advocate similar approaches in this latter stage: Prochaska and DiClimente suggest behavioural approaches and Livneh cognitive-behavioural and more action-orientated approaches, which she describes in more detail in a subsequent paper (1986b). Schlossberg (1984) views the phase as a time to promote coping, which Egan (1975) mobilizes by means of goal setting and the development of strategies to reach the goals. The counsellor and the client need to be clear as to which stage they are working on, as this stage represents a marked shift with a greater emphasis on objective methods. Robertson (1992) also advocates setting concrete and time-limited goals that are followed by rehearsal of possible outcomes. Reinforcement of earlier learning (e.g. concerning self-defeating thoughts or passive behaviour) may be combined with the promotion of self-esteem and a sense of empowerment. Bolton and Brookings (1996) have begun to develop a valid measure of empowerment which may become a useful asessment tool at this stage. A review of the extent and quality of the client's support system as well as deepening a recognition of a new sense of values are also recommended. These strategies must also be balanced with a real recognition of the client's permanent loss and limitations, possibly highlighting the client's shift in perspective since the commencement of counselling, in order to embrace a wholeness of experience.

Carers and the multidisciplinary team

Systems theory has been developed over the last few decades to explore interactions in a range of fields. It recognizes the interdependence between the constituent parts of the whole. A system is dynamic and self-regulating. We exist within a series of systems, e.g. family and community.

The rehabilitation team comprising health-care staff, client, the client's carers and family may be considered one such system. Crisis and disturbance to any part of the system can affect the whole system. Counselling intervention to the group or to part of the system may be valuable in re-establishing balance and effective functioning.

The remit of a rehabilitation counsellor varies. Some hospice staff teams have regular group counselling to help support their work. In a burns unit for children in Belgium the counsellor is available for carers, staff and patients. The counsellor found that his approach has helped to humanize the technical procedures by pointing out the importance of the relationship between the child, his or her family and the staff team. In a head injury and rehabilitation unit in the UK a rehabilitation counsellor has extended her role to train the multidisciplinary team in co-counselling as a supportive measure. This approach has helped to change the staff's reaction to stress, which can keep a system in a state of imbalance.

A model that is particularly adaptable to raising the consciousness of the system is transactional analysis. Eric Berne's model has grounded psychodynamic theory in observable behaviour and can be used to examine patterns of communication between people. The induced dependence in many hospital patients, for example, can evoke the dynamics of authority-dependence relationships from the past. It can be used to recognize what Berne called the 'transference drama' in life (Stewart, 1992) and to bring psychological game-playing into awareness. Such awareness can be reinforced with support groups, training sessions, keeping a journal and co-counselling.

Psychological game-playing may exist between patient and staff, patient and carer and between the health-care staff. It may be the rehabilitation counsellor who can initiate or focus strategies to bring these dynamics into awareness. Berne (1964) chose whimsical names for the games he describes to help them be readily understood. 'Gee you're wonderful, Professor' can be played by any health professional. The patient may be meeting the staff's need for praise or power; however, amid the admiration the health professional may not notice that the patient is not actually getting better. Staff may also play a form of this game regarding their perceived roles. An experienced nurse may feed information to a junior doctor so that the patient is led to believe that the doctor is 'wonderful', although the nurse may be left feeling resentful and the nurse's training and experience are obscured.

Several other games, including 'I'm only trying to help you', are applicable to the healthcare field. Psychological games are 'an ongoing series of complementary ulterior transactions progressing to a well-defined, predictable outcome' (Berne, 1964: 44). As the games take place out of awareness they may be repeated regularly until a strategy to explore the situation is put in place. An understanding of the dynamics of the games can enable a player to, in Berne's words, 'name the game' or 'leave the field'.

Berne's method of examining the transactions between people can be useful in understanding how a team is operating. A staff team working under high stress can tend to split the world into 'them' and 'us' as a means of protection from enormous anxiety. Berne construed such a position as the child ego state, which may lead to very indirect forms of communication such as leaving equipment in front of staff doors as a way to express frustrations at imbalances in space availability. Strategies to encourage staff to reflect on these dynamics in a support group, for example, can help to bring the whole system into balance, which often has the result of improved patient care as well.

Training of rehabilitation counsellors

There are two aspects to the training of rehabilitation counsellors. One is the need to be aware of the nature of various disabilities and illnesses, to understand current models of adjustment to disability and illness, and to explore our understanding of social and medical models regarding health, illness and disability. The second aspect relates to our personal response to illness and disability. To become aware and sensitive to our response entails examining such areas as our experience of, and reaction to, grief and loss, and our desire to work in the rehabilitation field. Eadie (1975) has characterized the 'helping personality' as 'one based on the ideal of being loved and lovable, with often a primary need to be loved' (p.109). Such aspirations lead to self-denial and self-effacement. Other motivations may include a need to control an area of great fear: the threat of becoming disabled or chronically ill. Following training, these areas may be revisited in supervision and support groups.

Supervision may be particularly useful in helping the rehabilitation counsellor to recognize feelings and attitudes towards the client which may be out of awareness (counter-transference). Segal (1996) describes some negative effects of counter-transference: the counsellor may avoid challenging the client due to the counsellor's fantasy that the disabled client has no emotional strength, or the counsellor may see only his or her construction of disability. Such notions may involve psychological changes including splitting, denial and idealization. As a result, a counsellor could, for example, collude with a client's, or a carer's, denial of the disability.

Coping with a carer's denial of a disability may already be a significantly difficult aspect of a child's life, as French (1993a) has shown. Shearer (1986) writes that in society there is a conflict or a 'paradox at the very heart of the relationship between the able-bodied majority and the disabled minority. They are both essential to our sense of our "able" selves and the people we consistently reject as the ones we neither want nor need' (p.107, see also Shearer, 1981). Counsellors working closely with illness and disability need to confront their phantasies and work to heal the potential split, which may be as much within ourselves as in the society in which we live. As Guggenbuhl-Craig (1980) reminds us: by accepting our 'incompleteness', our 'completeness' is fulfilled.

More conscious aspects to be examined include assumptions about clients, which may be reflected in the goals of rehabilitation. Traditionally these have emphasized independence. But French (1993b) argues that this notion has been taken too far and may lead to inefficiency, stress and isolation. Some clients may choose to have help with domestic chores that are a struggle, and to use a wheelchair even though they can walk, because it is more efficient. Staying close to the client's experience and true choices will help the rehabilitation counsellor to be more effective.

Conclusions

People with chronic illness and disability are not a homogeneous group and will experience the vagaries of human experience with a range of responses. Although we have strong indications from research of the stages within a transition of adaptation, together with indications for counselling interventions, we must respect that each person's journey is unique. Our response therefore needs to be flexible and integrative. In this respect a rehabilitation counsellor's skills are similar to those of counsellors working with other mixed population groups. The distinguishing aspect is that the counsellor has explored his or her own responses to illness and disability.

Areas of current debate in this field include whether only disabled people can effectively counsel disabled clients. Oliver (1993) comments from her research findings that 'a disabled counsellor may be too subjective; however, a non-disabled counsellor may be too objective'. She concludes that as no two experiences are the same, a 'good' non-disabled counsellor could empathize effectively with a range of experiences. Vehement discussion, originating in the disability rights' lobbies, finds much of the rehabilitaton services oppressive and seeks for rehabilitation counselling to be seen as an empowering activity (Holmes, 1993). Another area of debate centres around how to actualize a systemic conception of rehabilitation with more integration of physical and psychological approaches. This development would entail greater recognition of the interrelationship between these two aspects. For example, a person in shock and confusion will not be able to learn new skills in physiotherapy sessions. Increasing insights into the correlation between emotional and physical health (e.g. Sinatra and Lowen, 1987) and psychoneuroimmunology developments may contribute to this area. A recognition of counselling intervention as a resource for carers, the multi-disciplinary team, and the person with the illness or disability could foster further understanding of this interrelationship and a move towards greater integration.

Acknowledgements

The author wishes to thank two students on the MSc in rehabilitation counselling at Brunel University – Sue Gray and Mary White – for the opportunity to discuss their research and incorporate it in this chapter, and also IRTAC conference colleagues Kerstin Hagg and Jean Petit.

References

Ashley, J. (1973) *Journey into Silence*. London: Bodley Head.
  An autobiographical account of coping with total deafness.
Ben-Sira, Z. (1983) Loss, stress and readjustment: The structure of coping with bereavement and disability. *Social Science Medicine*, 17, 1619–31.

Bennet, G. (1984) The wounded healer in the twentieth century. *British Journal of Holistic Medicine*, 1, 127–30 quoted in: A. Shearer (1986) Wholeness and Handicap. *Holistic Medicine*, 1, 105–13.

Berne, E. (1964) *Games People Play*. Harmondsworth: Penguin.
An inspired exploration of the psychological games played between people – heavily coloured with 1960s jargon!

Bolton, B. and Brookings, J. (1996) Development of a multifaceted definition of empowerment. *Rehabilitation Counselling Bulletin*, 30, 256–64.

Campling, J. (Ed.) (1981) *Images of Ourselves: Women with Disabilities Talking*. London: Routledge and Kegan Paul.
Insightful and honest insights into women's experience of disability.

Dossey, L. (1991) *Meaning and Medicine: Tales of Breakthrough and Healing*. London: Bantam.
A cardiologist's new approaches to healthcare.

Eadie, H. (1975) The helping personality. Contact 49 quoted in A. Shearer (1986) Wholeness and handicap. *Holistic Medicine*, 1, 105–13.

Egan, G. (1975) *The Skilled Helper: A Model for Systematic Helping and Interpersonal Relating*. Monterey, California: Brooks Cole.

French, S. (1993a) 'Can you see the rainbow?' The roots of denial. In J. Swain, V. Finkelstein, S. French and M. Oliver (Eds) *Disabling Barriers – Enabling Environments*. London: Sage in association with The Open University.
Challenging and inspired perspectives on the experience of disability.

French, S. (1993b) What's so great about independence? In J. Swain, V. Finkelstein, S. French and M. Oliver (Eds) *Disabling Barriers – Enabling Environments*. London: Sage in asociation with The Open University.

Griffiths, P. (1993) Rehabilitation counselling: the development of a new course specialism in British counselling. *British Journal of Guidance and Counselling*, 21, 82–94.

Guggenbuhl-Craig, A. (1980) *Eros on Crutches*. Dallas: Spring Publications.

Holmes, G. (1993) The historical roots of the empowerment dilemma in vocational rehabilitation. *Journal of Disability Policy Studies*, 4, 1–19.

Kübler-Ross, E. (1969) *On Death and Dying*. New York: Macmillan.
The book which pioneered the exploration and deeper understanding of a taboo area.

Lenny, J. (1993) Do disabled people need counselling? In: J. Swain, V. Finlelstein, S. French and M. Oliver (Eds) *Disabling Barriers – Enabling Environments*. Sage in association with The Open University.

LeShan, L. (1990) *Cancer as a Turning Point: A Handbook for People with Cancer, their Families and Health Professionals*. Bath: Gateway Books.
New England physician who developed new approaches to working with people with cancer.

Livneh, H. (1986a) A unified approach to existing models of adaptation to disability: Part 1 – A model of adaptation. *Journal of Applied Rehabilitation Counselling*, 17, 5–16.
Clear and comprehensive accounts.

Livneh, H. (1986b) A unified approach to existing models of adaptation to disability: Part 11 – Intervention strategies. *Journal of Applied Rehabilitation Counselling*, *17*, 6–10.

Livneh, H, and Antonak, R. (1991) Temporal structure of adaptation to disability. *Rehabilitation Counselling Bulletin*, *34*, 298–319.

Lyons, R., Sullivan, M., Ritvo, P. and Coyne, J. (1995) *Relationships in Chronic Illness and Disability*. London: Sage.
Excellent study with good reference list.

Matson, R. and Brooks, N. (1977) Adjusting to multiple sclerosis. *Social Science Medicine 11* 245–50.

Morris, J. (1989) *Able Lives: Women's Experience of Paralysis*. London: The Women's Press.

Oliver, J. (1995) Counselling disabled people: a counsellor's perspective. *Disability and Society 10* 261–79.

Oliver, M. (1993) Re-defining Disability: A Challenge to Research. In: J. Swain, V. Finkelstein, S. French and M. Oliver (Eds) *Disabling Environments – Enabling Environments*. London: Sage Publications in association with The Open University.

Prochaska, J. and DiClimente, C. (1982) Transtheoretical therapy: Toward a more integrative model of change. *Psychotherapy: Theory, Research and Practice 19* 276–88.

Robertson, S. (1992) Counselling adults with physical disabilities: a transitions perspective. In: S. Robertson and R. Brown (Eds) *Rehabilitation Counselling: Approaches in the Field of Disability*. London: Chapman & Hall.
A valuable source book.

Rogers, C. (1967) *On Becoming a Person: A Therapist's View of Therapy*. London: Constable. Rich material for the client-centred counsellor.

Schlossberg, N. (1984) *Counselling Adults in Transition*. New York: Springer Publishing.

Segal, J. (1996) Whose disability? Countertransference in work with people with disabilities. *Psychodynamic Counselling*, *2*, 155–66.

Shearer, A. (1981) *Disability: Whose Handicap?* Oxford: Basil Blackwell.

Shearer, A. (1986) Wholeness and handicap. *Holistic Medicine*, *1*, 105–13.

Siegel, B. (1990) *Love, Medicine and Miracles: Lessons Learned about Self-healing from a Surgeon's Experience with Exceptional Patients*. London: Harper Collins.
An American surgeon pioneering new approaches to patient care.

Sinatra, S. and Lowen, A. (1987) Heartbreak and heart disease: the origin and essence of coronary-prone behaviour. *Holistic Medicine*, *2*, 169–72.

Stewart, I. (1992) *Eric Berne*. London: Sage.
Clear and comprehensive acount of Berne's life and an introduction to his theories.

Sutherland, A. (1981) *Disabled We Stand*. London: Souvenir Press.

Teel, C. (1991) Chronic sorrow: analysis of the concept. *Journal of Advanced Nursing*, *16*, 1311–19.

Trieschmann, R. (1988) *Spinal Cord Injuries: Psychological, Social and Vocational Rehabilitation*. New York: Demos.

219

Vargo, J. (1992) A cognitive approach to counselling clients with physical disabilities. In: S. Robertson and R. Brown (Eds) *Rehabilitation Counselling: Approaches in the Field of Disability.* London: Chapman & Hall.

Wood, P. (1981) *International Classification of Impairments, Disabilities and Handicaps.* Geneva: WHO.

This model has been discussed in many professional health journals.

Index

Compiled by Mary Kirkness

WITHDRAWN